What Your Colleagues Are Saying

"I have read two books that give me hope that the CCSS may improve both teaching and learning, especially for struggling readers and writers. This book, written by ReLeah Lent and Barry Gilmore, is one of those two books (the other was written by Lucy Calkins and her colleagues). . . . So, read this book and then begin to adapt your instruction in the manner described so artfully."

—RICHARD L. ALLINGTON

Professor of Education, University of Tennessee,
and Author of *What Really Matters
for Struggling Readers,* Third Edition

"This is a very helpful and very timely book. Lent and Gilmore provide a very smart yet workable and commonsense approach to not only engaging struggling learners, but then assisting them through collaborative activity in a meaningful context of use to greater facility as readers and writers, speakers, and listeners. The approach will certainly help teachers help their students to meet the next generation of standards and assessments, but also so much more than that."

—JEFFREY D. WILHELM

Professor of English Education and
Director, Boise State Writing Project

"*Common Core CPR* is a powerful text. . . . [It] offers commonsense suggestions for successful work with the standards in all classrooms, especially with students who struggle. Using an interdisciplinary approach to literacy, the authors do not view the standards as isolated skills to teach, but as natural outcomes as they scaffold learning."

—SHARON DRAPER

Author of *Panic* and *Tears of a Tiger*

"Finally! A practical and comprehensive guide for teachers who want to ensure that the needs of all students are met in this age of Common Core Standards, including reluctant and struggling readers and writers. Thank you, ReLeah Lent and Barry Gilmore, for helping ease one our greatest fears about the Common Core—that struggling students will struggle even more."

—DEBORAH APPLEMAN

Author of *Critical Encounters
in High School English,* Second Edition

Common Core CPR

Common Core CPR

What About the Adolescents
Who Struggle . . . or Just Don't Care?

ReLeah Cossett Lent

Barry Gilmore

Foreword by Richard L. Allington
Afterword by Sharon M. Draper

CORWIN
A SAGE Company

FOR INFORMATION:

Corwin
A SAGE Company
2455 Teller Road
Thousand Oaks, California 91320
(800) 233-9936
www.corwin.com

SAGE Publications Ltd.
1 Oliver's Yard
55 City Road
London EC1Y 1SP
United Kingdom

SAGE Publications India Pvt. Ltd.
B 1/I 1 Mohan Cooperative Industrial Area
Mathura Road, New Delhi 110 044
India

SAGE Publications Asia-Pacific Pte. Ltd.
3 Church Street
#10-04 Samsung Hub
Singapore 049483

Publisher: Lisa Luedeke
Development Editor: Julie Nemer
Editorial Assistant: Francesca Dutra Africano
Production Editor: Melanie Birdsall
Copy Editor: Melinda Masson
Typesetter: C&M Digitals (P) Ltd.
Proofreader: Laura Webb
Indexer: Karen Wiley
Cover and Interior Designer: Gail Buschman

Common Core State Standards (CCSS) cited throughout the book are copyright © 2010 National Governors Association Center for Best Practices and Council of Chief State School Officers. All rights reserved.

Printed in the United States of America

Library of Congress Cataloging-in-Publication Data

A catalog record of this book is available from the Library of Congress.

ISBN: 978-1-4522-9136-9

This book is printed on acid-free paper.

SUSTAINABLE FORESTRY INITIATIVE
Certified Chain of Custody
Promoting Sustainable Forestry
www.sfiprogram.org
SFI-01268
SFI label applies to text stock

13 14 15 16 17 10 9 8 7 6 5 4 3 2 1

Contents

Chapter 2. Why Scaffolding Complex Text Is Crucial

Chapter 5. Why Evidence Matters: From Text to Talk to Argument 135

Chapter 6. How Using Diverse Media and Formats Can Ignite Student Learning 171

Chapter 7. Why a Culture of Reading Is Critical—and How to Create One 211

Visit **www.corwin.com/commoncorecpr** for a complete Professional Learning Guide, PowerPoints, and reproducibles designed to be used in conjunction with *Common Core CPR*.

Foreword

Over the past year or two I've read far too many books and articles about the Common Core State Standards (CCSS). With all that reading I now have read two books that give me hope that the CCSS may improve both teaching and learning, especially for struggling readers and writers. This book, written by ReLeah Cossett Lent and Barry Gilmore, is one of those two books (the other was written by Lucy Calkins and her colleagues).

What has worried me about the CCSS, and most of the material I've read on the CCSS, is that there are folks who seem to interpret the message of the CCSS as doing what we have been doing while replacing current texts with more complex texts. One thing we know for sure is that giving struggling readers difficult text is no solution.

I live and work in a textbook adoption state, and this year has seen schools across the state replacing their commercial reading programs with newer commercial reading programs—new programs with "CCSS compliant" printed across the covers of the teacher manuals! However, these new programs typically present the old one-size-fits-all lesson design.

Too many people reading the CCSS documents seem not to have noticed the emphasis on problem-based learning, the emphasis on differentiated instruction, the emphasis on reading multiple texts, and the emphasis on wide and independent reading. Take, for example, this quote from the Publishers' Criteria for Common Core State Standards (Coleman & Pimentel, 2012, p. 4):

> *Students need access to a wide range of materials on a variety of topics and genres both in their classrooms and in their school libraries to ensure that they have opportunities to independently read broadly and widely to build their knowledge, experience, and joy in reading.*

What seems clear to me, and to ReLeah and Barry, is that implementing the CCSS will require much more than simply purchasing a new one-size-fits-all commercial curriculum package.

It is not just the CCSS expectation that students will be reading and writing much more frequently than is the case today, but that they will be reading and writing for personal reasons, not just for reasons a teacher has set for them. CCSS practitioners envision classrooms where students engage each other in literate conversations about what they have been reading and writing—classrooms where students don't just learn a few basic skills but acquire the proficiencies necessary to become literate and engaged citizens.

In this small book the authors provide a clear view of what CCSS classrooms might look and sound like. They provide examples of student work and lesson plans from a variety of teachers working in a variety of schools across the nation. The point that is driven home so succinctly in this book is that the CCSS may stimulate many more teachers to do exceptionally well, as do the exemplary teachers described here.

However, as the authors note, simply giving struggling readers more complex texts and more complex assignments will be more likely to drive them toward dropping out. The examples provided of the differentiated work that struggling readers might be doing in CCSS-guided classrooms, coupled with the sorts of growth these students exhibit when the lessons fit them, offer a sharp contrast to too much of what now passes as CCSS-informed instruction.

So, read this book and then begin to adapt your instruction in the manner described so artfully by its authors. If more classrooms begin to look like the classrooms offered here, it will be a good thing for American students and for the ultimate goal of improving the literacy proficiencies of all of our students.

—Richard L. Allington
University of Tennessee

Introduction

Meeting the Common Core With Common Sense

The Common Core State Standards (CCSS) have been maligned, extolled, dismissed, and microanalyzed, sometimes simultaneously—especially when groups come together for the specific purpose of understanding the standards and how they may substantially change teaching practices. The national rhetoric online, in journals, and at educational conferences reflects a significant amount of discord reminiscent of the reading wars a decade ago. Not surprisingly, when sweeping changes are mandated from outside a school, dissonance often follows that is long-lasting and harmful not only to students, our first priority, but to the school community or district at large. Reason is often subjugated to near-panic as decisions are made, money is encumbered, and mandates are created without anyone asking what is practical and doable with a given set of students. If ever there was a time for a calm and reasoned response to sweeping changes, it is now.

Many books have flooded the market recently offering an analysis of the standards, strategies for implementing the standards, and a Pandora's box full of secrets to mastering the CCSS. These books have a place in our professional library because without an understanding of the standards, we can't even fairly discuss them. We need appropriate strategies to help us implement the many new competencies in the standards. What we also need, however, is permission to move the students we have—not the ones we wish we had—higher up the ladder toward success in a reasonable manner rather than naively insisting that all students can and will meet a set of standards created by people who have never assessed their abilities, skills, or life circumstances.

If we envision the standards as a starting point rather than a finishing line—a goal that, in fact, may not be attainable for everyone—our

> If ever there was a time for a calm and reasoned response to sweeping changes, it is now.

expectations and blood pressure will return to a normal range. Much like the first model year of a new car, the CCSS will have kinks to be worked out, feedback to be analyzed, and maybe even a recall or two. That's the nature of anything new, and a commonsense approach involves not only examining the standards but examining the students, resources, faculty, and data that are unique to each school and district. With a picture of who we are, we can then take appropriate steps to use the standards in a way that will help us move all of our students forward instead of fearfully allowing them to push us places where we simply can't afford to go.

> A commonsense approach involves not only examining the standards but examining the students, resources, faculty, and data that are unique to each school.

Defining "Standards"

In thinking about standards, the word itself might well be the first topic for faculty or professional learning community (PLC) dialogue. Consider, for example, sharing responses to these questions:

- What is the purpose of standards?
- Generally, what are the benefits of standards? The disadvantages?
- How have standards shaped education or classroom practices in the past?
- To what extent have such standards been successful and/or unsuccessful?
- What latitude is there within any given set of standards? Within the CCSS?
- When thinking of standards in areas other than education, when are they most necessary, such as standards for constructing bridges or inspecting meat processing plants? In what areas might standards be counterproductive, such as when standards are applied to aesthetics or creativity?

Everyone may agree that standards are necessary for safety or to ensure the quality of products or processes, as in factories, but we might find some disagreement when talking about standards for education. Then again, we may have little to say about standards in general, but solidly approve of a certain standard or vehemently disapprove of a different one.

While some argue for the inherent value of standards, one of the dangers is a tendency toward "standardization" of every point on the continuum toward one commonality. This tendency was seen, for example, when Impressionist art in the late 1860s deviated from the art standards of the day with its rather "messy" style of short visible strokes that created an impression of reality rather than the accurate, lifelike paintings that defined the standard. Many Impressionist painters died under the shadow of ridicule from the standard-bearers without knowing how much their works would be valued in the future. When standards are implemented without regard for variations, we run the risk of excluding works (and people) of enormous value.

} What happens to students with limited English language skills?

The idea of creating standards that will move students toward "college and career readiness" sounds reasonable, and implementing the standards may, indeed, help the majority of students move higher on the learning continuum, but we also risk leaving behind hundreds of thousands of students who may never be able to fit the mold. These same students, however, may have much to offer the workplace, society, or their own community. So, what happens to students who come from a literacy-impoverished background, students with limited English language skills, students who are disengaged or unmotivated, students who are not able to devote the time necessary to master the CCSS, or students who see and respond to the world, like the Impressionist painters, in a different way?

Teachers all across the nation have stories of students, even capable students, who simply will not do work outside of class, refuse to read assigned texts, write as little as possible, skip school until they are on the verge of dropping out, and are not motivated by grades or other extrinsic rewards.

"My students' real lives exist outside of this building, and we are doing everything we can just to get them to show up," a high school English teacher told us recently, literally wringing her hands as she talked. "If they can make a D—and in our district, teachers aren't allowed to give a grade below a D—many of the kids are completely satisfied. Challenging text? Analyzing how an author 'draws on and transforms source material in a specific work'? Writing using precise language? *Please.*"

While it may seem that this teacher, typical of many others, is making excuses for not being able to meet the CCSS, our take is that she is overwhelmed by the vast amount that is being required of her, especially since she felt she wasn't successful *before* the CCSS were mandated. The state might as well tell her to transform her students into giraffes. She sees no way that it can possibly happen, and the discouragement that accompanies such realization contributes to the problem. To insist that all students conform to a set of standards outside their present abilities or mind-sets is to significantly reduce their chances of ever becoming college or career ready. It is a paradox that the same set of standards has the ability to stretch some students and limit others.

> It is a paradox that the same set of standards has the ability to stretch some students and limit others.

This book is about those students who *will not* or *cannot* readily adapt to the challenges inherent in the CCSS. Each chapter focuses on how to scaffold such students' learning through active and engaging, research-based practices that will help those who have not been successful in the past. As with most important documents, the CCSS have within them room for interpretation, and it is incumbent upon districts to make time for teachers to work together as they adapt the standards in light of their students' backgrounds, abilities, motivations, and learning rates.

An Introduction to the Standards

While the standards explicitly delineate goals for what students should learn, we argue that it is the spirit of that learning, not blind adherence to the standards, that should be uppermost in our practice. In the introduction to the standards, there is carefully crafted language that offers much reassurance. Unfortunately, many workshops about CCSS go directly into opening the large package of nuts and bolts before looking at what the standards are hoping to build. This picture or "vision," as the CCSS authors refer to it, emphasizes what it means to be a literate person in the 21st century, noting that such skills have wide applicability outside the classroom or workplace. Specifically:

- According to the authors, "Reading is at the heart of understanding and *enjoying* complex works of literature." The language in this sentence does not say that students should be *forced* to read complex works of literature but, rather, says that they be led to *enjoy* them. And what does "complex" mean? The ideas in Lois Lowry's *The Giver* or Veronica Roth's *Divergent* are certainly complex. Are we to jump immediately to the conclusion that "complex" means "difficult" or reading beyond the level of the reader? We suggest that the words "complex" and "challenging" need discussion among faculties before they attempt to create tasks based on the terms. Challenging text and complex works of literature can mean one thing to a proficient reader and quite another to a striving reader.

> Challenging text and complex works of literature can mean one thing to a proficient reader and quite another to a striving reader.

- Students who meet the standards "are able to pick carefully through the staggering amount of information available today in print and digitally. They seek the wide, deep and thoughtful engagement with high-quality literary and informational texts that builds knowledge, enlarges experience, and broadens worldviews." This statement rings with possibilities for engagement and implies that we have the *opportunity* to present students with a wide variety of texts, freeing us from the constraints of a single textbook series or program. It also speaks to making learning relevant and meaningful for each student.

- Students will "learn to reason in a cogent manner and use evidence that is essential to private deliberation and responsible citizenship in a democratic republic." These skills are developed over time—a lifetime, actually. The authors of the standards surely expect us to give students enough time to not only use but come to value these skills.

Important Considerations

Perhaps the most important sentence in the entire set of standards is this:

> *The standards leave room for teachers, curriculum developers, and states to determine how these goals should be reached and what additional topics should be addressed.*

The next most important may be this:

Teachers are thus free to provide students with whatever tools and knowledge their professional judgment and experience identify as most helpful for meeting the goals set out in the Standards.

While many feel they are being cookie-cut into a "standard" educator, whatever that is, or must follow lockstep through the CCSS, the intent of the standards appears to be just the opposite. It's been a long time since teachers have been encouraged to use their "professional judgment and experience" or given the freedom to do so. Administrators and district or state staff who overlook this most important directive will certainly fail to meet the inherent goals of the standards.

We appreciate the fact that the authors advocate an interdisciplinary approach to literacy and that they suggest that the standards not be seen as isolated skills. For example, the authors note that, "often, several standards can be addressed by a single rich task." The term "rich task" is especially pleasing to us because it denotes more, much more, than having students fill out worksheets, answer questions at the end of chapters, or complete the types of assignments that have caused rampant disengagement across the disciplines. The language in this section, such as "gather," "synthesize," "report," "conduct original research," and "solve problems," suggests active, innovative teaching based on inquiry—with "research and media skills" embedded. Good teachers have long been utilizing just such an approach.

Those students for whom school has been a challenge not because it was too difficult but because the test-prep culture bored them into dropping out at last have a chance to engage in learning as it should be—*if* schools embrace the introductory material of the standards as seriously as they do the rest of the document.

Using Common Sense: What Is Not Covered by the Standards

Just as a nonexample is important when defining what *is,* the information on page 6 of the CCSS is important in understanding not only the language of the standards but their intent. As the standards are evaluated and interpreted, some may take liberties in narrowing the curriculum and standardizing instructional approaches. The following items caution against that approach.

- "The standards define what all students are expected to know and be able to do, not how teachers should teach." Teachers can take heart in the fact that they can try out new practices, engage students in creative and innovative activities, and expand their teaching repertoires while still meeting the standards. Further, this first item reassures readers that the standards "do not—indeed, cannot—enumerate all or even most of the content students should learn." Those who insist that the literature exemplars, for example, or content that is mentioned in the standards should be an iron-clad part of the curriculum are simply wrong. All that is required is a "content-rich curriculum"—one that teachers should have a role in creating.

- "A great deal is left to the discretion of teachers and curriculum developers." Many teachers have told us that in the past they have been directed to spend hours engaged in test prep and have had little say in that mandate. This item seems to let teachers off the "test prep" hook. "While the Standards focus on what is most essential, they do not describe all that can or should be taught."

- The standards do not dictate the "nature of advanced work for students who meet the Standards prior to the end of high school." This item goes on to mention "literature, composition, language and journalism" as topics available to such students. One could easily infer that individually directed studies and electives such as debate, creative writing, and drama could fill this gap.

- The authors of the standards do provide flexibility in the support and intervention offered to students who are well below or well above grade level. Thankfully, they state that "no set of grade-specific standards can fully reflect the great variety in abilities, needs, learning rates, and achievement levels of students in any given classroom." That admission opens the door for students who need extra support or more challenging assignments,

> Teachers can take heart in the fact that they can engage students in creative and innovative activities while still meeting the standards.

offering an antidote to what often happens when standards are used to standardize students.

- The standards allow for accommodations for those students needing them and clearly state that the standards do not "define the full range of supports appropriate for English language learners and for students with special needs." And the authors also admit that students acquiring English do not need to display "native-like control" of conventions and vocabulary, a huge relief to teachers of students whose first language is not English.

- Lest anyone think the standards exclude affective components of learning, a last item notes that "attention to such matters as social, emotional, and physical development," especially in the early grades, is a component of the standards. The authors did not intend that PE, art, and music be eliminated from the curriculum, and districts that are considering such a move in favor of a more academic approach to schooling should think again.

> The authors of the standards do provide flexibility in the support and intervention offered to students who are well below or well above grade level.

A Portrait of a Young Student: What We Cover in This Book

Page 7 of the introduction to the CCSS offers a portrait of students who "exhibit with increasing fullness and regularity these capacities of the literate individual." In our quest to capture the spirit of the standards as well as the specifics, we've paid close attention to the characteristics of a successful student presented in this part of the document—and we've considered where students and teachers may feel challenged by these goals. These items create the skeleton on which the standards hang and, thus, provoke the questions and statements that we pose as the titles of each chapter of this book.

Below, we offer a brief overview of the chapters and our purpose for raising these eight questions and challenging statements. In the chapters themselves, however, you'll find that every discussion of these areas begins with an anecdote drawn from a real classroom and continues with practical strategies for applying the standards to our work with real students. We also include, in each chapter, a variety of material, from quotations to book lists to suggestions for classroom activities, in shaded boxes that accompany the text. We hope you'll approach each of the following areas with the understanding that the questions we pose, the statements we offer, and the practices we suggest as responses to those statements and questions all offer not absolute answers but possibilities for continual inquiry by teachers as they seek to engage and motivate students.

Chapter 1. How Do We Reach Reluctant Students?

The first characteristic of college- and career-ready students offered on page 7 of the standards states that such students "demonstrate independence." But what about students who have never learned such independence and who might not know what to do with it if it were given to them?

Students such as these often do not participate in learning because they are not engaged in that learning. In this first chapter, therefore, we introduce "Our Standards for Motivation and Engagement," which we refer back to throughout the rest of the book. In addition, we focus on creating "self-directed" learners. Teachers of reluctant learners tell us that their students lack the self-efficacy and the necessary skills to become independent or even interdependent learners. Literate individuals, according to the CCSS, have the ability to find and use resources to assist them in their tasks. Many students have become victims of "learned helplessness" as they sit in class passively, dependent upon the teacher or another student to help them complete tasks or assimilate new learning. With the standards in our back pockets, we can make conscious decisions to throw away the worksheets and help students learn how to ask relevant questions, seek clarification, and articulate their own ideas. This requires that teachers become more facilitators than instructors as they help students move toward independence by utilizing practices that foster the engagement that can lead to self-direction and self-efficacy—the belief that one can accomplish a task and the determination to do so. While this will be a new way of working with such students, it is foundational in meeting the standards.

{ Teachers of reluctant learners tell us that their students lack the self-efficacy and the necessary skills to become independent or even interdependent learners.

Chapter 2. Why Scaffolding Complex Text Is Crucial

This second characteristic in the CCSS introduction's portrait of a college- and career-ready student describes one who is actively learning in order to "build strong content knowledge"—researching, speaking, listening, writing, and reading purposefully. It does not describe a student who takes notes as the teacher lectures, simply watches a PowerPoint, or reads an assignment for the sole purpose of answering questions from a textbook. In this chapter we look at scaffolding as a way to build content knowledge and skills. We also discuss text complexity and what it means for learners who are not yet able to unlock difficult complex text. It is telling that this item is written not to suggest that the *teacher* build strong content knowledge for the student but to require that *students* do the building. This, too, may require a shift in practice for many teachers of striving learners.

Chapter 3. How Do We Engage *All* Students in Reading and Writing?

In many schools of the 20th century, students completed an assignment for the purpose of having the teacher, usually as the only audience, read it, evaluate it, and post a grade. Because the technology-based, global communication of the 21st century requires an entirely new way of looking at classroom tasks, the third characteristic of a successful student presented in the CCSS introduction notes that such a student responds "to the varying demands of audience, task, purpose, and discipline." Students must now take into account not only various audiences beyond the teacher but how their goals and strategies for communication will vary according to the audience, especially when writing or speaking. When writing, they must also consider how to use language correctly and appropriately, as literate individuals do. Helping students communicate through reading, writing, speaking, and listening is the job of each teacher in a school where everyone works together to build the literacy skills of *all* students. This chapter provides engaging practices that create opportunities for students to interact with readers, writers, and peers as they use literacy skills for a variety of tasks.

Chapter 4. How to Go Deeper: Creating Analytical Thinkers

The focus on comprehension presented by the CCSS introduction, which suggests that students "comprehend as well as critique," is not new. Reading strategies abound in books, articles, webinars, conferences, and in-service workshops, but we have come to realize that the act of comprehending, especially comprehending complex text, is not as simple as applying a strategy. Additionally, current thinking advocates replacing one set of skills that students use ubiquitously across the disciplines with instruction regarding reading and writing *within* the disciplines. Students must learn how to use literacy skills unique to science, social studies, English, and math and, at the same time, understand how such skills are related.

The introduction of critique also brings to the table a new way of looking at comprehension and analysis. While we have always paid lip service to "thinking critically," the 21st century definition includes critical literacy, a type of literacy where students understand how language is used to accomplish social ends. Students who engage in critique see literacy as more than just decoding a text or gaining surface understanding of the author's ideas. Critical literacy reshapes comprehension as a tool for understanding nuances of meaning and interpretation. Thus, students must learn to read and research as skeptics, question the author's assumptions, and assess the veracity of claims. As they present their research and arguments in written or oral form, they reinforce the skills they learned while reading thoughtfully and critically.

Once again, the CCSS introduction paints a portrait of a student who reads actively with individual purposes instead of scanning merely for information or to answer questions. Unfortunately, many striving learners are victims of the beliefs by educators that they must first be able to read on "grade level" before reading critically. Striving learners who engage in critical literacy deepen comprehension of all texts and, more importantly, become empowered as readers. Chapter 4 offers suggestions for teaching critical literacy, deep comprehension, and argumentative writing.

> Students must learn how to use literacy skills unique to science, social studies, English, and math and, at the same time, understand how such skills are related.

Chapter 5. Why Evidence Matters: From Text to Talk to Argument

The fifth characteristic of college- and career-ready students, according to the introduction, is that "they value evidence." Students love to prove their points as they argue persuasively, often with the goal of leaving those who disagree in the dust. Teachers can use students' inherent love of argument to teach them how to use evidence in all aspects of their academic and social lives. As they read informational text, they will evaluate claims that are presented in terms of validity and sound reasoning. They will also learn how to use evidence in speaking and writing to support assumptions, make points, and bolster arguments. This chapter offers activities that will help students see evidence as something that can be useful and relevant rather than as a box of dry facts dropped into an assignment in order to meet their teachers' requirements. Students who learn to use evidence in meaningful ways discover the intrinsic value in it.

> These activities will help students see evidence as something that can be useful and relevant rather than as a box of dry facts dropped into an assignment in order to meet their teachers' requirements.

Chapter 6. How Using Diverse Media and Formats Can Ignite Student Learning

In the past, teachers have had to drag striving readers to the textbook and often end up reading the text to students, many of whom seem incapable of making their fingers turn a single page. Now, the same content that was "boring" in print is suddenly engaging in a digital format. This is perhaps the one area where intrinsic motivation is built into the goal of the standards, expressed in the introduction as the ability to "use technology and digital media strategically"; all we need to do is help students *learn* how to use this media strategically. That means rethinking how to implant technology into our daily classroom practices as an integral tool of learning.

This chapter will help teachers use the tools of technology and digital media to infuse literacy in all its forms—reading, writing, researching, speaking, and listening—into presentations and projects that deal with inquiry and essential questions, thus heightening student engagement and building independence.

Chapter 7. Why a Culture of Reading Is Critical—and How to Create One

The idea of creating a culture of reading brings joy to the hearts of English language arts teachers everywhere, especially when they read the following sentence that may epitomize their belief about literature: "Through reading great classic and contemporary works of literature representative of a variety of periods, cultures, and worldviews, students can vicariously inhabit worlds and have experiences much different than their own." Yes, the standards do dictate that content-area teachers in upper grades use informational text more than fiction, but this element clearly shows the CCSS value literature, both classic and contemporary, and see it as an essential resource for helping students become responsible and sensitive citizens in a world of increasing divergence. In this last chapter, we provide examples of how texts can be used to foster deeper understanding of other perspectives and cultures through inquiry and literature circles as well as through independent reading. There are also tips for creating text sets, classroom libraries, and environments that allow students to "vicariously inhabit worlds and have experiences much different than their own" as the last descriptor of successful students suggests they should.

Chapter 8. What Do We Do About the Language Standards?

The seven characteristics of successful students we address above, those outlined on page 7 of the introduction to the CCSS, mention language and conventions in passing. There is not a specific description related to language, nor should there necessarily be one—we believe that conventions are one tool students use to communicate and think deeply, not an end in themselves. Yet the presence of the language standards in the CCSS demands our consideration. How do we teach to and with these standards? What do we know about grammar and vocabulary instruction? In this final chapter, we discuss the need for integrated and engaging instruction in these areas that allows teachers to support students as they make progress toward the characteristics we've discussed here.

Keeping the End in Mind

ReLeah once knew a kid who was a promising soccer player. In the "standards" of soccer he had mastered every competency and, what's more, he could demonstrate proficiency. The summer of his sophomore year, right before he was to go to soccer camp, however, he announced to his parents that he was quitting the team—dropping out. His parents tried to get him to reconsider, but he was adamant. During hours of discussion, they came to understand—and to help him understand—why he had made that decision and what had prompted it.

The coach had failed to keep the end in mind. His unilateral focus on achieving the skills of the game without a great deal of regard for the "human" side of the sport left the boy feeling that his accomplishments had no real intrinsic value. He had mastered the discrete skills necessary to become a solidly good player, but the camaraderie so important in any team sport was missing, and he couldn't shake the feeling that the time he spent in practice wasn't relevant to his "real" life. His original purpose for playing soccer—not only to learn how to play, but also to enjoy the sport, develop relationships with other athletes, and feel good about his abilities—had somehow been subjugated to simply winning. Further, it seemed to him that no matter what he accomplished, it was never good enough; he felt he was always just under the mark no matter how hard he tried. In pushing for excellence, his coach had failed to give this boy the autonomy he needed to grow as an athlete and as a person.

In discussing this unfortunate scenario, we become concerned that in our push to have students "master the standards," we may lose those students altogether, especially those for whom school has never been easy. In the end, it isn't most important that students "analyze how and why individuals, events, and ideas develop and interact over the course of a text" or that they "determine or clarify the meaning of unknown and multiple-meaning words and phrases." What *is* extremely important is that students learn how to be productive, responsible, and literate citizens who come to see education as a valuable stepping-stone to all of life's endeavors. If we use the standards to win the game at any cost, we may well see an increase in dropout rates and a widening of the achievement gap as many students, especially those on the precipice, come to disdain education rather than value its usefulness and take pleasure in its offerings.

As we turn this next corner in American schooling, we must not lose this opportunity to redefine how we will help those students who are most at risk. In the end, however, it is not the standards that will make a difference; it is the vast expertise and solid common sense of educators who know their craft, care about their students, and are willing to take on the hard work of change that will increase learning for *all* students.

Acknowledgments

The authors wish to thank photographers Leigh Northrup and Lee Travis for supplying many of the photographs that appear in this book. We also thank the students of Cannon School and Hutchison School for their assistance, as well as Jennifer Futrell and Alicia Quattlebaum for providing access to anchor charts, classroom libraries, and other classroom features.

Numerous teachers shared classroom activities that we describe in the text, including Ivy Phillips, Amy Lawrence, Chaney Cruze, Dr. Matthew Rush, Pam Ayers, Susan Kelly, and Nick Yeager. We are also grateful to teachers at Asheville Middle School, particularly Amanda Swartzlander, Jeff Dewhirst, and Carrie Buchanan who allowed us access to their classrooms and shared not only their students but their ideas. We also acknowledge the contributions of their principal, Cynthia Sellinger, and instructional coach, Melissa Hedt, who paved the way for our visits and helped us learn about the value of Paideia seminars.

Our brilliant editor, Lisa Luedeke, oversaw this project from conception to publication, and we thank her for her insightful suggestions and commitment to students. We also thank Maura Sullivan for her creative contributions to this book (such as the title!) as well as the other top-notch professionals at Corwin who made the process enjoyable and efficient: Julie Nemer, Francesca Dutra Africano, Melinda Birdsall, and Melinda Masson, copy editor.

1 How Do We Reach Reluctant Students?

> Students can, without significant scaffolding, comprehend and evaluate complex texts across a range of types and disciplines, and they can construct effective arguments and convey intricate or multifaceted information. Likewise, students are able independently to discern a speaker's key points, request clarification, and ask relevant questions. They build on others' ideas, articulate their own ideas, and confirm they have been understood. More broadly, they become self-directed learners.
>
> —Description of College- and Career-Ready Students, CCSS Introduction

Let's begin with the story of an actual student—we'll call him Daniel. An eighth grader whom Barry taught early in his career, Daniel arrived in Barry's classroom each day focused not on what he would learn but on how he could get through the day without trouble until the final bell rang and he could finally get on to basketball practice.

Daniel also fit the profile of a reluctant learner squarely. He wrote poorly and spoke with little command of formal English—but when he cared about a subject, he could show insight and depth in his

© yellowdog/cultura/Corbis

thinking. He read with alarming difficulty, rarely finishing (or even starting) reading assignments. Between daily basketball practice, helping his single mother care for three younger siblings, and a daily homework load he never managed well, Daniel started the year behind and never fully caught up. Daniel's highest aspiration was simply to *pass* English

Common Core and Common Sense: What Do We Do About the Exemplar Texts?

Examining Appendix B of the CCSS is something like knowingly walking into a minefield. This appendix contains the exemplar texts both for language arts and for content-area classes, along with a few general teaching ideas, or "performance tasks," as samples.

So what's wrong with that? In one sense, it's a great resource. Anyone reading the standards would naturally wonder what "complex literary and informational texts" (R.10) might be; it's good to have an example. On the other hand, the exemplar texts strike many teachers as beyond the scope of their students, more a reflection of a traditional canon than a relevant and engaging textual landscape, or just plain hard to teach.

The first paragraph of Appendix B, of course, is crucial; it states explicitly that the reading selections "expressly do not represent a partial or complete reading list" (p. 2). That's not always how this addition to the standards is interpreted, however. We've heard of teachers who have been forced to teach the works in the appendix or who have been forbidden to teach a work in ninth grade that's labeled in Appendix B as a sample text for Grades 6–8.

Our position on Appendix B is simple, and we believe it aligns with the intentions of the CCSS. The exemplar texts are just that: examples. They offer guideposts, not destinations. Throughout this book, therefore, while we'll occasionally refer to these texts, we'll far more often offer lists of relevant and engaging works that we have found appeal to learners of all types. We encourage teachers and principals to work together to formulate their own such lists of highly involving texts that are appropriately challenging for the learners in the classroom—texts that offer both the chance for students to stretch and learn and opportunities for success.

in eighth grade so that he could play sports and please his demanding mother, but he was as happy with a grade of D as an A if it would allow him to remain on the basketball court.

Understanding Reluctance: Why Daniel Struggled

If we're going to understand both how challenging and how rewarding it can be to align the expectations of the Common Core State Standards (CCSS) with our real work in the classroom, we must understand what makes a student such as Daniel reluctant to learn in the first place. Daniel was so far away from the skills of constructing "effective arguments" and conveying "multifaceted information" described in the introduction to the standards (see the opening quotation for the entire description) that Barry, as a young teacher, hardly knew where to begin. What's more, Daniel wasn't the only struggling learner in his class; he was one of several such students Barry wanted to reach—and that was just in one of Barry's five sections of eighth-grade English.

Close to the start of the school year, for instance, Barry asked the class to write a response to the Robert Frost poem "The Road Not Taken" (one of the illustrative texts for Grades 6–8 suggested by the Common Core).

First, the class spent a period discussing the poem, examining details and what might be inferred from them. The discussion was lively, but Daniel remained silent throughout it. The next day, Barry allowed around 30 minutes in class for each student to write an interpretation of the poem's final stanza using evidence from throughout the work. Barry knew students in the school had completed similar writing at the end of seventh grade, and he meant for the assignment to yield formative impressions of each student's writing ability. Here, however, is the entirety of Daniel's response:

> *Robert Frost poem talk about two roads that meet in a forest. The poem mostly says he is standing there thinking. He don't know which road to take. Frost poem at last makes a choice. He take the road less travelled. Then he is happy with his choice.*

Barry thought long and hard about how to respond to Daniel's paragraph (many of his students had produced at least a page in response to the assignment). He even pulled Daniel aside between classes before he tackled grading the paragraph and asked Daniel why he hadn't written more.

Daniel shrugged. "I didn't have nothin' else to say," he answered.

"Do you remember the discussion we had in class?" Barry asked. "Can you think of any details from the poem that would explain the choice you're writing about?"

Daniel just shrugged again. "I don't know," he said.

Later in the year, with several writing assignments to refer to, Barry would see that Daniel regularly wrote as little as he thought he could get away with. Like many students, Daniel saw writing in school as a task rather than a skill, as a chore to complete for a grade rather than a path to learning or self-expression. He supposedly revised his writing when it was required of him (really, he merely corrected at a minimal level), but he did not develop cognitive strategies as a result of that revision. He was focused, at best, on an extrinsic reward—playing basketball, getting his teacher and his mother off his back—and not at all on the process.

At first, however, Barry missed the real issue with Daniel's writing. He honed in on development and mechanical errors and wrote a lovely paragraph as feedback explaining the importance of these areas of writing. He conferenced with Daniel in class later that week and focused mainly on issues of length and structure, trying to help Daniel find more to write about, to draw out intellectual ideas from a student who really wasn't interested in the poem intellectually. In short, he focused on Daniel's writing skills, but not on whether or not he cared.

What Barry didn't comprehend, at first, was that at the core of Daniel's underperformance wasn't a problem with writing at all—it was a problem with learning.

Active Learning: The Student as Center

If we were to boil all of the research, thinking, and change in pedagogy over the past few decades down to a single, simple truth, it would

> Like many students, Daniel saw writing in school as a task rather than a skill, as a chore to complete for a grade rather than a path to learning or self-expression.

probably be this: Students learn best when they are both motivated and active. Our use of the word "active" here, of course, is not limited to physical movement; we're referring to participation and involvement of all kinds. A student who is taking notes rather than simply listening to a lecture might be described as active, but a student who shares her own ideas about a text in a classroom discussion, who presents her thinking formally in front of a class, or who teaches another student a skill is far more active. It's important to remember, of course, that activity alone does not equate to learning (confusing the two is a mistake that can lead, at its worst, to what might be termed "poster peril"— interminable classroom craft projects without substantial learning outcomes). Yet active involvement, coupled with caring about material, is still a key to greater learning.

A classroom that offers activity and increases motivation places the student at the center of learning. Teachers in such classrooms are guides. They may occasionally deliver content in a traditional lecture format, but more often, their classrooms include elements that draw students in and allow them to take an operational role in learning.

Below are 10 areas of student learning that we believe are crucial to any classroom. You are probably familiar with the four main areas of the language arts standards in the Common Core: reading, writing, speaking and listening, and language. Think of these standards as a fifth area—in addition to content-specific skills, every teacher should strive to include what we'll call "Standards for Motivation and Engagement."

Clearly, this isn't a list of learning goals that you achieve by handing out stacks of worksheets. These elements require teachers to involve students throughout a class period in substantive activity. They reflect the need for a teacher's work to involve planning classroom activity as much as or more than classroom content.

Indeed, we believe that these 10 areas of student engagement are so crucial to reaching all learners—and disengaged or reluctant learners in particular— that whenever a particular activity or approach in this book exemplifies one of these 10 goals, we'll mark it with an arrow in the margin, like the one shown in the margin here. We hope that in this way, you'll see that many classroom strategies, including those that many language arts teachers

> Activity alone does not equate to learning. Yet active involvement, coupled with caring about material, is still a key to greater learning.

Our Standards for Motivation and Engagement

Learning Goal	Standard
Active learning	Students interact with material in ways that provoke critical thinking and questioning.
Autonomy	Students' encounters with choice and opportunities for input increase their interest and create a sense of control over their own learning.
Relevance	Students form bridges and connections to content even when it seems, at first, distant from their own lives.
Collaboration	Learning takes place in pairs and groups in which multiple participants and points of view are engaged.
Technology use	Students use technology not as a toy or distraction but as a tool to increase learning opportunities and to increase depth of study.
Multiple learning methods	Students encounter material in a variety of ways that increase "stickiness," appeal to various learning preferences, and connect disciplines.
Challenge and success	When learning, all students feel both challenged and successful in ways that increase self-efficacy.
Differentiation and scaffolding	Instruction is individualized, builds upon prior knowledge, and is carefully structured so that each student learns deeply and at an appropriate pace for the class and material.
Inquiry	Assignments and topics promote a sense of curiosity and a love of learning through problem solving and open-ended questioning.
Feedback	A variety of assessments (formative, summative, and self-directed) and a variety of timely responses (conferences, rubrics, written comments, and peer feedback) ensure that student learning capitalizes on strengths, limits or corrects weaknesses, and motivates ongoing learning.

have been employing for years, can both meet the standards and engage students. The standards, we believe, don't demand an entirely new definition of good teaching; rather, they demand that we pay attention to the outcomes of what good teachers have always done and continue to do.

Unfortunately, it may sometimes seem to teachers that they're not trusted to create the sort of active learning environment that is conducive to greater engagement. Instead, districts or principals, concerned about accountability, may prescribe programs and curricula in an attempt to make all teaching uniform. They may unwittingly push teachers toward the opposite of a student-centered approach. At their worst, they may mandate strategies that pretend to create a student-centered environment but that, because they dictate to teachers how a "student-centered" environment should come about, create just the opposite effect: a fear-based teaching system in which teachers rush to cover content and lose their own motivation.

The good news is that the language of the Common Core, in many ways, supports a student-centered environment. The CCSS do not, after all, tell teachers *how* to help students reach the benchmarks they identify. They do not prescribe curricula or particular approaches to teaching, nor do they demand, for the most part, that certain texts or content take precedence over others, even if they do provide *examples* of texts. The standards focus, instead, on skills, and in many places they even seem to privilege the sort of active learning that is suggested by our list.

One thing of which we can be absolutely sure is that rote learning and study drills by themselves will not lead to the sort of learning that inspires motivation and engagement from otherwise disengaged students. It may be tempting, as state tests loom closer or as accountability for scores increases, to veer toward coverage rather than the practice of skills, to hope students memorize enough to pass the test. But even if this approach worked for some students (and we don't believe, in the long run, that it does), struggling learners are precisely those for whom such classroom strategies have failed. Prior failure in settings where they are expected to memorize, repeat, and mimic without feeling any value or appreciation for the material they're learning is what can create a sense of learned helplessness in such students.

The Need for Self-Efficacy: A Key to Turning Daniel's Reluctance Around

Remember our initial description of Daniel? His only motivation was external. He just wanted to get through the day. He was not invested in

> Rote learning and study drills by themselves will not lead to the sort of learning that inspires motivation and engagement from otherwise disengaged students.

his own learning or achievement, and he didn't really seem to believe he was capable of learning.

The research on struggling learners—students such as Daniel—outlines a downward spiral rather than a journey. Especially in classrooms that don't emphasize the 10 areas of learning we outline in our additional standards, less motivated and less interested students such as Daniel can find themselves suffering through school year after year rather than enjoying it, experiencing repeated failure and a lack of connection to school material. This lack of connection lowers their motivation further and causes them to fail further—and to expect failure as a matter of course.

Who Are Our Struggling Learners?

What do we know about reluctant and disengaged learners? In particular, students who struggle in school:

- May be motivated externally but not internally (S. Ivey & Guthrie, 2008).

- Come to learning with an expectation of failure and a low sense of self-efficacy, or the belief that they can succeed in school (Margolis & McCabe, 2004).

- Feel that they have no power over their own learning or what happens in the classroom (Henry, Castek, O'Byrne, & Zawilinski, 2012).

- Exhibit lower self-control in their work habits (Tangney, Baumeister, & Boone, 2004).

- Often struggle as a result of socioeconomic, cultural, and learning differences between their out-of-school (home) environment and the world of school (Dressman, Wilder, & Connor, 2005).

- Avoid deep thinking or challenging cognitive processes (S. Ivey & Guthrie, 2008).

- May have developed general comprehension strategies but not the specialized strategies, vocabulary, and knowledge base for complex texts (Lee & Spratley, 2010).

This list of characteristics provides a sharp contrast to the profile of a college- and career-ready student as provided by the Common Core introduction. If you teach struggling learners, this might sound like familiar territory. But wait: Let's also not forget some of the most promising information we know about *all* adolescent learners, including those who struggle:

- All students spend time engaged in literacy both in and out of school, although those literacy practices may look different from formal work and include exposure to words through sources as diverse as magazines, graffiti, the Internet, and popular fiction (J. Gallagher, 2012).

  MULTIPLE LEARNING METHODS

- Struggling learners—and others—show increased motivation when their literacy experiences include peer interaction and reading as a social activity (Henry et al., 2012).

  COLLABORATION

- Given greater access to books, reluctant readers will often read more (Krashen, 2009).

- For at-risk students, active participation in learning can increase resilience and engagement and lower academic risk (Borman & Rachuba, 2001).

  ACTIVE LEARNING

- Relationships with teachers matter: In one study, middle school students with high levels of teacher support were almost 3 times as likely as their counterparts to have high levels of engagement in learning and were 74% less likely to feel disengaged (Klem & Connell, 2004).

  CHALLENGE AND SUCCESS

All of these facts offer guidance that could be useful in reaching students who seem not to want to learn. Translated into classroom practice, these characteristics of struggling learners offer the clear conclusion that merely suggesting to students that they focus on using correct verb forms or include more details in their writing will not engender long-term academic success. What students need, first, is a sense of ownership, motivation, and purpose. They need a *reason to learn*.

RELEVANCE

For a student such as Daniel, external motivation (basketball or his mother) may provide a valuable entry point for a teacher in efforts

Photographed by Comstock

to stop or reverse the downward trend. But when a student loses both external *and* internal motivation, the teacher's job—to engage that student in learning—is not just difficult; it may seem nearly impossible. Engagement in literacy, in particular, drops as students grow older, with many adolescents gradually becoming less and less connected to words and language as they move up from grade level to grade level.

How do we get such students to learn at all, much less to meet the demanding and expansive standards presented in the Common Core?

Even with our new 10 standards for engagement, there's no silver bullet, of course—no magical ingredient that suddenly engages a student in learning and makes standards instantly easy to meet. Still, consider the assignment Daniel completed in our earlier example. How actively involved was he? His initial essay response may have looked different, for instance, if he had:

ACTIVE LEARNING

SCAFFOLDING

AUTONOMY

RELEVANCE

- Played a key role in a small group discussion about the poem.

- Used a graphic organizer or another note system to organize his thoughts about the discussion before writing.

- Described his own plan for writing the essay to a partner or his teacher.

- Written about an aspect of the poem that he felt connected to or was curious about.

Any of these small steps might have helped Daniel feel a sense of success and self-efficacy. They might have drawn him into the assignment just a bit more.

Getting a student such as Daniel interested in reading and writing, much less meeting the Common Core State Standards, can seem daunting. After all, the teachers of students who are already college and career ready, those who are interested and eager to learn, often don't need a list of standards to tell them what their students need to learn. Teachers of reluctant learners, on the other hand, can find the sheer number and breadth of standards their students still need to reach overwhelming. But we believe, at heart, that most students ultimately find active learning—when it leads to success, when it is manageable, and when it seems relevant and meaningful—to be enjoyable.

We can't claim, unfortunately, that Daniel ultimately achieved a remarkable breakthrough moment that changed the course of his learning entirely. There were successes—along with numerous failures—during Barry's attempts to reach Daniel. But there *were* successes, and those successes may serve as a road map for thinking about getting disengaged learners more involved in their own learning.

Daniel's Struggles: Initial Strategies That Failed

Daniel fell further and further behind in his reading and writing as his eighth-grade year progressed. When the class read Walter Dean Myers's *Monster,* a work Barry thought might particularly appeal to Daniel, he nonetheless struggled in class and abandoned any real attempts to read the novel as homework. His first encounter with Shakespeare through *A Midsummer Night's Dream* (very possibly an overly ambitious reading selection for eighth grade, though there were students in Barry's class who enjoyed it) was nothing short of disastrous. In further conferencing with Barry, he politely agreed to work harder on his writing but then showed almost no actual development or increased effort from assignment to assignment.

Consider, for instance, a specific standard, one focusing on revision in writing at the eighth-grade level, and how Barry's efforts—and Daniel's motivation and engagement with material—did and did not matter. The standard suggests that eighth graders should:

> With some guidance and support from peers and adults, develop and strengthen writing as needed by planning, revising, editing, rewriting, or trying a new approach, focusing on how well purpose and audience have been addressed. (W.8.5)

Notice the all-important word "some" in this standard; while the standards recognize that guidance and support are necessary in the learning

We believe, at heart, that most students ultimately find active learning—when it leads to success, when it is manageable, and when it seems relevant and meaningful—to be enjoyable.

> While the standards recognize that guidance and support are necessary in the learning process, they also anticipate a level of self-government from students.

process, they also anticipate a level of self-government from students as they revise. But Daniel showed little of this ability to self-direct. Left to his own devices, he would change a few verb endings or spell the name of an author correctly in a second draft—then go on to make exactly the same mistakes the next time around. And many of the traditional revision activities Barry used with the class seemed to have very little effect with Daniel. He would dutifully, for instance, color-code every verb in a page of his writing, but when Barry asked for a second draft with only verbs improved, a technique that often strengthened the writing of other students, Daniel's work came back (if he turned it in at all) with *more* errors than it had the first time and little improvement in word choice. Late in the year, when Barry had the class insert quotations into an essay, despite a class of practice on how to smoothly integrate evidence into writing, Daniel turned in a very short response that included this scanty paragraph:

> *In MDSN Lysander quote "The course of true love never did run smooth" is based on real life situation. There are many ways such as: confusing, hurt, and happiness. Those are the things people that love go through. Lysander quote also applies to Midsummer night because even though it has a happy ending and deals with magical things, they still went through things to get what they wanted.*

Again, as tempting as it was for Barry to focus first on fixing the obvious needs Daniel displayed—syntax or even just getting the title correct, for instance—the more pervasive issue was that Daniel fundamentally didn't care whether he improved this paragraph or not. He got it on paper. Enough.

Daniel's Success: Strategies That Worked

By spring of Daniel's eighth-grade year, Barry wasn't certain he'd helped Daniel move much further along from the point where he entered the grade. Then things changed. To understand how, let's look at several steps of a process of learning that unfolded naturally and fortuitously late in the year:

Step 1: Harnessing Daniel's Interest

Daniel exhibited every sign of learned helplessness and a lack of self-efficacy—instead, he seemed to harbor the belief that, ultimately, he was doomed to fail in school. His encounters with class texts regularly reinforced this sense of impotence. While some of his classmates read books both in class and on their own, Daniel rarely read at all.

One initial moment of excitement came, however, near the end of the year, not in English class but in social studies, where Daniel encountered the Holocaust for the first time. At lunch one day, his social studies teacher mentioned how interested he'd become. Daniel's other teachers were skeptical; certainly none of them would have predicted this area of fascination. Later, in class, Barry asked Daniel why his study of the Holocaust had gripped him in this way.

"I guess it's cause they're real people," Daniel answered. "It ain't made-up stories like the ones we read. These stories matter."

RELEVANCE

"Have you been reading the stories of actual Holocaust survivors?" Barry asked.

Daniel shrugged. "Some. They're pretty good."

A few days later, Daniel made a B+ on a social studies quiz. It proved to be just the lever his teachers needed. It wasn't, in fact, the first time Daniel's interest had sparked better work from him; an earlier piece exploring his personal feelings about a Michael Jordan Nike commercial had been his longest piece of writing yet, though it was still riddled with mechanical errors, and a group presentation on a poem had gotten him moderately involved. But this was something new: Daniel was showing interest in a new, academic topic, and that interest was translating into academic success. His teachers did not want to let the opportunity slip by.

Barry and the social studies teacher pulled Daniel aside between classes. Daniel, clearly nervous at speaking with two adults at once, fidgeted.

"We want you to know that this quiz was fantastic," the social studies teacher said. "Not just because of the grade, but because you really show that you understand the material."

FEEDBACK

Daniel's eyes got a bit wider.

BOOKS

Books for Connecting Language Arts and Social Studies

Throughout this book, we'll offer lists of recent books that we believe will both engage and challenge adolescent readers of all reading levels. This list and those that follow aren't meant to be comprehensive; rather, they offer additional resources to the teacher looking to enrich a classroom with books that will work in literature circles, classroom libraries, and personal choice reading assignments. The list below, in particular, reflects books that language arts and social studies teachers might use to connect their curricula—as Barry did with Daniel's social studies teacher.

The Astonishing Life of Octavian Nothing, Traitor to the Nation: Volume I: The Pox Party and ***The Astonishing Life of Octavian Nothing: Traitor to the Nation, Volume II: Kingdom on the Waves*** by M. T. Anderson

This series, set in Revolutionary Boston, shows the paradox of patriots battling to win their freedom from an oppressor while African slaves remain in captivity. Both novels are complex texts and will require scaffolding for struggling readers, but students find the plot mesmerizing, and teachers value the realistic setting and events.

Between Shades of Gray by Ruta Sepetys

Many students think of the Holocaust as set in only Poland and Germany, but as Sepetys shows in this novel, those in other countries also suffered. In this riveting and disturbing story, a 15-year-old Lithuanian girl and her family are separated from their father and taken to a Siberian work camp where they struggle to survive. This beautifully written novel will help students understand the magnitude and cruelty of the Holocaust.

Bomb: The Race to Build—and Steal—the World's Most Dangerous Weapon by Steve Sheinkin

This may be a nonfiction title, but it reads like an exciting spy thriller. The creation of the atomic bomb was an event that began in 1938 in a German laboratory and continued into the desert of Los Alamos, New Mexico, with many unexpected events along the way. Readers will gain a clear understanding of World War II and experience quality writing, too.

A Break With Charity: A Story About the Salem Witch Trials by Ann Rinaldi

This engaging historical fiction is one of many by Rinaldi, author of works on such notable figures as Mary Lincoln and Phillis Wheatley. All of her books are well researched and introduce students to the history of the United States through interesting characters and engaging plots.

Chains and *Forge* by Laurie Halse Anderson

This well-researched series, set in the Revolutionary War era, is a perfect fit for social studies and English classes. The narrative is compelling and the characters complex, but the setting is what makes these novels perfect for the classroom. Students will learn about the Revolutionary War, the plight of slaves during this time, and the nuances of freedom.

Claudette Colvin: Twice Toward Justice by Phillip Hoose

Hoose, an award-winning author, explores the true story of Claudette Colvin, a teenager who lived in Montgomery, Alabama, during the Jim Crow segregation. When she refused to give up her seat to a white woman on a city bus in 1955, she found herself shunned by her community. She later became a plaintiff in a lawsuit that changed segregation laws forever. Primary documents such as photographs and interviews enhance this remarkable story.

Hitler Youth and *The Boy Who Dared* by Susan Campbell Bartoletti

Bartoletti's nonfiction account of the Hitler Youth phenomenon, appropriately titled *Hitler Youth: Growing Up in Hitler's Shadow*, will provide students with detailed background about Hitler's propaganda campaign and the part Germany's youth played in the Holocaust. In her novel *The Boy Who Dared*, Bartoletti imagines "what if" and puts her answer in a powerful book about a German boy who discovers the truth about Hitler.

T4 by Ann Clare LeZotte

Thirteen-year-old Paula Becker, who is deaf, is targeted for Hitler's T4 program where doctors euthanize the mentally ill and disabled as "unfit to live." This harrowing story of a young girl who is forced to leave her loving family to keep from being a victim of the T4 program engages reluctant readers with its first-person, free verse poems.

Titanic: Voices From the Disaster by Deborah Hopkinson

English teachers will love these compelling stories from *Titanic* disaster survivors and witnesses, and social studies teachers will appreciate the meticulous research Hopkinson has put into making this a fresh take on an oft-told story.

Words in the Dust by Trent Reedy

If your students liked *Shabanu: Daughter of the Wind* by Suzanne Staples, they will want to read this novel about the life of a young girl in Afghanistan after the Taliban have been defeated. Her dream is to have her cleft palate corrected, but life is not easy in this war-ravaged country. *Words in the Dust* is a perfect novel for interdisciplinary study. Other excellent novels for adolescents set in Afghanistan during and after the Taliban's reign include Deborah Ellis's *The Breadwinner* and N. H. Senzai's *Shooting Kabul*.

"We're going to do a crossover activity where we look at a piece of Holocaust writing in English class," Barry said. "We're going to be in groups of four, with a discussion leader for each group. Since you're doing so well with this unit, I want to give you the piece in advance and let you lead the discussion in one group. What do you think? All you need to do is read it and come up with two or three good questions—I'll supply the rest."

DIFFERENTIATION

Daniel warily agreed and said little, but that night both teachers received an email from his mother: Daniel, she said, had read the piece with her and asked for help coming up with questions. She was elated.

Note the parameters for Daniel's success: The gains could be modest, the goals reachable. Daniel did not need to do a great deal of extra work—two or three questions only on a short passage—and he was given the opportunity to come to class feeling prepared rather than surprised by material. This activity focused most on engendering a *feeling* of success. It was also about providing Daniel the appropriate tools to achieve success in class and to continue his success in follow-up work.

SCAFFOLDING

CHALLENGE AND SUCCESS

Step 2: Drawing Daniel Into the Class

Daniel didn't turn into a model student overnight, but he did perform adequately in the group discussion on a selection from *Night* by Elie Wiesel the next day. He led off the discussion with a straightforward question about the passage ("Why do you think Elie didn't react more when he was separated from his mother?") and quickly ran through the three questions he'd prepared before moving on to those supplied for the whole class.

COLLABORATION

After the class, Barry praised Daniel's participation and asked him how he thought things went.

FEEDBACK

"I guess it was OK," Daniel said. "I can do better next time."

Daniel's progress, modest as it was, was still progress. What's more, Daniel was making progress in more than one area of the standards at the same time. This is a central, crucial truth about the standards and student-centered teaching: When students are engaged by activity, they will in turn engage texts and topics in multiple ways.

Michelle Fine on Speaking and Listening

Michelle Fine (1988) points out how seldom reluctant learners encounter encouragement to discuss and talk in class; low-income students in particular, she notes, including many minority students, are more predisposed to and work stronger in groups, but schools pathologize these strengths by making them seem inimical to the work that excellent students should do:

> "Smart kids" get to participate; "remedial kids" get to memorize. "Smart kids" work in groups; "remedial kids" are accused of cheating. "Smart kids" are creative; "remedial kids" are right or wrong. When I interviewed high-school dropouts about their educational biographies, a number responded similarly to my question, "When you were younger, were you the kind of kid who participated in class a lot?" It took three independent responses for me to understand: "Not me. I was a good kid." (p. 95)

How we teach students to think about talk may thus determine the experience they have with talk; struggling students may struggle more with speaking in class because we've told them not to. If we wish to capitalize on the best benefits of having students such as Daniel speak, we need to give them practice, and that's what the Common Core speaking and listening standards aim to suggest. Get kids talking, and the classroom may get loud—but sometimes, learning is just noisy.

The speaking and listening standards are roughly divided into two sections—discussion and presentation—but in reality, they encourage us to focus on multiple approaches to student learning that mirror the active learning we've emphasized in this chapter: communication skills, collaboration, discussion, debate, presentation, and critical analysis of technology and media. Most of all, however, they encourage students to "probe," "reflect," "pose questions," and "engage" through talk—the very elements of learning that lead to more excitement about topics and texts.

We'll discuss the speaking and listening standards throughout this book; though a high-stakes test may not specifically reflect achievement in the areas of speaking and listening, we encourage you to remember how integral the results of a classroom that engages students through talk can be to all aspects of student learning.

When Daniel participated in the group discussion, for instance, the Common Core didn't yet exist. If the standards had existed, Barry might have recognized that Daniel had taken a step toward meeting the speaking and listening standards, which call specifically for eighth-grade students to:

> Engage effectively in a range of collaborative discussions (one-on-one, in groups, and teacher-led) with diverse partners on *grade 8 topics, texts, and issues,* building on others' ideas and expressing their own clearly. (SL.8.1)

INQUIRY

This standard includes coming to discussions "prepared, having read or researched material under study" and posing "questions that connect the ideas of several speakers and respond to others' questions and comments with relevant evidence, observations, and ideas." In the group discussion, Daniel posed his own questions and showed his preparation. The speaking and listening standards don't exist for their own sake, however; we don't want students to talk just because talking itself is good. *Meaningful* talk in class is a strategy, a conduit to processing and comprehension. It's a chance to turn one's own reflection into interaction and greater understanding.

Step 3: Allowing Daniel to Deepen His Study

AUTONOMY

DIFFERENTIATION

The final assignment of the year in Barry's eighth-grade class was an independent reading and writing project in which students compared two texts, one they'd read during the year and one they read on their own. After conferencing with each student, Barry allowed them to choose the outside text. With Daniel, he was fully prepared to accept a fairly easy and short text—maybe a magazine article—and probably one about sports, Daniel's primary interest. That would have been fine if it engaged Daniel, but it might not have prompted any gains when it came time to write about the piece.

DIFFERENTIATION

"Have you heard of this comic book about the Holocaust?" Daniel asked when he came to speak with Barry.

He was referring, it turned out, to the graphic novel *Maus*. Daniel's social studies teacher suggested it to the class.

Incorporating Choice Effectively

VOICES FROM THE
CLASSROOM

"A long time ago, I used to make an assignment where I'd put up a list of poems and have students sign up to study them one day in class—for instance, they could sign up to read one classic Wordsworth sonnet out of a list of 25 poems from the 19th century. I thought I was offering choice, but really, I was forcing students to choose between total unknowns. It didn't help them get interested in the poems at all. These days, I try to offer real choices. I allow time for students to read through poems first. I talk to them individually about their interests and what might get them involved. I let them bring in poems they find, and we discuss whether or not they'll work for the assignment. I've even let students use song lyrics—and sometimes, I've talked them out of using the pieces they want to use. It takes more time, but it's a better system, because in the end the students are attached to the poems they choose but also have accepted a certain level of challenge. And a nice by-product: If they've already started working on the poem by talking to me, they're less likely to plagiarize and more likely to continue the work on their own."

—Gloria Paronski, Little Rock,
Arkansas, tenth-grade teacher

"Sure," Barry answered. "Does that interest you?"

"Yeah. But does that count as reading?"

Barry nodded. "Wait until you read it. You'll see."

Remember that among the elements of a student-centered, active classroom, you're likely to find teachers who scaffold learning and who differentiate instruction. Daniel's reading was weak, but the pages of *Maus* offered opportunities for him to strengthen that reading in safe ways. The addition of visual material often made up for the lack of *schema*—background knowledge and previously learned information—that Daniel exhibited when reading a work such as *A Midsummer Night's Dream.* Those visuals also offered context clues for unfamiliar words. And at the heart of the matter is the fact that Daniel just liked the work.

Maus, as it turned out, served as a bridge to help Daniel better comprehend the work he was reading in his social studies class, Elie Wiesel's *Night.* The scaffolding provided by the visual elements of *Maus* also allowed the graphic novel to serve as scaffolding for *Night* and made it far easier for Daniel to tackle what was, for him, a very complex text.

We've already shared Daniel's writing and pointed out the lack of connection it displayed to texts. Here, by way of contrast, is an unedited entry from Daniel's reading journal:

> *In my opinion, Maus and Night are so far the best books that I have read. I'm glad I chose Maus and Night because they gave me a different view on life and I learned how things have changed over time. Both Vladek in Maus and Eliezer in Night helped me to fight through tough situations and to not give up Vladek and Eliezer have similar situations. They both survived in the Holocaust and both lived to tell the story about how they survived and what they had to do to get through it. The two characters taught me the meaning of hard work and fighting through tough situations). Although the two taught me how to overcome hard times, I still sometimes have to go through situations the same way that I used to go through them. The lesson they taught me really helped in a long run because I now know what to do in these situations. In <u>Maus</u> Eliezer and his little brother came out from the war alive and the rest of his family was gone. He had a responsibility's such as: watch over his little brother and protect him. In my opinion, Eliezer and Vladek are good role models. They are role models for people who must fight to protect their families. They have to work hard to keep food on the table, clothes on their backs, and a roof over their head. Though they have similar story lines, they have one thing that is different between the two. In <u>Night</u>, Eliezer's family dies and he and his brother were the only ones to survive while in <u>Maus</u>, Vladek family survives except for his wife. Family matters. Eliezer and Vladek have that inspired me to go out and do the same for my family. I'm not impressed with them just surviving, but it plays a big part because it teaches me how to not give up and to think about family when it gets tough down the road.*

CHALLENGE AND SUCCESS

AUTHENTIC ASSESSMENT

Daniel's writing in his journal had not improved mechanically from earlier pieces. But the increase in his engagement—the result, in part, of choice and autonomy—is clear. So too is the fact that he began to reflect more deeply about what he was reading—to latch onto, in fact, themes and points of comparison.

Personal reflection and connection are not explicitly addressed in the CCSS, but it *is* clearly indicated that students should connect with authors and narrators.

> Read and comprehend complex literary and informational texts independently and proficiently. (R.8.10)

Daniel had also engaged closely with two texts, and the Common Core asks eighth graders to attempt a deeper level of comparison:

> Compare and contrast the structure of two or more texts and analyze how the differing structure of each text contributes to its meaning and style. (R.8.5)

Given more time with Daniel, Barry might have sought ways to help him make rich connections between narrative style and nuance of meaning between *Maus* and *Night*. The door was open; Daniel needed more encouragement—and more time—to explore what lay beyond it.

In this case, however, the end of the year was fast approaching. Nonetheless, there are more pieces to Daniel's story—the culmination of active learning, motivation, and ownership.

Final Thoughts: Leaving Daniel (for Now)

We'll explore one important aspect of Daniel's continuing journey—his struggle with writing mechanics and standard English—at the end of this book, in Chapter 8. For now, let's consider where Daniel ended his eighth-grade year.

As part of his final exam, Barry asked each student to reflect on his or her learning in eighth grade with a short response that was both

Personal reflection and connection are not explicitly addressed in the CCSS, but it is clearly indicated that students should connect with authors and narrators.

What About Students Who Struggle Even More Than Daniel?

As his eighth-grade year ended, Daniel was becoming more engaged and was reading with greater interest.

Sadly (but understandably), Daniel's success is not replicable in every case. Though Daniel was hardly the only struggling learner in Barry's class, he functioned near the bottom of his class in terms of motivation and academic energy; in other settings, he may have been closer to the top. That's where the real danger lies, where group work is harder to imagine because it's just so hard to manage in a setting where most or all of the students are as disengaged as Daniel—or more so. What to do in such a case? The answer, of course, is not simply to have students return to learning by rote—that is, if we want to promote deep learning, which is closely tied to engagement.

Engaging extremely disengaged students, especially in groups, is hard; there's no question about it. But small steps add up. We suggest the following guidelines for how one might begin to engage classes of such learners:

SCAFFOLDING

- Start with interesting, manageable texts, then move slowly to more complexity.

COLLABORATION

- Let students talk—often.

- Focus on learning, not on what needs to get done.

- Share your enthusiasm.

ACTIVE LEARNING

- Get students moving when possible (even if it's just standing or raising their hands).

MULTIPLE LEARNING METHODS

- Alternate between lively interaction and quiet reflection, including writing.

AUTHENTIC ASSESSMENT

- Frequently include ungraded, short writing assignments and respond to them in meaningful ways.

- Look for signs of internal motivation and capitalize on them.

- Pay attention to external motivation, but don't overemphasize it.

FEEDBACK

- Support small accomplishments with positive feedback.

> - Provide problem-based instruction and projects in anticipation of our chapter on inquiry.
> - Build connections—with students and with material.
>
> Each of these approaches requires deliberate attempts by teachers to create a classroom that involves and invites students rather than imposing work upon them. It's a slow process, but one that is ultimately rewarded by giving students control of their own learning.

INQUIRY

RELEVANCE

metacognitive and, to some extent, forward-thinking. Daniel's response was neither lengthy nor particularly well-written, but it was illuminating:

> *I never liked English classes. I'm not a good reader or writer. I cant say I did so well all through this class, but I think I got better. Mainly, I got better at reading. Writings hard for me but I never thought I'd like a book like I did in this class at the end. My goal for high school is to like more books which I think I can happen if my teachers let me choose some of them. I hope to read more like Maus and Night and maybe some other books not about the Holocaust. When I read books like that I want to talk more about them and maybe even write about them (well not really with the writing). Thank you for this class and for getting me to read.*

Daniel's journey was not at an end. He did not reflect the college and career readiness embodied by the CCSS; he didn't even meet all of the standards for eighth grade. But Daniel also could have left middle school not only failing to meet those standards, but further than ever from wanting to meet them or from wanting to learn at all. Barry was lucky, in this case—Daniel found interests that led him to greater engagement. As we'll see in Chapter 8, when we encounter Daniel again, as well as in other examples of struggling students through this book, there's no more crucial first step for meeting the standards than this.

Through Daniel we see the results of strategies that work with reluctant students in general. For instance:

- Choice and personal selection in reading increase the ability of students to tackle texts that interest and engage them—and that they can actually read.

AUTONOMY

HOW TO Replicate Barry's Lessons

Barry's successes with Daniel came about through a series of classroom activities, not a single lesson. If we reflect on the steps of that process, however, we can see a general approach that can be replicated to reach disengaged learners in any language arts class:

- Look for quick moments of interest, such as Daniel's response to the Holocaust.

- Capitalize on students' interests by creating individualized writing or reading assignments that allow students to explore those areas.

- Deliberately structure an opportunity for a student to be successful—a brief discussion or personal writing assignment, for instance.

- Create opportunities for peer interaction in which a student can build on that success by sharing and hearing from others.

- Deepen study for the student by connecting these small successes to a more sustained or complex assignment that involves choice and ownership.

- Allow for self-reflection so that the student can measure and learn from his or her own successes.

AUTHENTIC ASSESSMENT

- Frequent freewriting and journaling can provide a platform for students to write and connect to texts in ways that formal essays might not.

COLLABORATION

- Discussion can offer chances for students to engage in thinking about texts—if they take an active role in the discussion.

In the rest of this book, we'll investigate these and other specific strategies as they connect to the Common Core State Standards. Every part of our discussion, however, rests on the central idea that meeting the standards with common sense entails having students *do* learning in class rather than *receive* learning. It means creating a supportive environment in which students are free to try out active inquiry and are invited to discover how exciting the material we teach can be.

Or, as one of our own teachers used to say: You can lead a horse to water. You can't make it drink. But if you let it trot around for half an hour, give it some encouragement, jump in the pool yourself and splash around, and let it make up its own mind, there's not a horse in the world that will choose, just *because*, to go thirsty.

2 Why Scaffolding Complex Text Is Crucial

Students establish a base of knowledge across a wide range of subject matter by engaging with works of quality and substance. They become proficient in new areas through research and study. They read purposefully and listen attentively to gain both general knowledge and discipline-specific expertise. They refine and share their knowledge through writing and speaking.

—Description of College- and Career-Ready Students, CCSS Introduction

Kallie was not happy that she had been placed in a remedial reading class, but she understood that she had scored poorly on the reading section of her state's standardized test the previous year and had no say in the matter. By all accounts, Kallie, a freshman, could read well orally, but she had difficulty comprehending. As a means of informal evaluation, the school's reading coach, Allyson Hart, asked her to read aloud a piece of text from Edward Bloor's *Tangerine*, a young adult novel that other students had enjoyed. The passage described a sinkhole that was sucking down the entire portable building where the main character was attending math class.

Photographed by Jetta Productions

The students were scrambling over splintering wood, swirling water, and each other in order to escape certain death. Ms. Hart asked Kallie what she "saw" in her mind as she read. The student looked at her with a questioning expression and replied softly, "Not much."

"Not much?" Ms. Hart repeated, amazed. "Don't you see a huge building collapsing into the muddy hole with students running like crazy to avoid being sucked in too?"

"I guess," she said, but it was clear that Ms. Hart's ramped-up visualization and Kallie's hazy image were quite different.

If there had been a standard concerning visualization, Kallie most certainly would have failed to achieve proficiency. As it was, she was facing some real challenges in high school, especially with the implementation of the Common Core State Standards (CCSS). Her content-area teachers were expecting her to read more complex text, but she was struggling with fairly easy text. "College and career ready," at this point anyway, wasn't even in the picture.

AUTHENTIC
ASSESSMENT

Ms. Hart began her work with Kallie by asking her about her reading habits, self-confidence as a reader, and past reading history. She then asked Kallie to complete a survey (see Student Reading Survey) in an effort to fill in the missing parts of Kallie's literacy portrait. Ms. Hart discovered that Kallie did not have a favorite book, believed reading anything other than text messages was "nerdy," and didn't consider "school" reading as relevant or meaningful to her in any way.

Kallie's strong oral reading skills had most likely convinced her previous teachers that she was also good at comprehending, especially since she had perfected a great trick: answering low-level comprehension questions by scanning the text and then filling in the blanks. She could make a passing grade by answering most of the questions correctly at the end of textbook chapters—and plenty of her friends belonged to this same club. Ironically, school had too often taught them that "reward" comes in finding answers, not in finding meaning.

School too often teaches struggling students that "reward" comes in finding answers, not in finding meaning.

Creating Proficient Readers: What's a Teacher to Do?

In the past, Kallie may have provided enough correct answers to pass most of her courses, but now, with the CCSS upping the ante, she will no longer be able to succeed by copying answers out of a textbook. Let's

Student Reading Survey

Instructions: There are no right or wrong answers to these questions—just answer as honestly as you can.

1. How difficult is it for you to pay attention when you're reading?

2. What type of book is easiest for you to read?

3. What is the last book that you enjoyed?

4. What subject gives you the most difficulty? Do you know why? Explain.

5. How do you study for a test?

6. How well do you remember what you read?

7. What do you do when you come to a part of the text that is confusing to you?

8. When you are reading and come to a word you don't know, what do you do?

9. Do you consider yourself a good reader? Why or why not?

10. What can I do to help you become a better reader?

This tool is available for download at **www.corwin.com/commoncorecpr**.

HOW TO Informally Evaluate Your Students' Reading Abilities

- Have students read 100 words from a book of their choice aloud. You can note reading rate and prosody, of course, but the real value of such an activity is to hear, as Barry puts it, "a student's reading voice."

- Use a metacognitive survey such as the one in the Student Reading Survey box or create your own. Encourage students to simply talk about their reading experiences. Dig into their reading histories by asking questions:

  ○ When did you first learn to read?

  ○ What are your positive and negative memories of reading in first grade, second, third?

  ○ What is the worst reading experience you've ever had?

  ○ Do your parents like to read?

  ○ What books do you own?

- Look at the student's writing and see if you note patterns, such as brief answers directly from the text, or a rambling narrative that fails to incorporate details from the text.

- Talk with the student's other teachers and ask them about how well she reads in their class and if her work reflects deep understanding of the content.

look at part of the introduction that is the focus for this chapter (see the shaded box on page 27). We are told that students must "establish a base of knowledge across a wide range of subject matter" not simply by reading but by *engaging* with "works of quality and substance." Students are expected to "become proficient," not merely adequate, in new areas through "research and study." They are to read purposefully to gain both general knowledge and discipline-specific *expertise*. Suddenly, the playing field has changed for Kallie and others like her who could get away with superficial reading just a few years ago.

Content-area teachers (and many English teachers as well) have not been trained as reading teachers and may feel panicky as they come to understand the expectations of the CCSS. How are they to teach the intricacies of their disciplines and, at the same time, help students who have difficulty reading? In this chapter, we hope to allay your fears. By adhering to our standards for motivation and engagement *and* incorporating practices that will help students such as Kallie become more active readers, you will be able to increase your students' literacy skills significantly. Let's return to Ms. Hart's class and see how she worked with Kallie on her reading challenges.

Reading: An Active Process

Ms. Hart's plan was to revert to less complex, highly engaging texts and show Kallie how to interact with the content by asking questions, making connections, and developing a relationship with the author. She wanted Kallie to discover that reading was not only enjoyable, but could also be a source of information for her own purposes. Ms. Hart began looking for just the right book to entice Kallie, starting with the obvious.

RELEVANCE

"Have you read *Twilight?"* she asked.

"No, but I saw the movie, and I didn't think it was all that great," Kallie replied.

"Is there *any* book that you've been wanting to read?"

"Well, I thought I might try *Hunger Games,* but then I thought it might be boring. I saw the movie, though; I *loved* the movie," she said, oblivious to the fact that if she loved the movie, she just might love the book as well.

Ms. Hart pulled off the shelf a copy of the popular young adult novel *If I Stay* by Gayle Forman, a story about a girl whose parents die in a car accident and who, although she is in a coma, can see and hear everything around her. "I think you'll like this," Ms. Hart said, although Kallie did not look convinced.

DIFFERENTIATION AND SCAFFOLDING

Armed with sticky notes, Ms. Hart asked Kallie to read orally and stop at designated intervals where she guided her into active reading by asking her to evaluate the characters' actions, predict what may come next, or talk about what she would have done in a similar situation. If Kallie replied with her favorite answer, "I don't know," Ms. Hart asked her to read the passage again until Kallie came up with even a glimmer of an answer.

ACTIVE LEARNING

Ms. Hart advised Kallie's reading teacher, Ms. Perry, to place her with a partner who also had difficulty staying with the text. They would read the same

COLLABORATION

book silently and use sticky notes to make their thinking visible, stopping often to talk through the events of the novel "book club" style. Ms. Hart also showed them how to help each other monitor their comprehension by giving them a guide with the following reminders:

- Is any part of the novel confusing to you? If so, stop and talk about it with your partner.

- If your mind wanders off, go back and reread what you missed.

- If you come to a word you don't know and you think it is important, ask your partner or teacher what it means.

- If you can't relate to what you're reading, try to think of experiences you've had (or something you've seen on TV or in the movies) to help you make a connection.

- If you're reading without thinking, ask questions as if you were talking to the author or make a prediction about what may happen next.

Each day the girls wrote responses to their reading in their notebooks as a way for their teacher to monitor their progress. After a few days, Ms. Hart came back to check on Kallie and her partner. She especially wanted to see if Kallie had begun to visualize what she read.

"What do you think of the book?" she asked Kallie.

"It's OK," Kallie answered in her usual low-key manner.

"How do you see Mia in your mind? What does she look like?" Ms. Hart asked.

"I don't know," Kallie answered immediately and then smiled as she pointed to the picture of the girl on the front of the book.

"I mean, what do *you* think she looks like, not some artist's version. Could you draw her? Do you have any friends who look like her?"

Kallie considered the question. "Can I use the computer?" she asked. Kallie did a search until she came up with a picture of a girl who was attractive but not "model" pretty, dressed in ratty jeans and a T-shirt with a band's logo on the front. "This is what I think Mia wants to look like when she comes out of the coma."

Kallie was on her way.

We will admit that most English and content-area teachers do not have time to work with individual students in the intensive way that Ms. Hart worked with Kallie. This type of deep work is usually done in a reading class or by a reading coach, but our point is that if Kallie's teachers had pushed her into more challenging text without finding out if she was capable of such reading, she might well have become another dropout statistic. For students like Kallie, moving into complex text is a process, not a mandate—and all of their teachers need to have a plan for helping them engage in that process.

Text Complexity: Difficult to Define

The phrase "text complexity" has become a current buzzword, especially when discussing the CCSS. Unfortunately, many educators who make decisions about curricula invoke this term to justify using *only* challenging texts and throwing out anything that may be seen as "easy." A superintendent in one district told us that he was purchasing all of the CCSS exemplars for use in language arts classes, but teachers would need to make the case for using any other texts. The teachers in that district were, indeed, vehemently making the case for other texts, but they were then accused of wanting "easier" materials so they wouldn't have to step up to the "text complexity" plate. As we pointed out in Chapter 1, it is important to note that exemplar texts mean only that: examples.

It may be helpful at this point to remind ourselves once again that the standards define what students are expected to know, not how teachers should teach or what materials they should use: "The aim of the standards is to articulate the fundamentals, not to set out an exhaustive list or set of restrictions that limits what can be taught beyond what is specified herein" (Introduction, "Key Design Consideration"). The CCSS Appendix A offers guidance in this area by specifically discussing factors that make texts complex.

Complex Texts: One Size Does *Not* Fit All

We know that what is a relatively simple text for one reader might be highly complex for another. Both Barry and ReLeah find Shakespeare enjoyable and complex, but not so complex that it is difficult to read. But remember Daniel, from Chapter 1? While some students in his class were

> Moving into complex text is a process, not a mandate.

able to master *A Midsummer Night's Dream,* he and others struggled with it to the point of frustration and surrender. Indeed, when we work with teachers who have degrees in areas other than English, they sometimes tell us that they, too, find Shakespeare extremely challenging as well as complex. When we ask what texts they find challenging but accessible, they offer all sorts of options. One teacher, for example, recommended what he described as a relatively "easy" book, *The Fabric of the Cosmos: Space, Time, and the Texture of Reality* by Brian Greene, when ReLeah expressed an interest in string theory. ReLeah began the book and discovered that she really wasn't all that interested in knowing more about string theory after all, mostly because she found the text extremely complex.

What, Exactly, *Is* Text Complexity?

We're not sure there is an adequate definition for "text complexity." The authors of the CCSS tried to help us out by including a three-part model in Appendix A, summarized below.

1. *Qualitative dimensions* refer to elements that human readers can identify: levels of meaning or purpose, structure, language conventionality, clarity, and knowledge demands.

2. *Quantitative dimensions* refer to the more objective, scientific measures: word or sentence length, text cohesion. Most of these elements are measured by computer software. Common measures include the Lexile Framework for Reading, the Flesch-Kincaid Grade Level test, the Dale-Chall Readability Formula, and the Coh-Metrix system.

3. *Reader task and considerations* refer to "variables specific to particular readers (such as motivation, knowledge, and experiences) and to particular tasks (such as purpose and the complexity of the task assigned and the questions posed)" (CCSS Appendix A, p. 4). The authors once again call upon teacher judgment in the area of reader task and considerations.

Text Complexity: Do Lexiles Make Sense?

To illustrate how quantitative measures don't provide a satisfactory method for evaluating text complexity, consider this. In Appendix A of the CCSS, the authors note that a quantitative assessment of the exemplar text *The Grapes of Wrath* by John Steinbeck places it within the Grade 2–3 text complexity band: "A Coh-Metrix analysis also tends to suggest the text is an easy one since the syntax is uncomplicated and the author uses a conventional story structure and only a moderate number of abstract words" (Figure 6, p. 14). Imagine Kallie learning to comprehend by reading this "easy" text.

Similarly, the Lexile score of Lois Lowry's popular and oft-taught *The Giver* is 760, which places it in a Lexile range aligned to career and college readiness expectations at the second- to third-grade level (fourth to fifth using the old Lexile ranges). Most English language arts teachers recommend this book for students in Grades 6–8 because of its mature concepts and the significant inferential thinking required by the reader. Even the ATOS system, a popular readability formula developed by the creators of the Accelerated Reader program, shows the disadvantages of relying on only one measure to determine text complexity. *The Crucible* by Arthur Miller scores a reading level of 4.9, the same exact level as *Twilight* by Stephenie Meyer, but Gary Paulsen's *Hatchet* is rated at 5.9! When we show such examples to teachers—who know better—they just shake their heads.

A Commonsense Approach: Text Complexity in Fiction

You probably already have plenty of quantitative data about your students provided by your reading or instructional coaches or even by test scores, but, as the Common Core recommends, these data need to be verified through qualitative means as well as reader considerations. After all, you, the classroom teacher, are the expert and ultimate judge of what your students are or aren't able to read; you are the one who must decide when and how to challenge learners and how to balance that challenge with engagement and texts that foster a love of reading. In looking at text in terms of qualitative measures, teachers can assess what makes it complex by considering the following.

Fiction

- **Levels of Meaning**

  ○ *Does the text have simple language that is complicated by levels of meaning that may be hidden or inferred?*

An example of such a text is George Orwell's *Animal Farm* or, for younger students, the picture book *The Stranger* by Chris Van Allsburg. Another

The Crucible scores a reading level of 4.9, the same exact level as Twilight, but Hatchet is rated at 5.9! When we show such examples to teachers—who know better—they just shake their heads.

interesting text that illustrates this paradox is *The Arrival* by Shaun Tan. The book has no words but incredibly complex levels of meaning and metaphor.

- **Language**
  - *Does the text use language that may be difficult to understand, such as ambiguous, figurative, or archaic language?*

Alice Walker's picture book *Why War Is Never a Good Idea* is a perfect example of a text that looks easy but is, in fact, very complex. Similarly, students who initially may be excited to read works by Edgar Allan Poe often find the language so difficult that they lose interest.

- **Point of View**
  - *Is the narrator unclear, unreliable, or untrustworthy, thus confusing the reader or forcing him to make sophisticated inferences beyond the obvious?*
  - *Does the point of view change unexpectedly?*

The best example of this component is probably William Faulkner's *The Sound and the Fury,* which anyone would recognize as complex. For kids, the Newbery Medal–winning young adult novel *When You Reach Me* by Rebecca Stead may fit into this category as might Lauren Oliver's *Before I Fall,* where the reader has to continually readjust her thinking as the narrator changes her attitude and perspective.

- **Plot Structure**
  - *Is the plot written through flashbacks or other structures instead of in a chronological way?*

Many young adult novels make use of different plot structures that may intrigue proficient readers but confuse reluctant readers. For example, in *Thirteen Reasons Why*, the popular young adult novel for older readers by Jay Asher, the text alternates quickly between the voice of a character (in italics) who exists only on tape talking about events in the past and the voice of the narrator who is listening to the tape and living in the present. Walter Dean Myers, a favorite author for male readers, also often uses unusual plot structures. For example, in his novel *Shooter* he uses various perspectives in the form of interviews, police reports, and a medical examiner's report to "tell" his story. Kelly Gallagher (2009) emphasizes this point when he talks about readers needing a tolerance for ambiguity when they begin reading many young adult novels; reluctant or inexperienced readers have yet to develop that skill.

- **Characters**
  - *Are the characters constantly changing?*
  - *Is there some tension between what is on the surface and what must be inferred about a particular character, or is there too little detail for readers to come to know characters well?*

Laurie Halse Anderson's *Speak* may fall into this category as readers try to figure out what is behind the main character's thoughts and actions. *Code Name Verity* by Elizabeth Wein exemplifies a novel where there are many characters with unusual names (and nicknames). In addition, the reader must infer a great deal about the characters and their actions in order to make sense of the plot.

And that's just fiction! Nonfiction has a whole different set of measures.

Nonfiction

- **Language**
  - *Does the text contain so much academic vocabulary that students are unable to comprehend what they are reading?*
  - *Is the text inconsiderate; that is, does it fail to support the reader's comprehension through clear sentence structure, logical flow of ideas, and sufficient explanation of key vocabulary?*

The Fifth Amendment of the U.S. Bill of Rights, an exemplar text in the CCSS, is a good example of an important but difficult nonfiction text: Besides the specialized vocabulary such as *presentment, indictment,* or *just compensation,* the amendment includes syntactical subordination that can be very tricky for students to unravel. The language of such texts, as fundamental as they may be to the study of history, may erect barriers to student comprehension before discussions about higher concepts can even begin.

> Many young adult novels make use of different plot structures that may intrigue proficient readers but confuse reluctant readers.

- **Conceptual Density**

  ○ *Are there so many ideas in the text that they are difficult to synthesize?*

  ○ *Are the ideas seemingly unconnected or stacked upon each other without adequate explanation?*

The most common example of this type of complex text is content-area textbooks, especially those in science and social studies, where too many concepts are presented over too few pages with insufficient explanation for students to fully comprehend the ideas embedded in the text.

The content of many English language arts texts falls into this category, too. For example, after famously telling readers that he "went to the woods to live deliberately," Henry Thoreau continues to tell us that his purpose was "to live so sturdily and Spartan-like as to put to rout all that was not life, to cut a broad swath and shave close, to drive life into a corner, and reduce it to its lowest terms." Even if students can understand each phrase in this sentence individually, understanding them in tandem with one another might prove a frustrating challenge.

- **Prior Knowledge**

  ○ *Are the concepts or ideas beyond the knowledge base of the reader?*

We recently heard from a teacher who used *The 9/11 Report: A Graphic Adaptation* by Sid Jacobson and Ernie Colón to help students understand the findings of the National Commission on Terrorist Attacks Upon the United States. While reading the text, several students asked about the meaning of "al-Qaeda," and the teacher found himself spending a whole class period explaining the term, one he assumed his students would know well.

- **Unity**

  ○ *Does the text include so many irrelevant details that it is difficult for the reader to sort out what's important?*

Here again, we cite both textbooks and Thoreau's *Walden* as examples of this characteristic of complex text. Textbooks include every detail that might possibly be found on a standardized test, leaving many readers overwhelmed and confused. Thoreau's work offers a variation of this problem. Chapter 6 of *Walden*, for example, describes Thoreau's bean-fields in great detail. Even students who take meticulous notes and read carefully might miss the larger point of the work when reading such a chapter; reluctant students are unlikely to read it at all. A reader of great maturity, of course, will find the links between Thoreau's philosophy and his in-depth description; struggling readers are likely to feel as bored and frustrated as they would if we asked them to plow a field of beans themselves.

- **Structure**

    o *Is the arrangement of ideas in the text unclear or random, making it difficult for readers to grasp a content thread?*

    o *Are there few signal words to alert readers to organizational changes?*

Some high school students love Tim O'Brien's personal accounts of his service in Vietnam, while others find his nonchronological style and abrupt transitions confusing and jarring. While O'Brien's use of structure is in and of itself a part of conveying his experience, struggling readers might find it difficult to manage the challenges of style and content at the same time.

Text Complexity: No Easy Answers

Note that we do not suggest that teachers merely avoid any text that contains the challenges we describe here. Many students look forward to (and even enjoy) the experience of reading a difficult text. A high school senior once complained to ReLeah that her English teacher was only showing the movie version of *Macbeth* because she felt most of the students were incapable of reading the play. This student wanted the opportunity to unravel Shakespeare's complex language, even if she had to do it alone. At the same time, we know struggling students may find such works to be a challenge for the precise reasons that other students (and their teachers) love them—because they use complex elements of language and structure to convey ideas—and, therefore, you may need to take extra care as you work through such texts with students.

> Note that we do not suggest that teachers merely avoid any text that contains the challenges we describe here.

DIFFERENTIATION

What If Your Students Have Little Experience Reading Nonfiction?

Struggling readers often have not read much fiction—and have read even less nonfiction. That's why it is important to talk with them about how to approach nonfiction by pointing out text structures, use of vocabulary, and strategies for determining the veracity of claims, for example. Such students need more than explicit instruction, however, when approaching informational text; they need a lot of practice reading a wide variety of nonfiction.

AUTONOMY

- Ask for a class set of current event magazines written specifically for students, such as *The New York Times Upfront*. Allow students to read the magazines freely but also use at least one article a week for the purpose of instruction.

TECHNOLOGY USE

- Once a week have designated students bring in an article (from an online or a print source) to share with their group. Everyone will eventually have a chance to present an article.

- Provide text sets of nonfiction books, articles, and websites to accompany each book of fiction students are reading.

- Work with other content areas and choose an article a week that can be taught across disciplines. Have students develop questions they have about the article to encourage inquiry and active reading.

INQUIRY

- Provide primary documents for every unit of study. The Library of Congress is a good source for written artifacts.

So, identifying "complex" texts of "quality and substance," much less having students read them, is quite a task, one that requires a close look at readers' skills as well as at the subtle and obvious demands of the text. The reader, especially the reluctant reader, brings to the process of reading many variables that complicate the goals of the standards, such as interest, motivation, knowledge, and experience. No program or textbook series can determine what is complex text for your class of unique students. Think again about the unusual way in which text was challenging for Kallie. It took some digging by a knowledgeable teacher

Kylene Beers and Robert Probst on Rigor

"More rigor is probably a good idea. There is surely a lot of wasted time in the school day—too many minutes spent on drills and pointless worksheets; too much time spent making sure students are prepared to pass high-stakes tests; countless days wasted on Accelerated Reader quizzes. The problem is that rigor is a term too easily misinterpreted by critics who have little direct contact with schools. A careless and ill-conceived effort to increase rigor in the classroom is likely to have exactly the opposite effect. If we infer, from the Common Core [State] Standards' call for the teaching of more complex texts at all grades, that we simply need to teach harder books, we will make a serious mistake."

—Kylene Beers and Robert E. Probst (2013, p. 20)

to uncover her reading issues. How is a teacher to move students toward reading challenging text when there are so many variables to consider?

Scaffolding: Building the Bridge

Scaffolding, a metaphor created by Wood, Bruner, and Ross (1976), describes a process that helps students build skills and accomplish tasks and is an important component in engagement. Many educators describe scaffolds as instructional practices that support learning; others see the process of scaffolding as building a bridge from what students know or can do to what we want them to know or do. The word *scaffold* is mentioned several times in the standards, presumably because of scaffolding's clear advantage in helping students become independent, self-regulated learners, a major goal of the CCSS.

Lest we begin to *push* kids across the bridge to more challenging reading, consider Richard Allington's (2002) caution: "You can't learn much from books you can't read" (p. 16). If students are misreading or skipping as many as 5 words out of every 100, that's 10%–25% missed words on every page (Allington, 2002). They should be missing only one or two words per hundred at their independent reading level—and it is at this level that we *begin* the trek across the bridge.

VOICES FROM THE
CLASSROOM

The Five-Finger Rule

"I picked up the five-finger rule from an elementary teacher. When she took her students to the library to choose books, she'd have them pick a random page in the book before they checked it out and count the unfamiliar words on the fingers of one hand. One to two unfamiliar or challenging words meant the book was pretty easy, three to four meant it would be difficult, and five or more meant it was too hard. Now my ninth-grade students do the same thing when we start a challenging text—we count the unfamiliar words on a random page. Sometimes we still have to read the text even though we'd be using our fingers and our toes to count all the words, but it lets us start talking about reading strategies and what we'll have to do to comprehend a difficult work."

—Andy Harwell, high school
teacher, Los Angeles, California

DIFFERENTIATION ▶

Scaffolding typically occurs when the teacher (or a peer) helps the student with a task that she is unable to grasp independently, often by tapping into what the student already knows about the topic. As the student learns and gains the required skills or knowledge, the teacher backs off, only offering assistance when the student is unable to do any part of the task alone. Such deliberate, often intermittent, support helps students gain the confidence they need to complete a task or to approach new or challenging learning. The trick is to provide enough assistance, especially in the beginning, that the student moves toward independence, but not so much support that the student feels disempowered. This balance also lies at the heart of differentiation—providing the amount and type of instruction to meet individual learning needs.

COLLABORATION ▶

Too much scaffolding with an entire class defeats the purpose, boring some students and outpacing others. This is why we are such avid proponents for organizing classes into small groups. See Chapter 7 for more information about creating a structure for group work. We must also remind ourselves that the process of scaffolding, like all important processes, *takes time.*

Scaffolding: A Model That Works

In their work on scaffolding, Hogan and Pressley (1997) present five scaffolding techniques:

- Modeling

- Offering explanations

- Inviting student participation

- Verifying and clarifying student understandings

- Inviting students to contribute clues

ACTIVE LEARNING

Let's take a look at how scaffolding might be employed with Anchor Standard for Reading 2, where students must:

> Determine central ideas or themes of a text and analyze their development; summarize the key supporting details and ideas. (R.2)

Anyone who has ever taught language arts knows how difficult it is for students to grasp themes or central ideas. Students confuse summaries with themes and confuse themes with morals; in addition, they have difficulty separating their own opinions from what they have read in the text. Students may also get off track if teachers are incorporating tasks from Anchor Standard for Reading 8 since students may have difficulty differentiating between how to evaluate a claim and how to determine a central idea:

> Delineate and evaluate the specific claims in a text. (R.8)

Ms. Hart Scaffolds With a Picture Book

Let's return to Ms. Hart's work with Kallie as an example of scaffolding. Ms. Hart knew that Anchor Standard for Reading 2 addressed a basic reading skill that Kallie and others like her needed to master if they were to succeed in their content-area classes. She used Hogan and Pressley's (1997) techniques to scaffold the process by first modeling how students could find a central idea or theme in a simple text, such as a picture book

SCAFFOLDING

for older students. She had found that such texts allowed her to illustrate the process *before* having students transfer the skill to more complex texts. Ms. Hart chose a picture book by Pulitzer Prize–winning Poet Laureate Ted Kooser, *House Held Up by Trees* (2012), a narrative about how nature actually lifted an abandoned house from its foundation and protected it from falling apart.

TECHNOLOGY USE

MULTIPLE LEARNING METHODS

In a whole-class mini-lesson with Kallie's reading class, Ms. Hart read the book aloud to students, showing them the pictures with a document camera. Although students at first appeared to be bored—some, in fact, were insulted at the very idea of being read a "children's" book—Ms. Hart soon captured their attention through the book's lyrical language and stark images that seemed to zoom in and then zoom out, as if through the lens of a camera.

"What are the most important events in this story?" she asked when she had finished reading. As is often the case, most students wanted to include *all* the events. She took her time and allowed them to work through the messy process of creating a summary, first with their learning partners, then in small groups. Ms. Hart, ever the facilitator, wandered around the room, interacting with students as they worked. She was pleased to hear one group engaged in a rather heated discussion—all centered on creating a summary.

FEEDBACK

COLLABORATION

ACTIVE LEARNING

> *"I don't think it is important that the man was getting old. That doesn't have anything to do with the house, and the story is about the house, not the man."*
>
> *"But the man is getting old, and the house is getting old—don't you get that?"*
>
> *"I get it, but we're writing a summary of what's most important, not every little detail."*
>
> *"If the man didn't get old and move out, the house wouldn't have been abandoned."*

The group finally decided to include in their summary a mention of the main character growing old, although some members still disagreed.

Each group shared their summaries, and Ms. Hart led the class in developing a whole-class summary from the offerings of the six groups. The next day, Ms. Hart began the class by discussing how a summary differs from a theme. She asked questions that required students to examine the text more closely:

- What message was Kooser trying to convey to his readers? How do you know?

- Which words specifically support this message?

- Which images support this message?

Ms. Hart reread the book aloud and encouraged students to consider "how and why individuals, events, or ideas develop and interact over the course of a text" (R.3) by giving them hints about how Kooser used characters and events to make a statement about the passage of time and the role of nature in our lives. As she verified and clarified students' thinking, Ms. Hart helped the students uncover the central idea in Kooser's book and posted it for the class to see. She asked students to write the theme in their learning logs and then revise it in their own words to encourage ownership.

CHALLENGE AND SUCCESS

The next day, Ms. Hart divided the students into groups, allowed each group to choose a picture book for older readers, and had them reinforce their skills by working together to write a summary and theme.

AUTONOMY

AUTHENTIC ASSESSMENT

By this time, the students had forgotten to complain about reading a "children's" book because Ms. Hart had put into practice essential elements of engagement: active learning, autonomy, collaboration, opportunities for success, *and* scaffolding.

Scaffolding: From Picture Books to Poetry

Ms. Patterson, Kallie's English teacher, taught most of the students in Kallie's reading class third period, and she often worked with Ms. Hart in planning lessons. She wanted to take advantage of the students' exposure to the poet Ted Kooser, so when her students came into class, she placed them in groups and provided each with a couple of Kooser's poems. Her goal was to address the "Craft and Structure" Anchor Standards for Reading.

MULTIPLE LEARNING METHODS

BOOKS

Picture Books for Scaffolding the Teaching of Theme

Blues Journey by Walter Dean Myers

Beautiful images illuminate the "blues" as readers consider loss through slavery, poverty, lynching, love, and fear. An author's note provides additional information.

The Butterfly by Patricia Polacco

Set in a French village occupied by Nazi troops, two little girls, one of them Jewish, become friends when the Jewish child is hidden by the other's mother. Together, they come to understand the great tragedy that is tearing their world apart.

14 Cows for America by Carmen Deedy

Maasai warriors in Kenya offer a gift to the grieving people of America who have not yet recovered from the attacks on 9/11. This beautiful story of generosity and compassion reminds readers about the importance of crossing boundaries of cultures, nations, and customs. Additional information about the tribe is offered in an afterword.

Fox by Margaret Wild and Ron Brooks

This complex allegory about a one-eyed dog, a bird with only one wing, and a cunning fox reveals truths about friendship, loyalty, and betrayal.

INQUIRY

TECHNOLOGY USE

RELEVANCE

Many students expressed surprise that Kooser, "a 'kid's' picture book author," could write such deep poems. One student even looked Kooser up online and reported to the class that he had won almost 50 awards. Ms. Patterson, excited that some of the students were expressing an interest in poetry, brought up Kooser's website on her SMART Board, and they listened to him read a poem she thought they would like, "If You Feel Sorry." In it, Kooser chastises people who feel sorry for themselves on Valentine's Day. Her students laughed at the way he personifies the little papers that hold pieces of Valentine candy in boxes as "dried out, brown and sad."

The Man Who Walked Between the Towers by Mordicai Gerstein

This true story of Philippe Petit, the Frenchman who strung a cable between the Twin Towers and then walked on the tightrope as the city watched, can be used with the documentary film *Man on Wire*. The book contains poetic language and a strong plot.

Planting the Trees of Kenya: The Story of Wangari Maathai by Claire A. Nivola

This true story of Maathai's commitment to the land of her people tells how her connection to nature helped her to become an activist for the environment. Maathai was awarded the Nobel Peace Prize in 2004.

Patrol: An American Soldier in Vietnam by Walter Dean Myers

This gripping narrative takes the reader into the jungles of Vietnam as a soldier describes his fear and uncertainty about what he is required to do.

Smoky Night by Eve Bunting

The Los Angeles riots set the stage for a story of prejudice and racism that unexpectedly turns into one of compassion and understanding. Powerful images support the theme.

The Wolves in the Walls by Neil Gaiman

Read this book to your students for the sheer fun of it. Lucy hears something scratching in the walls of her house, and what else could it be but wolves? When the family manages to remove the pesky (and scary) animals from their home, guess what appears next?

Ms. Patterson ended the lesson with one of Kooser's famous quotes that she intended to use as a writing prompt the following day: "One thing poets can do for us . . . is give us fresh new ways of looking at the world." As the bell rang, she heard one of her students wonder aloud if that's what Kooser was trying to do when he wrote *House Held Up by Trees*.

Untangling Complex Text: A Commonsense Approach

We know what you might be thinking at this point. A creative lesson using picture books and poetry is all well and good—and does meet some of

HOW TO Replicate Ms. Hart's Lesson

1. Choose a picture book that has a clear theme.

2. Use a document camera to show students pictures as you read the book.

3. When you finish reading, ask students to work with a partner and list the most important events in the book.

4. Allow pairs to share with the entire class and defend their choices.

5. Place students in groups of four, review the steps in writing a summary, and ask each group to create a summary of the book from the students' lists of "important events."

6. Have each group present a summary, and then work with students to create a whole-class summary.

7. Discuss how theme differs from summary.

8. Pose questions such as "What message is the author trying to convey? How do you know?" as a way of helping students understand theme.

9. Have students individually write the theme of the book in their learning logs. Check for understanding.

10. Give each group a different picture book and have students write a summary and theme, which they will share with the class.

the standards—but where does that leave us when trying to meet Anchor Standard for Reading 10 that demands students "read and comprehend complex literary and informational texts independently and proficiently"?

Challenging text, the very text that the standards say we should be teaching, may sometimes be too difficult for students to tackle without considerable frontloading. It is this very frontloading, along with scaffolding and differentiated instruction, that will *show* students how to learn to read such text. As always, practices that create engagement should be front and center.

Anchor Standards for Reading 4, 5, and 6

Interpret words and phrases as they are used in a text, including determining technical, connotative, and figurative meanings, and analyze how specific word choices shape meaning or tone. (R.4)

Analyze the structure of texts, including how specific sentences, paragraphs, and larger portions of the text (e.g., a section, chapter, scene, or stanza) relate to each other and the whole. (R.5)

Assess how point of view or purpose shapes the content and style of a text. (R.6)

As an example, we'll look at one of the trickier illustrative texts mentioned in the Common Core for Grades 9 and 10: George Washington's Farewell Address. Here's a paragraph from the end of the speech (one of the easier paragraphs in the text!):

> *It is our true policy to steer clear of permanent alliances with any portion of the foreign world; so far, I mean, as we are now at liberty to do it; for let me not be understood as capable of patronizing infidelity to existing engagements. I hold the maxim no less applicable to public than to private affairs, that honesty is always the best policy. I repeat it, therefore, let those engagements be observed in their genuine sense. But, in my opinion, it is unnecessary and would be unwise to extend them.*

Now let's look at the sample performance task associated with this speech in the standards:

> Students compare George Washington's Farewell Address to other foreign policy statements, such as the Monroe Doctrine, and *analyze* how both texts *address similar themes and concepts* regarding "entangling alliances." (Appendix B, p. 129)

Common Core and Common Sense: What About Prereading?

Since the early days of the introduction of the CCSS, debate has swirled around the topics of frontloading and prereading. Should teachers throw students into the deep waters of complex text so that they immediately encounter ideas and concepts through the author's own words? Should they bolster comprehension by preteaching aspects of the text ranging from an outline of the story to themes, background information, or structural elements? Proponents of the first approach argue that an emphasis on challenging texts means students must learn to grapple with difficult reading material independently; it's also common for pundits to complain that teachers who frontload the text do so at the expense of student interest, spending 20 minutes setting up a 5-minute read. Proponents of prereading, on the other hand, suggest that many readers are simply ill equipped to make sense of texts without some understanding of historical context, for instance, or difficult literary styles.

As with so much about the Common Core, we turn back to a simple question: What does common sense tell us? For one thing, there's no one approach to frontloading that will always work. You know your students, and you know the texts you teach. While we never wish to underestimate or bore students, we also seek healthy challenge without unhealthy frustration. Teaching a Naomi Shihab Nye poem? Try plunging students right in and allowing them to figure out what they need to know to understand the poem. Sharing a section of Homer's *Odyssey* with students? You might want to frontload some concepts about mythology, epic poetry, or ancient Greece. The trick, of course, is thoughtfulness—what will draw students in and help them read successfully without doing the heavy lifting for them?

There's a caveat we wish to offer, here. It's not just struggling readers or language learners who need frontloading. Sure, a student with a limited reading background might struggle with comprehension. But consider: Elsewhere in this chapter we mention the deceptive reading Lexile score of Miller's *The Crucible*. Many students could tackle the words and sentences of this play without difficulty, but could even advanced students easily make sense of the complicated nuances of social life in 17th-century Salem, Massachusetts, without some historical prior knowledge? Moreover, every teacher who presents this play to a class must decide whether information about 1950s communism is best given before, during, or after a study of the play. Is there a right approach? Not within the wording of the standards themselves. Classroom teachers, we believe, should have the autonomy to decide, text by text and class by class, what the students with whom they work need to know—or don't.

As with *all* of the sample performance tasks in Appendix B of the standards, this one is linked to the reading standards. None of the informational texts are linked to tasks involving, for instance, the skills outlined in the speaking and listening standards. They ought to be, however, because one of the best ways to help students unpack this difficult speech and comprehend it is through engaging collaborative discussion. Students would certainly benefit from helping one another untangle the difficult phrases and word meanings in the passage. Even so, when Ms. Hart thought about this text and Kallie's skills, she said honestly that she wasn't sure Kallie could stay with the text long enough to unlock its meaning. And Kallie wasn't the only one, of course; this text would be challenging for almost all of the 10th-grade students in Kallie's school. Ms. Hart decided to work with Kallie's social studies and English teachers in an effort to create an interdisciplinary lesson around this text, an approach advocated in the CCSS.

COLLABORATION

MULTIPLE LEARNING METHODS

An Interdisciplinary Lesson: Social Studies and English

Ms. Patterson, Kallie's English teacher, and Mr. Branch, Kallie's social studies teacher, read the passage and looked at each other in dismay. "I'm having trouble comprehending this passage myself," Ms. Patterson laughed.

"First we have to build background knowledge," Mr. Branch said, noting that the students probably had no context for this passage. "I can do that and tie it into my curriculum."

SCAFFOLDING

"How will you create relevance?" Ms. Patterson asked, always on the lookout for engagement. "You could compare it to the speech of a recent president so the language will be more familiar."

RELEVANCE

"That's a good idea," Mr. Branch said. "George W. Bush was president during 9/11. His Farewell Address could be contrasted with Washington's." The teachers contributed their content-area knowledge as they created a plan.

Exemplar Text: A Social Studies Lesson

The lesson began in Mr. Branch's class. He did not give the passage to the students; instead he placed students in groups and asked them what they remembered about foreign policy in Washington's time. As he expected, they didn't remember much.

INQUIRY

TECHNOLOGY USE

With the librarian's assistance, he had collected books about this time period. "Use these books, textbooks, your computer—anything you can to become familiar with the 1790s—and remember that your goal is to find out about our relationship with other nations at that time."

Kallie's group went directly to Wikipedia and, becoming distracted by the hyperlinks, ended up spending most of their time reading about inaugural addresses, especially since they had watched Obama's inauguration recently. When all the groups came back together to discuss their findings, Mr. Branch was surprised at what they had learned and distressed that many of the groups, like Kallie's, had totally ignored foreign policy. Ms. Patterson noted that they would need to work on focusing their searches to the target questions. Mr. Branch, however, took the information the students provided and filled in the gaps.

FEEDBACK

He first introduced the topic of Farewell Addresses and explained how presidents use these speeches to remind citizens of their achievements, reinforce their ideas, and pass along their hopes for the future. He passed out copies of George W. Bush's Farewell Address and assigned one of 24 paragraphs that made up the address to each student—who would then be responsible for reading his or her paragraph aloud to the class. With their learning partners, students practiced reading their paragraphs.

COLLABORATION

RELEVANCE

MULTIPLE
LEARNING
METHODS

Encouraged by Kallie's group's interest in Barack Obama's inauguration, Mr. Branch planned to show the class part of Obama's Inaugural Address to help them "deliver" their paragraphs. He discussed characteristics of a good speech and pointed out how speakers use their voice and body language to deliver speeches, thus creating a persona or presence that can make or break the effectiveness of the speech. He passed out evaluation sheets, explained each term, and asked students to comment on President Obama's delivery in each of the following areas:

- Voice inflection
- Gestures
- Pacing
- Eye contact
- Repetition of words or emphasis of key points

- Tone

- Audience awareness

- Sincerity

- Facial expression

The next day, Reader's Theater style, students delivered Bush's speech, one paragraph at a time. Each student also had to point out one way Bush's farewell speech was different from one that Washington might have made and one way it might have been similar. Note that this is a perfect way to address Reading Standard 9.

ACTIVE LEARNING

AUTHENTIC ASSESSMENT

> Analyze how two or more texts address similar themes or topics in order to build knowledge or to compare the approaches the authors take. (R.9)

The Grade 9–10 strand for this standard in informational text is:

> Analyze seminal U.S. documents of historical and literary significance (e.g., Washington's Farewell Address, the Gettysburg Address, Roosevelt's Four Freedoms speech, King's "Letter from Birmingham Jail"), including how they address related themes and concepts. (RI.9–10.9)

Kallie read her paragraph:

> *So around the world, America is promoting human liberty, human rights, and human dignity. We are standing with dissidents and young democracies, providing AIDS medicine to bring dying patients back to life, and sparing mothers and babies from malaria. And this great republic born alone in liberty is leading the world toward a new age when freedom belongs to all nations.*

Because Kallie practiced reading her paragraph with her partner prior to the presentation, she had a good sense of its meaning. After her recitation, she said, "Here's one difference between Washington and Bush. Washington wouldn't have talked about AIDS because it didn't exist then. And a similarity? Bush was talking about freedom in the

CHALLENGE AND SUCCESS

HOW TO Incorporate the Speaking and Listening Standards

Kallie's teacher, Mr. Branch, knew that students need models for speaking and listening just as they need models for reading and writing. His exercise first involved careful analysis of how a strong public speaker—in this case, President Obama—delivers to an audience. In doing so, Mr. Branch was also addressing the third speaking and listening standard in the ninth-grade strand:

> Evaluate a speaker's point of view, reasoning, and use of evidence and rhetoric, identifying any fallacious reasoning or exaggerated or distorted evidence. (SL.9–10.3)

The fact that Mr. Branch immediately asked Kallie's class to put these lessons into practice by delivering their own paragraphs orally allowed him to incorporate the next standard, as well:

> Present information, findings, and supporting evidence clearly, concisely, and logically such that listeners can follow the line of reasoning and the organization, development, substance, and style are appropriate to purpose, audience, and task. (SL.9–10.4)

Indeed, if you look at the paragraph Kallie actually read to her class, you might also notice that her audience awareness and careful work beforehand prompted her to write—and speak—with a different sense of purpose. This task, too, is reflected in the standards:

> Adapt speech to a variety of contexts and tasks, demonstrating command of formal English when indicated or appropriate. (SL.9–10.6)

Thus, Mr. Branch harnessed the power of students both as audience and as presenters to propel understanding of what seemed, at first, an inaccessible text.

21st century, and Washington also cared about freedom since he had just fought the Revolutionary War for America to get its freedom from Britain."

Exemplar Text: An English Lesson

Mr. Branch turned the lesson over to Ms. Patterson the following day. For the first time, students heard the sample passage from Washington's Farewell Address as Ms. Patterson read it aloud. She then read it again and asked students to jot down questions as she read. Many of their questions concerned vocabulary:

INQUIRY

- What does "patronizing infidelity" mean?

- What is a maxim?

- Is the "foreign world" any nation outside of the United States?

- What were their existing engagements then?

- What is real liberty?

Ms. Patterson made sure that her questions were included as well:

- Should the United States involve itself in foreign alliances?

- Is honesty in fact the best policy in foreign affairs?

- Who are our permanent alliances today?

- To what extent does Washington's policy position reflect or not reflect societies and personal relationships in novels such as *The Hunger Games* or *Divergent*?

- Should our foreign policy today reflect Washington's ideas?

Ms. Patterson then provided the students with a list of 20 questions, many of which the students had contributed. In pairs, they rushed to claim the question they wanted to answer. The room was buzzing with activity as the teams began researching their own questions. Some of the students used computers to look for information, others got passes to the library, and still others simply talked about their questions in small groups. The next day each pair read their question and shared what they had discovered as Ms. Patterson contributed information they may have left out. Finally, she gave the students the text from George Washington's address and had them first read it silently and then take turns reading it aloud to their partners. She reminded them about monitoring their comprehension through rereading, asking questions, and paying attention to what confused them.

ACTIVE LEARNING

COLLABORATION

TECHNOLOGY USE

SCAFFOLDING

ACTIVE LEARNING

CHALLENGE AND
SUCCESS

Amazingly, Kallie and her peers did come to understand the sample passage, probably one of the most difficult passages they had ever read in their lives. Their feeling of self-efficacy increased as did their understanding of foreign policy.

Difficult Texts: One Step at a Time

As we stated previously, we are not advocating that anyone teach every one of the exemplar texts in this way—or, in fact, teach them at all. Neither is that the intention of the standards. But this peek inside Kallie's classrooms is an example, one that illustrates what can be accomplished when we take the time to scaffold instruction. What about time? For those who contend they simply don't have time to go into such depth, take a look at all the standards that were covered in this lesson:

Anchor Standards for Reading: 1, 2, 4, 5, 6, 7, 8, 9, and 10

Anchor Standards for Speaking and Listening: 1, 3, 4, 6

AUTHENTIC
ASSESSMENT

And, if the teachers had decided to have students choose another president and write a Farewell Address for him, they could have covered many of the writing standards as well.

Taking the Time to Build the Bridge

Even when we show teachers all of the standards that can be covered through such an activity, many fear that taking the time to scaffold a concept, especially for only a few students who are having trouble, may slow down their momentum in "covering" the standards. But covering more doesn't mean more learning is taking place—quite the contrary. In lessons that we have learned from countries whose students are scoring higher than ours on international tests, we are finding a "teach less, learn more" approach (Darling-Hammond, 2010). Darling-Hammond (2010) writes about model high schools in New York City that are "graduating students at twice the rate of the factory-model warehouses they replaced" (p. 235) through a "teach less" approach that embraces a challenging and engaging curriculum involving careful scaffolding for the learning of complex skills. "In contrast to many high school curricula,

HOW TO Replicate This Lesson

Scaffolding the skills necessary to tackle extremely difficult text can often seem like a crab walk. One day you advance forward with some students; the next day you slide back with others; some days it seems like you don't budge an inch with anyone. The secret to making progress is a great deal of patience—and constant monitoring of what students understand and what still eludes them. The teachers who created the plan to help students comprehend Washington's Farewell Address were smart to approach this task together. They were able to reinforce important skills in each class and talk to each other about the progress specific students were making.

Here's how they did it.

Social Studies

1. Students built background through inquiry and an Internet search.

2. Mr. Branch took what the students found and worked it into a lesson, correcting misinformation and building on accurate findings.

3. As a way of making the lesson relevant and scaffolding learning, Mr. Branch gave students George W. Bush's Farewell Address and assigned each student one of the 24 paragraphs in the address to read aloud to the class. Students were given time to practice with their partners.

4. Prior to delivering their paragraphs, students watched Obama's Inaugural Address and talked about the qualities of good delivery.

5. After each student read a paragraph, he or she had to explain how the text may have compared to a similar address given by Washington in the 1790s.

English Language Arts

1. Ms. Patterson read Washington's Farewell Address to the class twice. First, she asked the students to simply listen. The second time she read the text, she asked them to write down any questions they might have.

2. The next day, Ms. Patterson provided students with 20 questions, many of which students had contributed.

3. In pairs, students chose a question and researched its answer.

4. Students shared what they had discovered in their research with Ms. Patterson filling in additional information when necessary.

5. Students finally read Washington's Farewell Address silently and then took turns reading it aloud to their partners as they monitored their comprehension.

which assume that students have already mastered skills of reading, writing, and research, the schools construct a curriculum that explicitly teaches students how to study, how to approach academic tasks, what criteria will be applied and how to evaluate their own and other's work" (Darling-Hammond, 2010, p. 252).

Covering more doesn't mean more learning is taking place—quite the contrary.

If other schools want to garner such success, they must move away from a lecture-centered classroom and toward one that is student-centered, even if such a shift takes more time. "Faculty [at these model high schools] voice the belief that students learn by tackling substantial tasks and getting feedback against standards that guide their efforts to improve. Their beliefs are borne out by a large body of research showing very substantial gains in achievement for students" (Darling-Hammond, 2010, p. 252). Especially for students who have difficulty with traditional schooling, this authentic approach to learning is imperative.

Scaffolding in Action: Practices That Support Learning

Teachers are good at scaffolding; they do it all the time, often without realizing it. The following practices are examples of how scaffolding can be used to help students become independent thinkers, readers, and writers.

Employ Formative Assessment to Target Learning Needs

AUTHENTIC ASSESSMENT

Formative assessment occurs when teachers assess students' progress on an ongoing basis and then use that knowledge to adapt their teaching to meet students' needs. Formative assessment practices are easy and can be embedded in classroom instruction by simply

DIFFERENTIATION

- observing students;

- listening to classroom or small group discussions;

- engaging students in mini-conferences; and

- looking at tests, homework, entrance/exit slips, student surveys, or any other student work with an eye toward altering instruction based on what students have and have not learned.

And guess what? Using formative assessment to guide instruction produces significant gains in student learning (Black & Wiliam, 1998).

Offer Feedback Regularly

Teachers who scaffold offer appropriate feedback at appropriate times. As students engage in tasks, teachers watch for frustration and provide individual assistance if they deem it necessary with, for example, a little modeling, an explanation of how an argument can be strengthened with a quote, or a conversation with a student about why he finds a certain passage difficult.

Think of when you are doing something that frustrates you, say your taxes, and you consult a relative who is an accountant. You don't want him to do your taxes for you or evaluate your efforts; you just want some feedback on what you've done—maybe regarding itemized deductions. Through such feedback, you will fill in the gaps in your knowledge and learn to do the task better in the future.

Authentic feedback doesn't begin with value judgments, advice, or even positive, generalized statements such as "Good job!" Instead, it offers timely and continuous information that moves students toward their learning goals. Effective feedback practices include

- making *specific* comments regarding a student's work, such as "The point you made about friendship in this story is a new way of looking at relationships. It shows that you thought this through";
- offering two or three areas of particular need without overwhelming the student;
- focusing on major needs first (such as content) and minor errors last (such as punctuation);
- helping students keep their goals in mind by targeting feedback to those goals; and
- linking feedback to specific revision tasks that students can easily understand.

Remember to consider the most important component of engagement, intrinsic motivation, when offering feedback—the goal is learning, not getting a grade or simply finding the right answer. Indeed, some research even suggests that grades combined with teacher comments produce

FEEDBACK

AUTHENTIC ASSESSMENT

less learning than teacher comments alone (William, 2011). Feedback may be especially important for reluctant students because it helps them understand that they can improve through effort; that they are not "doomed to low achievement due to some presumed lack of innate ability" (Boston, 2002).

Use Read-Alouds to Build Literacy Skills

MULTIPLE LEARNING METHODS

Reading fiction and nonfiction aloud to students from your discipline is one of the best ways to scaffold content-area knowledge. When we talk about reading aloud, we do not mean spending an entire period reading a book to students, of course. We mean choosing passages to read aloud that model the skills you want students to learn as you show them how you, as the expert in your field, comprehend text. One seventh-grade science teacher we know used the novel *Code Orange* by Caroline Cooney as a read-aloud the last five minutes of class each day. She found that students would do most anything she asked if she would add a minute or two to her end-of-class reading.

Building Background Knowledge to Make Learning Stick

DIFFERENTIATION AND SCAFFOLDING

As Mr. Branch wisely noted when introducing students to Washington's Farewell Address, he needed to build their schema or background knowledge before introducing them to the primary text. Many reluctant students enter the classroom with little prior knowledge about the topic of study, and this one deficiency can have devastating effects on their learning. Prior knowledge is the "Velcro" to which new information sticks. And why should we devote time to building background knowledge as a way of helping kids access content knowledge and skills? Take a look at the research:

- Background knowledge is a prerequisite for comprehending new information (Guthrie & Anderson, 1999).

- What students already know about content is one of the strongest indicators of how well they will learn new information (Marzano, 2004).

Frank Serafini and Cyndi Giorgis on Reading Aloud

VOICES FROM THE FIELD

Serafini and Giorgis, authors of *Reading Aloud and Beyond* (2004), contend that reading aloud

- increases test scores;
- introduces readers to new titles, authors, genres, and text structures;
- builds a sense of community;
- provides opportunities for extended discussions;
- connects readers with content-area subjects;
- demonstrates comprehension strategies;
- increases readers' interest in independent reading;
- provides access to books that readers may not be able to read on their own;
- offers demonstrations of oral reading fluency;
- helps readers make connections and build background;
- provides demonstrations of quality writing; and, best of all,
- shows students that reading is pleasurable.

- Students who lack background knowledge struggle to access, participate in, and progress throughout the general curriculum (Strangman, Hall, & Meyer, 2009).

- There is a strong correlation between prior knowledge and reading comprehension (Langer, 1984; Stevens, 1980).

- Background knowledge increases students' interest (Tobias, 1994).

How to Build Background Knowledge

There are many ways to help students build or activate background knowledge. Look at the following list and consider how these practices not only provide background for students but also engage them in learning.

VOICES FROM THE
CLASSROOM

The Power of Read-Alouds

"I make my kids thirsty for reading by beginning each day with a read-aloud. Sharon Draper's 'Bandaids and Five Dollar Bills,' Sara Holbrook's 'Naked,' Shel Silverstein's 'Sick,' or Kwame Alexander's 'In My Closet, on the Top Shelf' instantly creates a desire to read. A powerful first line from a novel can also be engaging. One of my favorite first lines is from K. L. Going's Fat Kid Rules the World: 'I am a sweating fat kid, standing on the edge of the subway platform staring at the tracks. I am seventeen years old, weigh 296 pounds, ready to jump. Would it be funny if the fat kid got spattered by the subway?' As I read this, I ask students to think about the kinds of pain Troy Billings must feel. Shared literature provides a portal into the literate world not often viewed through the lens of a teenage reluctant reader. The only requirement I have of the students with regard to read-alouds is that they must simply listen. No quizzes, no written response, nothing; I tell my students that my only purpose is to share good literature with them."

—Pam Ayers, high school reading and
English teacher, Port Charlotte, Florida

DIFFERENTIATION

MULTIPLE LEARNING METHODS

COLLABORATION

- Consider what content students need to know before they can make sense of a particular reading (see Mr. Branch and Ms. Patterson's lesson, earlier, on George Washington's Farewell Address).

- Read aloud text related to the new information to be learned and help students make connections.

- Have students record what they already know about a topic and engage in a discussion with a learning partner or in a small group. Then, give students a piece of text related to the topic, have them read it individually, and ask them to come back to the group to share what they have learned. You'll gain the added bonus of addressing Anchor Standard for Speaking and Listening 1.

Anchor Standard for Speaking and Listening 1

Prepare for and participate effectively in a range of conversations and collaborations with diverse partners, building on others' ideas and expressing their own clearly and persuasively. (SL.1)

- Tap into digital literacy and find articles, pictures, videos, and primary documents associated with the content. Better yet, have students research areas related to the topic and present their findings to the class, which would address Anchor Standard for Reading 7 as well as Anchor Standard for Speaking and Listening 5.

TECHNOLOGY USE

Anchor Standard for Reading 7; Anchor Standard for Speaking and Listening 5

Integrate and evaluate content presented in diverse media and formats, including visually and quantitatively, as well as in words. (R.7)

Make strategic use of digital media and visual displays of data to express information and enhance understanding of presentations. (SL.5)

- Have students create questions about the topic and use the questions as research topics before reading. If this is in the form of a written report, you will also be addressing Anchor Standards for Writing 2 and 7.

INQUIRY

- Utilize a KWL (What I *Know*, What I *Want* to Know, What I *Learned*) chart, or a variation of it, perhaps one that students create.

- Keep a varied and current classroom library and provide time for independent and self-directed reading. Wide reading creates wider background knowledge to draw from when encountering new topics.

AUTONOMY

Anchor Standards for Writing 2 and 7

Write informative/explanatory texts to examine and convey complex ideas and information clearly and accurately through the effective selection, organization, and analysis of content. (W.2)

Conduct short as well as more sustained research projects based on focused questions, demonstrating understanding of the subject under investigation. (W.7)

Final Thoughts

Let's return to Kallie as we conclude this chapter. Our student who had difficulty visualizing a compelling scene in a novel still contends that reading is only something she does when there is nothing better to do; nevertheless, she *is* reading. Her absentee records indicate that she is in school more often than she was in ninth grade, and all of her teachers report that she generally participates in class, especially in social studies and English, her favorite subjects. It's true that she is still considered "at risk"; she struggles with comprehension, especially as the text becomes more complex, and she rolls her eyes when Ms. Hart tells her that she is turning into a great student. But it's also true that she is beginning to understand what it means to explore a topic in depth, think about complex ideas, and communicate her opinion on important issues. If Kallie's 11th- and 12th-grade teachers scaffold her learning by using the standards as a guide rather than a prod, she *will* graduate—and she may even decide that she likes this learning business so much that college might not be such a bad idea after all.

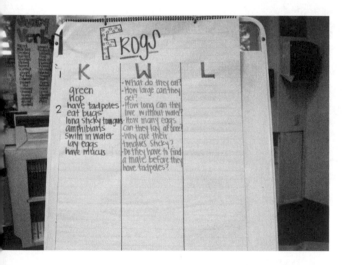

A KWL Chart in Progress. KWL charts, or variations of them, can be used with any topic, from the fifth-grade introduction of frogs shown here to sophisticated areas of literary understanding.

3 How Do We Engage *All* Students in Reading and Writing?

Students adapt their communication in relation to audience, task, purpose, and discipline. They set and adjust purpose for reading, writing, speaking, listening, and language use as warranted by the task. They appreciate nuances, such as how the composition of an audience should affect tone when speaking and how the connotations of words affect meaning.

—Description of College- and
Career-Ready Students, CCSS Introduction

Each year, Mark Levine, a middle school language arts teacher, assigns his sixth-grade students to write and peer-edit a short paper describing the process for making a peanut butter and jelly sandwich. Mr. Levine says that the students grumble but usually come in the next day with their hastily scribbled pages. Here's what Mr. Levine describes happening next:

> *Unbeknownst to them I'm prepared to make the sandwiches—all 95 of them. I bring all of the materials to class and put them on a table at the front of the room. Over the course of three or four days, they read the papers out loud. I make sandwiches according to their exact instructions, and they see the effect of their writing and how an audience perceives it. There are disasters and successes. It's a lot of fun,*

© darrenwise

but they also get that being specific and clear, thinking about purpose and who you're writing for, and even reading aloud as an editing tool are all important pieces of writing and the writing process. They find out that communicating with your audience matters.

Mr. Levine's students probably write their initial drafts in the same way most students write assignments for school, without giving much thought to audience or context. You can't blame them, entirely; most of the time, the audience for student writing is unspecified or conceptual, at best. The *real* audience in these cases is the teacher, and the teacher comes to the piece with multiple agendas, ranging from genuine interest to an uninspiring focus on mechanics or rubric items related to techni-cal aspects of writing more than to content. Mr. Levine provides visible

FEEDBACK

evidence of the need for clarity and turns himself and the class into an actual audience. "We refer to that lesson throughout the year," he tells us. "Even when they are writing narrative pieces or poetry, it helps to circle back to the sandwiches and why you have to be deliberate."

In describing literate students, the introduction to the Common Core State Standards (CCSS) focuses not just on an awareness of audience, task, and purpose, but also on *adapting* communication to fit a variety of situa-tions. In other words, it's not enough to write for one audience—student writers need to learn to change how they write for different purposes.

What if Mr. Levine's students had written their sandwich-making instructions for a third-grade class? For a college philosophy professor? As preparation for creating an online video demonstration? What if they'd turned their instructions into a narrative? How might they have adjusted their steps or language, and what process might have helped them do it?

In this chapter, we explore how literacy in all of its forms allows students to interact with a broader world—with authors, with readers, with one another. But how do we start? How can we teach students to understand audience and purpose as a reader? What about the more difficult tasks of writing with intentionality and voice? We take a look at both infor-mational text and narrative text, and we examine learning through the eyes of two students—Lorenzo, a middle school boy for whom school and reading held little meaning, and Vanessa, a ninth-grade girl who struggled to express meaning in her own words.

Starting With Reading: The Importance of Audience and Purpose

Just five minutes into Rebecca Randolph's seventh-grade English class, almost any observer would be hard pressed not to intervene when Lorenzo, a lanky boy Mrs. Randolph had placed in a seat near her desk, disrupted the class for what seemed like the 10th time since the bell rang. The school had placed Lorenzo in the standard-level language arts program because of his midrange test scores, but his energy and need to interact with others clearly drained the energy of both his fellow students and his instructor.

Moments after Mrs. Randolph began the mini-lesson that would precede a group reading activity, Lorenzo bounced out of his seat—supposedly to throw away a piece of paper—but couldn't resist playfully whacking another student on the head as he passed. He was chastised by Mrs. Randolph and returned to his seat, where he then began to thump his pencil on the desk in an obvious attempt to gain the attention of the students around him. It worked; soon, another boy began to mimic the thumps, and Mrs. Randolph was forced to stop her lesson again.

To make matters worse, Mrs. Randolph was a good teacher. She'd planned her class carefully, was not a lax disciplinarian, and included a variety of engaging activities in her lessons. Lorenzo, however, pushed her to her limits. He was a poor reader, his parents resisted having him tested for learning disabilities (Mrs. Randolph suspected some form of attention deficit disorder), and he almost never completed homework. He also had trouble following directions or instructions, especially in assignments with multiple steps. Unlike Daniel, the student from Chapter 1, or Kallie, from Chapter 2, Lorenzo's trouble in school stemmed as much from behavioral issues as from learning issues, but his increasing disinterest in learning and his academic failure reinforced—or were reinforced by—his behavior. Rather than withdrawing from school, Lorenzo reacted against it by acting out and seeking attention, further removing himself from actual learning.

DIFFERENTIATION

Fostering Writing as a Process

Many teachers *direct* students through the process of writing, from prewriting to a first draft to a finished product. We suggest that both English language arts and content-area teachers can help students *guide* themselves through a cycle of writing in a variety of ways:

- Create a writing process guide in your classroom where every student can track his or her writing at various stages: brainstorming, prewriting, first draft, conferencing, finished draft, and publishing, for instance. Students can move name cards from stage to stage as they work on a piece, then start over at the beginning of the cycle.

A Classroom Writing Process Organizer

- Have each student keep a writer's notebook and practice instituting daily quick-writes at the start or end of classes. Periodically ask students to turn one of these quick explorations into something more polished.

- Invite students to read work not only when it's finished but at all stages, emphasizing positive comments on drafts intended to help inspire writers as they revise and edit.

- Don't grade early drafts—give credit for completion until final drafts are due.

- Help students understand what writers *do*, not just what they produce. Watch interviews with successful authors as they talk about craft and the discipline of writing.

- Model *your* writing process for students, sharing not only finished work but your drafts in progress. Invite comments.

- Let students explore with various tools, discovering how technology, oral discussion, and presentation can be useful stages of thinking and revising.

FEEDBACK

AUTHENTIC ASSESSMENT

RELEVANCE

MULTIPLE LEARNING METHODS

Though clearly Mrs. Randolph's first priority was to set limits on Lorenzo's classroom behavior, it was also clear that discipline would remain an ongoing issue unless Lorenzo became more engaged and motivated in class. A classroom of 30 students just didn't sync up with Lorenzo's 13-year-old comportment; his behavior and his academic failure weren't malicious so much as they were the result of boredom, disconnection, and, in Mrs. Randolph's opinion, years of a home life that did not enforce real consequences. And, if you'd asked him, he probably would have told you Mrs. Randolph was his favorite teacher. Lorenzo's actions were directed not at her so much as at the general role of teacher and authority in the classroom—Mrs. Randolph's priority was teaching and learning, while Lorenzo's priority was finding a way to make school fun. His lack of interest wasn't personal, but it was almost impossible for her not to take it that way.

"I've talked to his parents," Mrs. Randolph said. "He and I have met with the principal. He was suspended last spring and may be again this fall. The thing is, I know he's not a terrible kid, but if he can't manage himself, he won't learn, and if he doesn't learn, he's going to have to repeat seventh grade. He's failing every class, not just mine, and failing badly."

We choose to tell Lorenzo's story because of the successes Mrs. Randolph saw during the year in which she taught him. As with many stories involving struggling learners, however, Lorenzo's is one not of total transformation, but rather of a break in the pattern of disengagement with gains made in small steps. And these gains came primarily for Lorenzo as a reader—and, thus, as a student—through addressing three critical conditions for learning: motivation, ownership, and interest.

Introducing Elements of Informational Text: Lorenzo's Response

If one were to examine only the exemplar texts from Appendix B of the CCSS, it might be easy to draw the conclusion that informational texts include only nonfiction documents of historical significance such as speeches from Winston Churchill or essays from George Orwell. Fortunately, Mrs. Randolph knew that in addition to such texts the category of informational text might include a number of more accessible options:

> Lorenzo's trouble in school stemmed as much from behavioral issues as from learning issues, but his increasing disinterest in learning and his academic failure reinforced—or were reinforced by—his behavior.

- Magazine and newspaper articles (including both the words and visual elements of these articles)

- Primarily visual texts such as advertisements or graphics

- Commercials, documentaries, or other videos

- Online texts of many kinds, ranging from formal websites to Wikipedia pages to social media posts

- Instructions, manuals, and technical information

- Speeches, broadcasts, and interviews

- Practical texts such as maps, signs, brochures, catalogs, warnings, surveys, and schedules

If you think about this list, you'll notice not only that it is full of documents that all students need to be able to read (in a very immediate sense), but also that it offers a range of avenues through which to capture student interest.

Consider, for instance, Lorenzo. The first grading period of Mrs. Randolph's class had passed without improvement—Lorenzo managed to do fairly well on a few early grammar refreshers, but failed the unit test on the short stories they'd read, failed every vocabulary assignment, and did not turn in his writing assignments at all. His grade fell below the 50% mark. The second grading period included a focus on informational text—a new area of the curriculum for the teachers at Lorenzo's school and one that Mrs. Randolph worked hard to implement with her department after the Common Core prompted its introduction.

Perhaps because she had few preconceived notions about how to teach informational text, she decided, without great optimism, to use the new unit as yet another opportunity to attempt to engage Lorenzo. Mrs. Randolph began her unit by "reading" two movie trailers with the class, one for a popular romantic comedy and the other for an award-winning drama. After a few minutes spent figuring out (with the help of a seventh-grade girl) how to circumvent the school's firewall so that she could access online video content and project it, Mrs. Randolph showed the class each trailer once, then asked the students to consider two main questions:

TECHNOLOGY USE

INQUIRY

- Who was the primary audience for each trailer, and what specific details from the trailer suggested that particular audience?

- What was the tone of each trailer, and what visual elements or words contributed to that tone?

She then showed each trailer again while students used a simple graphic organizer with three columns (one for details related to audience, one for visual elements of tone, and one for words related to tone) to make notes.

ACTIVE LEARNING

While Mrs. Randolph ultimately aimed to help students *write* and *communicate* with an awareness of audience, purpose, and tone, she knew her students needed to *read* and *comprehend* models of those elements first. In doing so, she also managed to meet a variety of the reading standards for seventh grade as they relate to information text, including:

> Determine an author's point of view or purpose in a text and analyze how the author distinguishes his or her position from that of others. (RI.7.6)

Unsurprisingly, however, Lorenzo barely wrote any words on his graphic organizer and made a few lame comments about the particular movies Mrs. Randolph had chosen. She then put her class into several small groups. While the groups compared their notes, she also designated a student in each to choose a recent movie, then invited the group to watch the trailer for that movie on her computer. When it came time for Lorenzo's group to approach, Mrs. Randolph had Lorenzo choose the trailer. Clearly excited, he immediately named his favorite movie: the violent and semihistorical *300*.

COLLABORATION

AUTONOMY

"I hadn't seen the movie, and I was sure it was inappropriate for seventh-grade boys," Mrs. Randolph said. "At the same time, the students in the group had all seen it, and we were just watching the trailer. I was nervous, but I knew this was a make-or-break moment with Lorenzo. I decided to take a gamble and use the online trailer with that group."

DIFFERENTIATION

The gamble worked, to an extent. The group's work over the next several minutes was punctuated by discussion about bloodshed in the movie and key action scenes ("Dude, remember when it showed that guy

Movie Trailer Note Guide

Name: _____

Audience	Tone (Visual Elements)	Tone (Words)
• What specific visual details from this trailer suggest a particular audience? • What words suggest a particular audience?	• What specific visual details suggest a particular tone?	• What specific words used in the trailer suggest a particular tone?

Conclusions

Based on your observations, how would you describe the ideal audience for this trailer?

Based on your observations, what adjectives would you use to describe the tone of this trailer?

getting sliced in half?"), but when it came time for the group to share its findings, Lorenzo himself spoke up. He discussed both audience and tone and shared details from the trailer.

Lorenzo stayed engaged, moreover, the next day, when Mrs. Randolph took the class to a computer lab and had partners work on an assignment that probed the concept of audience and purpose further. Using the Internet, she asked each pair to find five documents related to a movie of the pair's choice. Each document, she told them, must appeal to a different audience and convey a different purpose or tone—and they must be able to choose details that specify how and why this happened. Although much of the video content on the computers was inaccessible to students and the school firewall was active, Mrs. Randolph nonetheless spoke to students about appropriate and inappropriate content before beginning.

Lorenzo and his partner, Andre, stuck with *300*. Mrs. Randolph circulated throughout the room but returned to these two boys regularly, concerned about both their progress and whether or not they would stay on task. However, by the end of the class, Lorenzo and Andre had gathered and discussed several sites related to the movie:

- An interview with Gerard Butler, the starring actor
- A review of the graphic novel on which the movie was based
- A Wikipedia entry on the historical event on which the movie was based, the Battle of Thermopylae
- A fan page devoted to trivia about the movie
- An image of the movie poster with its slogan, "Prepare for Glory"

The two boys did a decent job of isolating both images and words from these entries that indicated tone, audience, and purpose.

The next day, Mrs. Randolph asked students to describe findings from their group work on the computers the previous day. Then she asked the students to volunteer possible guidelines for determining audience and purpose while reading informational text. Lorenzo and Andre contributed to the discussion by pointing out that while their movie clearly appealed to adolescent boys, the review of the graphic novel

RELEVANCE

COLLABORATION

TECHNOLOGY USE

ACTIVE LEARNING

AUTONOMY

they'd found was written with an adult audience in mind; they pointed out the long sentences and more difficult words as an example. Then, Mrs. Randolph asked students to choose any one of their sources—even a video or image, though she made sure some groups chose text-based documents—and consider its organization and structure. How, she then asked of the entire class, do specific words, especially in a written text, give us clues about how to read and interpret the information?

After school that day, Mrs. Randolph used the notes from all of her classes to create a single anchor chart focusing on the structure of informational text. Below is a version of the chart. By highlighting differences across types of informational text, and specific features of such texts, students get closer to understanding how each type might affect an audience. This helps students consider who the members of an audience for a piece might be and how they might respond to the text.

It's equally important for students to understand the *tools* authors use to construct their ideas, especially in informational text:

- Captions
- Titles and subtitles
- A table of contents
- Charts and graphs
- A glossary
- An index
- Sidebars
- Bulleted lists
- Fonts
- Illustrations and photographs

Such textual features, which teachers may take for granted, can elude or overwhelm struggling readers such as Lorenzo rather than aid them in reading. Mrs. Randolph offered explicit instruction concerning these features, explaining how informational text operates and offering examples of the features from real-world texts. This type of instruction is a critical aid for students as they work to understand this type of material.

Mrs. Randolph's Anchor Chart for Informational Text

Text Structures How does the author organize information?	comparison and contrast	description	cause and effect	sequences	problem and solution
Graphic Representation How can I portray this information visually?	Venn diagram	outline or idea web	flowchart	timeline	columns or flowchart
Clues to Structure What signal words are used in this kind of text?	although, unlike, similarly, just as, on the other hand, same, different	for example, for instance	because of, outcome, resulting in, the result of	first, next, then, after, finally, meanwhile	therefore, resulting in, one response to, a possible answer
Sample Thesis/ Introductory Sentence What kind of key sentence can we look for in the introduction?	"Although the earth and the moon are the same shape, there are key differences between them."	"The moon is the most barren and sterile environment one can imagine."	"Because of the gravitational effects of the moon, the actual length of our days is increasing."	"In order to make a moon landing, astronauts must follow a number of crucial steps."	"Many hospital workers believe that more women give birth during a full moon, but this is not actually the case."

Because he was engaged in the material he was studying, Lorenzo flourished during these classes. "This was the most involved I've seen him," Mrs. Randolph said. "That's not to say he didn't still act out, but he seemed genuinely interested and able to follow the class discussion for what might have been the first time."

The No-Escape Classroom: Creating a Culture of Reading

Granted, Lorenzo did not rush out the day after the above assignment and read *Hamlet* with a newly critical eye and a desire to analyze Shakespeare's language deeply. Nor did he suddenly produce eloquent essays that explored the nuance of a Wordsworth poem. Indeed, he didn't even necessarily finish any of his reading assignments in seventh grade.

But he did make progress.

Other students in Mrs. Randolph's class, we should note, were able to springboard easily from the movie trailer assignment to other reading tasks involving consideration of audience, purpose, and tone. In one follow-up assignment, for example, Lorenzo's partner Andre made a PowerPoint exploring how language forged connections to an audience using the lyrics of a popular hip-hop song. Mrs. Randolph experienced success in her class, but Lorenzo, despite a few days of engagement, was not yet a shining example of that success.

Nonetheless, it was important to Mrs. Randolph that all of her students, Lorenzo included, read texts not merely as consumers of information but as thinkers and communicators. As she moved from short informational texts to short stories and novels later in the semester, she kept in mind the need for students not just to *experience* text passively but to *interact* with it in a direct manner. To a large extent, helping students connect to texts meant continuing to help them understand how and why texts work, what authors seek to communicate, and how authors make choices with an audience in mind.

Mrs. Randolph also knew that such rich reading experiences don't result from merely assigning pages out of a textbook or samples from test preparation materials. Like most teachers, she did rely on these resources, but she also enlivened reading in her classroom by creating a reading culture. What are key elements of creating such a culture?

Use Real-World Mentor Texts. It's vital for disengaged readers in particular that a variety of texts be used as guides and bridges to positive reading experiences. Indeed, the very label "mentor text" implies that reading selections can act, to a degree, in the same way the best teachers

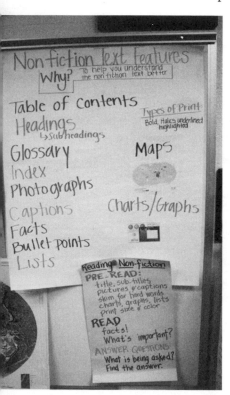

An Anchor Chart for Reading Nonfiction Text

SCAFFOLDING

Common Core and Common Sense: How Much Informational Text?

Perhaps the most controversial element of the CCSS appears at the very beginning, in the introduction (p. 5), when the authors of standards present specific percentages of all text taught to students that should be informational. The small chart below, drawn from the 2009 NAEP (National Assessment of Educational Progress) Reading Framework, has produced more indignant blog entries and online postings than perhaps any other aspect of the standards:

Grade	Literary Text	Informational Text
4	50%	50%
8	45%	55%
12	30%	70%

What do these numbers actually mean for teachers? Some critics have charged that this emphasis on nonfiction, in the name of preparing students for careers, robs English language arts teachers of the opportunity to engage students through the rich language and possibilities for critical thinking that great literature offers. Others are quick to point out that reading informational text *is* a necessary skill for the workplace and that the standards clearly indicate that the 70% of reading that is informational text is meant to take place not entirely in English class but across all reading in a school setting.

A commonsense approach ought to tell us that regardless of specific numbers, it's probably important for students to encounter a variety of texts and to understand how to read them. *We* certainly don't keep such close track of the balance of our reading, tracking minutes spent reading the newspaper against minutes spent reading a novel—do you? Let's put it like this: Before we worry about the exact percentage of time kids, especially struggling readers, spend reading specific types of text, let's worry about getting them reading at all.

How much informational text is enough? We'd say that it depends on your students and what you, as the expert in your classroom, observe. Certainly, you should introduce classes to both fiction and nonfiction. Just how you balance the two for individual students ought to revolve around the questions we've asked throughout this book. What engages, motivates, and gives ownership to the learners you teach? What mix of genres best serves the overall learning needs of your classes?

BOOKS

Books for Teaching Informational Text

Amistad: A Long Road to Freedom by Walter Dean Myers

Based on the true Amistad story, Myers offers primary documents to support the episode. Photographs, newspaper accounts, and correspondence bring to life the events surrounding the Africans who mutinied against the captain of their slave ship.

The Boy Kings of Texas: A Memoir by Domingo Martinez

This memoir about a smart boy who grows up in the border town of Brownsville, Texas, helps readers come to understand the difficulties that Hispanic teens face while simply trying to survive in America. The stories Martinez tells will make readers both laugh and cry as they accompany him on a memorable journey.

They Call Themselves the KKK: The Birth of an American Terrorist Group by Susan Campbell Bartoletti

This fascinating, well-researched book traces the evolution of the Ku Klux Klan from its beginnings as a small social club to a powerful, angry group of men bent on the destruction of a struggling group of people whose color is different from their own. The primary documents, annotated bibliography, and source notes make this an invaluable resource on the topic and will help students think again about the meaning of "terrorism."

Getting Away With Murder: The True Story of the Emmett Till Case by Chris Crowe

In 1955, Emmett Till, a 14-year-old black teenager from Chicago, took a trip to Mississippi to visit family. During that historic visit, he was brutally beaten to death by men who accused him of whistling at a white woman. Crowe painstakingly reviews the crime as well as the dramatic trial that many think was a catalyst for the civil rights movement.

The Great Fire by Jim Murphy

What caused the great Chicago fire of 1871? Murphy offers readers an insight into how the fire could have been prevented, starting with class discrimination and ending with bad communication. Primary documents make this event come alive for readers.

The Immortal Life of Henrietta Lacks by Rebecca Skloot

Henrietta Lacks was a poor black woman whose cancer led to one of the most important tools in medicine, HeLa cells—cells taken from Henrietta's body without her knowledge. Though her cells have led to important medical advances that have saved millions of lives, the ethical question of stealing and then selling cells lies at the heart of this compelling book.

Moonbird: A Year on the Wind With the Great Survivor B95 by Phillip Hoose

This engaging account of a shorebird, named B95 for the black band on his leg bearing his name, also includes facts, photographs, maps, and source notes. The book could be used by science and English teachers alike since Hoose offers not only research but also a strong theme and terrific prose.

We've Got a Job: The 1963 Birmingham Children's March by Cynthia Y. Levinson

Four thousand black teenagers voluntarily went to jail in Birmingham, Alabama, in 1963 as a statement against the segregation and police brutality they and their parents had experienced. This action drew national attention to their cause and helped ignite the civil rights movement. The clear organization of this compelling true account will help students understand the structure and features of informational text.

The very label "mentor text" implies that reading selections can act, to a degree, in the same way the best teachers act.

act. If you think about the best teachers you ever had, you probably remember that they challenged you appropriately but also engaged you by connecting to both your emotions and your sense of logic. Mentor texts ranging, for instance, from short passages of fiction to longer articles on high-interest subjects engage and challenge students in a similar fashion at the same time that they allow students to learn and reflect on uses of language.

Construct a Classroom Library. The research on classroom libraries provides clear evidence that they matter and that they work (Fielding, Wilson, & Anderson, 1986; Neuman, 1999; Routman, 2003). But let's be clear: A true classroom library is more than a bunch of books on a shelf in your room. Classroom libraries need to contain exciting literature at an age-appropriate level, they need to be used by the teacher and students, they need to be organized and accessible, and they should ideally provide the very mentor texts that teachers use to teach craft and mechanics. Indeed, classrooms containing active libraries achieve their results because teachers and students offer frequent book talks based on titles available in the classroom, because teachers pull mentor texts from those same titles, and because student excitement is raised by any means possible—book trailers, peer conversations, or author visits and online videos of authors, for example.

Model Reading. Simply put, teachers who don't read don't inspire students to read. Moreover, teachers can model reading of many different types—newspaper articles, young adult fiction, classical literature, contemporary nonfiction books, or much more. At Barry's school, for instance, every literacy classroom includes a prominently displayed sign (or just a spot on a board) where the teacher can write three titles under these categories: What I'm Reading, What I Want to Read, and What I Recommend (content-area teachers are invited to post their current reading selections, as well).

One week, the first category might include the title of a popular young adult book, and the next, it might be changed to a teaching resource book. Those postings in turn offer a chance for both spontaneous and planned conversations about books to take place daily.

Classroom Library

Similarly, ReLeah often advises professional learning communities and faculty groups to take a few minutes to share their reading selections with one another—and then to share them with students, as well. This allows students to experience, firsthand, what and how someone in a "field" reads. Teachers might also invite visitors from the community to do the same—not a full period, of course, but for 10 minutes once a week, in person or through recorded or live technology use, including email, video, or a phone call. What does the mayor, a doctor, the postal worker, or the sports store owner read, and why?

TECHNOLOGY USE

Make Reading a Community Experience. As valuable as it can be for teachers to model reading, it's probably even more valuable for students to see their peers reading. The "What I'm Reading" placards described earlier can be powerful when each student completes one and displays it in the classroom; just posting titles in this way can engender rich conversation about books. So can student-led book talks; as soon as a student finishes a book, an article, or another text, invite him or her to share with the class for just a minute or two. And it's also worthwhile to engage others in such an experience; try inviting a school administrator, a math teacher, or any other adult to come in and offer a book talk.

CHALLENGE AND SUCCESS

A true community of readers also extends beyond a single classroom. At Barry's middle school last year, for instance, every student and adult—including many parents—read and discussed the book *Wonder* by R. J. Palacio. Intergrade discussion groups, online blog entries, graffiti walls, and reflections offered at school assemblies by students and teachers all helped to unite and energize students about reading together. Did every student actually finish the book? Probably not. But the contagious excite-ment created by hundreds of readers enjoying a story together encouraged many traditional non-readers to take a stab at it.

COLLABORATION

Scaffold Reading Experiences. All reading is valuable. Quite often, teachers are torn between the twin goals of creating lifelong readers and preparing students to read more and more challenging and

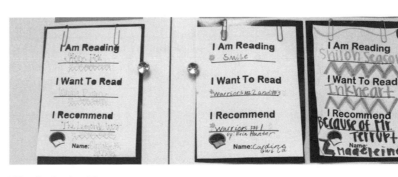

What I'm Reading Charts

VOICES FROM THE
CLASSROOM

The Community Reading Experience

Three teachers from Barry's school offered reflection on the experience of reading *Wonder* with nearly 300 students and teachers at the same time:

"It was wonderful to see groups from different grades reading the same book side by side, math or science teachers reading aloud to groups of students, and discussions where the book seeped into other classrooms and disciplines, from PE to art. It really brought us together."

—Seventh-grade teacher

"By using Palacio's masterpiece as a community book, we were able to tackle many sensitive issues with regard to being kind to others. Our students were mesmerized by the poignant moments as they watched Auggie persevere in spite of the emotional crippling he encounters. While Wonder was relevant and meaningful to the entire middle school, it had a phenomenal impact on many students who could personally identify with the story."

—Sixth-grade teacher

"The highlight of our reading was the time spent in small groups discussing character traits and how these characters were also seen in our real lives. For example, the students all had similar stories of the friendships shown in Wonder *as well as the difficulties of overcoming middle school drama. It seemed that each student found at least one piece in the book that really stuck with her and served as an excellent takeaway."*

—Fifth-grade teacher

academically rewarding texts. The danger comes from seeing those goals as mutually exclusive. Such thinking leads to the belief that students shouldn't read *Twilight* because they need to read *Pride and Prejudice,* or the more subtle message teachers often deliver that Meyer is fine for weekends but Austen is what belongs in school. If we want to encourage reading, we need to remember that every text a student encounters successfully leads to greater success in reading later on. Appropriate scaffolding can be a slow process, and students' needs regarding when and how much they need will differ. Individualized reading experiences, thus, are key in encouraging success.

DIFFERENTIATION

Encourage Reading Across Genres. A strong classroom library, like an actual library, should include more books (or magazines or other texts)

than only those a teacher likes. Graphic novels, for instance, should have a place in your library, as should both fiction and nonfiction and realistic and nonrealistic writing. Consider populating your classroom library intentionally, and possibly even organizing the library, using categories such as Realistic Fiction, Fantasy and Science Fiction, and Nonfiction. Ask teachers from other content areas to make suggestions of the texts they read or that relate to their subjects. And consider including student writing in your classroom library, as well—it's a great way both to validate the work students produce and to have peers model for one another.

CHALLENGE AND SUCCESS

In a classroom with a true reading culture, students such as Lorenzo find it hard to escape. They may still resist reading, it's true, but such resistance becomes less a matter of not doing homework and more a matter of refusing to fit in. They turn away from the textbook and see a bookshelf full of appealing titles. They turn to a friend and see the personal choice novel on her desk. They insist they only want to read magazine articles or comic books and find a teacher who not only allows them to read such material but insists on talking about it—or even on having the students themselves talk about the material to the class.

Beyond the First Step: What Happened to Lorenzo?

Reading with audience and purpose in mind is a skill reflected in the reading anchor standards, particularly when we look at specific standards by grade level. Note, for instance, the reading standard for seventh grade we cited earlier:

Determine an author's point of view or purpose in a text and analyze how the author distinguishes his or her position from that of others. (RI.7.6)

Now consider the same standard as it is written for Grades 11 and 12:

Determine an author's point of view or purpose in a text in which the rhetoric is particularly effective, analyzing how style and content contribute to the power, persuasiveness, or beauty of the text. (RI.11-12.6)

Lorenzo and his classmates started down the road toward fulfilling this standard with the activity involving movie trailers and texts related to movies we described earlier. Were they ready yet to discuss the beauty of nonfiction text or the power of rhetoric? Perhaps not so directly as the wording of the 11th-grade standards might require. Their journey didn't end with that assignment, however. Later in the year, Mrs. Randolph asked each student to choose a full newspaper or magazine article to read and posed several questions for students to consider:

- Who is the audience for this document, and what two details from the document prove that this is the audience?

- Pick two elements of the document that demonstrate a *choice* made by the author, and explain how each choice contributes to the overall meaning.

- What is the central message of this document, and why might the audience need or wish to read about this message?

- How does this author's message or tone differ from the way someone else might write about the same subject? What words or phrases prove your point?

"I don't get it," Lorenzo told her. "What am I supposed to do?"

"Did you listen to my instructions?" she asked, clearly frustrated. "I also gave you a full sheet of directions typed out. Did you read those?"

"I did," he said. "I still don't get it."

In a classroom with a true reading culture, students such as Lorenzo find it hard to escape.

AUTONOMY

INQUIRY

Mrs. Randolph sighed. With Lorenzo, it would never be easy. But she breathed deeply and chose a different route for Lorenzo; she created a PowerPoint presentation with a single question on each slide. Then she made the same PowerPoint available to the rest of the class. As their assessment, the students were allowed to change or alter each slide in any way they wished as long as they clearly answered the original question. Graphics, charts, bullet points, and other forms of text were all allowed and encouraged.

"And don't forget our anchor chart," Mrs. Randolph called to her class. "Use the informational text features to read the article!"

A few days later, Lorenzo turned in a PowerPoint that answered every question fully, using the review of a superhero movie as his focus. He included pictures on every slide, but more importantly, he understood the assignment and connected to the text. It was a qualified success, but an important one.

It also allowed Mrs. Randolph to use the students' experience with informational text as a launching pad for reading narrative. Earlier we cited the sixth reading standard for seventh grade as it applies to informational text; here is the partner standard for seventh grade that focuses on narrative:

> Analyze how an author develops and contrasts the points of view of different characters or narrators in a text. (RL.7.6)

From considering purpose and audience in nonfiction, it wasn't a daunting leap for Mrs. Randolph's class to compare voices in popular young adult works with multiple narrators such as *Wonder,* the novel we described Barry's middle school reading earlier, or Rob Buyea's *Because of Mr. Terupt.*

The growth of Lorenzo's engagement as a reader and student didn't alter his personality or his problems in school. He still squirmed in his seat, found instructions difficult to decipher, and received little support at home. But he also experienced success and ultimately progressed as a reader in Mrs. Randolph's class. You probably have students much like Lorenzo in class, and we can't promise to transform them into model

TECHNOLOGY USE

MULTIPLE
LEARNING
METHODS

AUTHENTIC
ASSESSMENT

SCAFFOLDING

HOW TO Replicate Mrs. Randolph's Lesson

Consider again the steps Mrs. Randolph took to introduce her students to informational text, this time generalized to work across multiple types of document:

- Share a short, high-interest informational text with a class (Mrs. Randolph used movie trailers).

- Read or view the text twice, the second time having students focus on specific questions of audience, purpose, and tone. Use a graphic organizer with one column for each so that students can note specific details.

- Put students in pairs or groups and assign them—or have them choose—a similar informational text to examine. Have all groups share their findings with the class.

- Use online resources to find a variety of informational texts related to a single topic (Mrs. Randolph had students find reviews and other materials related to a movie).

- Using the students' observations of these texts as a guide, make an anchor chart with your class of the elements of informational text.

- Create a follow-up assignment (an essay, a presentation, a discussion, or a technology-based product) through which students examine a text individually to connect audience, purpose, and tone to the language of the text. Like Mrs. Randolph and depending on the maturity of your students, you may wish to direct students clearly in this process with a question-by-question approach—or you may wish to use a simple, open-ended prompt.

pupils through a simple reading exercise. We can, however, promise that the key for many disengaged students lies in their understanding of what they're asked to read, how to read it, and, most importantly, *why it matters*.

And the same is true, ultimately, if you substitute the word "write" for the word "read."

Audience and Purpose in Writing

Pam Metcalf, a ninth-grade teacher, routinely starts the year with a writing assignment that forces students to consider their tone and purpose. "Imagine you've just gotten into major trouble at a Friday night football game," she tells her students. "At the game, which took place at a rival school, you were with some friends who decided to break into and vandalize the school building. Although you resisted the idea and did not enter the school, you were with the group and waited outside for them, where you were caught by a teacher. Before you return to school on Monday, you need to write four messages explaining the situation—a text to your best friend, an email to your parents, a letter to your principal, and a letter to a judge."

AUTHENTIC ASSESSMENT

If reading as a form of communication requires an awareness of audience, context, and purpose, writing requires it even more stringently. After all, what's the point of writing if you're not writing *for* someone—yourself or someone else? Yet teachers routinely (and perhaps understandably) forget that writing in school is not the same as writing for real-world purposes and turn writing into a purely academic exercise that can rob the task of meaning. It's like asking students to shoot free throws for days on end without ever playing an actual game of basketball or to solve endless math problems about perimeter without ever needing to figure out the perimeter of an actual object.

RELEVANCE

The goal of assignments such as Mrs. Metcalf's is to help students shape informational writing—and, eventually, arguments and narratives—in a deliberate, conscious manner that takes context into account. It's an approach driven, in part, by the tendency of today's students to neglect modes of discourse in their writing, to compose essays that include the language of texting ("romeo went 2 see juliet, lol") and that tend to circumvent the conventions of what the CCSS refer to as "standard English." Yet while the Common Core clearly privileges standard English as a goal of instruction in the language standards, helping students to write with purpose and intentionality is the practice most central to effective writing. (For a more in-depth discussion of the place of conventions and grammar in writing and learning, see Chapter 8.) The Anchor Standards for Writing, for instance, first lay out three kinds of text students should write—arguments, informative/explanatory texts, and narrative—and then immediately suggest that students should be aware of audience as they start the process of writing:

Produce clear and coherent writing in which the development, organization, and style are appropriate to task, purpose, and audience. (W.4)

A problem with this standard for teachers of disengaged or striving learners, however, is that it might suggest that the foremost priorities in writing instruction are to hold students accountable for clarity, organization, and style (which, for some teachers, could translate to mechanics and writing structure) rather than for reaching an audience effectively. Let's put that another way. Some teachers, reading the fourth anchor standard, might believe that the most important part of teaching writing is *how* students construct a piece rather than *why* they're constructing it in the first place.

No doubt, the *how* matters. But removing the *why* from writing is a recipe for disaster with students who are already uninterested in learning; what's more, such students will likely resist any lessons about style, organization, or clarity even more than they would otherwise when the purpose of the writing task is unclear or is seen as a mere pretense. By way of example, consider Vanessa.

Removing the *why* from writing is a recipe for disaster with students who are already uninterested in learning.

The Problem of Voice

"I hate writing," Vanessa, a 10th-grade student, told us. "I don't like reading, but I really hate writing." Pressed further, she added this reflection to her comment: "It's like I know what I need to say, but I can't get it to be the way my teachers want. It always sounds fine to me when I read it, and then I fail."

Vanessa's sixth-grade science paper—written four years before she made the comments above—exhibits much of the same awkwardness that continued to characterize her later writing. In the excerpt that follows, phrases such as "answers on" instead of "answers to" demonstrate a struggle with idiomatic language that sometimes corresponds with antipathy for reading. The third sentence, moreover, is a good example of Vanessa's attempts to sound the way she thought her teacher expected to her to sound—to sound smart, in other words, rather than clear:

Science means finding answers on what needs to be searched for. Scientists found out four factors that evaporation occurs. Learning everything about distillation was interesting in this project towards the relation of evaporation and the understanding about condensation happening. Distillation is an interesting concept of evaporation and condensation.

Vanessa struggled, in short, with voice. Although she wasn't disengaged in learning generally, Vanessa had disengaged from reading and writing—she enjoyed her language arts classes but hated the homework, for instance. It's tempting not to think of such a student as a struggling learner; after all, Vanessa behaved better than Lorenzo and made far better grades than Daniel from Chapter 1. Yet Vanessa's difficulty with voice and the resulting awkwardness of her written communication arose from the same source: a general lack of engagement in writing. Vanessa, like Daniel, looked on writing assignments as a task, not an opportunity. She felt that she had to communicate in a way she didn't understand for teachers who wanted something she couldn't achieve. The opening of this ninth-grade essay provides further evidence of her struggle to communicate effectively:

Essays are concepts that try to explore the mind and it tries to get a student to gain more knowledge in their writing than they would not have understood. It is required to choose books and think of a common theme that would allow us to see a relationship between books. All types of books have some relation to one another, which can enhance the thought of others considering each one has a different view on most things. For this research essay, I have chosen the selection of books which are based upon the common theme of containing characters who resist authority in various ways.

It's telling that Vanessa writes that "it is required" in introducing her topic, as if she saw herself as the passive receptor of this subject, not the instigator.

There's probably nothing harder to teach in writing than the concept of voice. It's a concept that's fluid at best, one that we're often tempted to chalk up to natural ability; some writers have voice, some don't. And it's

> Vanessa felt that she had to communicate in a way she didn't understand for teachers who wanted something she couldn't achieve.

true that there are writers, from Mark Twain to A. A. Milne, whose voice is inimitable. But problems with voice in student writing often reflect concurrent issues. The first is mechanical: As a nonreader, Vanessa had not filled her literacy toolbox with solid tools for writing. The second involves purpose and audience: Vanessa was writing, essentially, to no one and for no reason that mattered to her.

Narrative Writing: Vanessa's Route to Success

Unfortunately, years of enforced and restrictive creative writing assignments—and a resulting sense of inadequacy based on teacher comments on those assignments—had left Vanessa so wary of such writing that she wouldn't even consider voluntarily composing a poem or personal essay.

"I'm not a creative person," she stated firmly. "I know I'll never be a good writer. I just want to figure out how to get a B– on my essays instead of a C or a D." Vanessa's idea of creative writing, when she explained it to us, included prescriptive assignments; in ninth grade, she'd been forced to write a sonnet in iambic pentameter, a shape poem, and a poem in rhymed couplets. The lackluster response of her teacher to these canned assignments led to her self-assessment of her own lack of creativity.

In 10th grade, however, Vanessa encountered Jason Hall. "He reminded me of that teacher from *The Outsiders,* Mr. Syme," she said. "The one who told Ponyboy that he could write anything he wanted." Each day, Mr. Hall began his English class with a few minutes of writing. He offered daily prompts for students, but had two rules. First, students did not have to write to the suggested prompt, but did have to write. Second, every day, each student had to begin writing by addressing the piece to someone specific, from "Dear Mom" to "Dear Mr. President"— the subject was the student's choice and could even be a fictional or historical figure.

AUTONOMY

MULTIPLE
LEARNING
METHODS

RELEVANCE

At first, Vanessa trudged through the daily writing activity much as she approached all other writing assignments—as a chore. The turning point came the day Mr. Hall's prompt involved a visual: "Draw a map of a neighborhood you lived in as a child. Include one specific object taller than you were on your map. Then write the story of that object."

Donna Alvermann on Self-Efficacy

VOICES FROM THE
FIELD

"The potency of one's beliefs about the self is phenomenal. In adolescence, as in earlier and later life, it is the belief in the self (or lack thereof) that makes a difference in how competent a person feels. Although the terms self-concept and self-efficacy are sometimes used interchangeably in the research literature, they actually refer to different constructs. For example, an adolescent may have a good self-concept of herself as a reader, but her answer 'Not very' to the question 'How confident are you that you can comprehend a primary source on the Boston Tea Party?' would indicate low self-efficacy for that particular reading task. A statement about self-concept is domain specific, whereas one about self-efficacy is task specific (Pajares, 1996). Moreover, instructional conditions that are known to increase students' capacities to feel competent in dealing with difficult reading tasks have been linked to their willingness to work harder to achieve success on those tasks (Schunk & Zimmerman, 1997)."

—Donna Alvermann (2003, p. 4)

Vanessa's story, drawn from a map of her neighborhood, centered on an experience that had happened with a friend of hers in another class:

Dear Mr. Hall,

So look, once I was at Barbara's house. Well, I go there a lot. Anyways, we were outside sitting on her porch looking at this tree in her yard, right? So we're sitting outside, and we're talking about the tree, then the conversation lags and we just sit there. But what's that we hear? We both turn around to each other and stare at each other with intensity and our mouths are just totally open. And so then Ashley goes, "Is that the ice cream truck . . . ?" And Then I'm like "OH MY GOSH. IT IS. RUN RUN RUN!!"

So Barbara runs into her room and I start to follow her then I'm like NO, and I go throw open the front door and run down the street to the ice cream man and I'm running after him like "WAIT!!" And then he waits, and we get Spongebob popsicles. It was pretty grand.

HOW TO Teach Voice in Writing—More Ideas

There's no mass production of voice, no one assignment that will get every student to sound original, authentic, and unique in his or her writing. Here, however, are a few more ideas and tips for bringing voice to student writing.

Use Mentor Texts. Whether your students are working on fiction, essays, poetry, or other texts, there's no better way to learn about voice than modeling and emulation.

Try this:

- Have students highlight particular phrases that create voice or character and discuss them in groups or as a class—do this regularly. A tip: First sentences of young adult novels are great for zeroing in on voice; collect several, identify the voice, and discuss.

Trust the Process. Prewriting and revision are essential steps for creating voice. Experienced authors know that voice is sometimes crafted; it doesn't always emerge in a first draft.

Try this:

- Guide students toward voice by asking them to make a list of words or phrases or to envision points of view and characters before they write.

- In revision, try having partners read and describe the voice of a piece paragraph by paragraph (you might supply them with a list of descriptors, such as "scholarly," "flat," or "casual," before they try this).

Use Letters. Letters demand a specific, particular audience, and audience leads to particular ways of using language. Even essays or poems can start life as a letter, then be revised.

Try this:

- Take a letter to the editor from your local paper and ask students to write a response from another point of view, *or*

- Analyze the voice of such letters and discuss what you can surmise about the authors from the language they use.

- Allow students to compose or critique emails as part of a discussion about voice and tone. Not only will you reinforce the concept of voice and why it matters; you may prepare students for future communication with teachers or employers.

Use Illustration. Pictures and paintings have their own voice and provide interesting discussion starters; in addition, students can use illustration to reflect or inspire their own voice. What does the narrator, speaker, or reader look like?

Try this:

- Have students read a passage out loud to a partner, then have the partner draw a picture—a symbol, a stick figure, or just a smiley face, for instance—that illustrates the voice in the paragraph. If it's tough to come up with an image, it may be time to reconsider voice.

Teach Point of View and Perspective. Use mentor texts to review the effects of first-, second-, and third-person narration, as well as the difference between omniscient and limited perspective in narration. Point out that informational text also includes points of view and biases. Even outlining or discussing as prewriting from these points of view can be useful in determining what kind of voice a piece might have.

Try this:

- Have students write about the same topic, but from the point of view of a different character.
- For informative writing, have them try writing from a different philosophical perspective (these perspectives need not be complicated: the hopeless romantic, the scientific genius, the professional daredevil).

Focus on Small Parts. Voice arises from sentence structure and variety, from verbs, from punctuation, from similes and metaphors, and from many other small elements of language.

Try this:

- Focus revision on one area at a time—have students highlight (in print or on a computer) one area throughout a draft—every verb, for instance. Then ask them to revise only that area with voice in mind. Read the before and after pieces aloud at the end to see the difference.

Most writers spend a lifetime trying to nail down their own voice, or that of the characters they develop. Interestingly, voice is not mentioned in the CCSS (except in reference to active and passive verbs), but it is a key piece of engaging students in reading and writing and deserves practice and attention both as they read and as they write.

But then, just when I thought the experience was pretty stupendous, I was so intent on my popsicle that I tripped and sprained my ankle. I couldn't run track for two weeks, my coach got mad, and it was all Spongebob's fault (and the ice cream guy). So the lesson is: it's okay to run, but sometimes you have to be careful how you walk.

"It wasn't just, 'That's pretty good, keep working on it,'" she said. "Mr. Hall conferenced with me about it, then asked me every day if I'd written another draft. He really liked some of the words I used, especially *stupendous*. He also said he liked my last sentence. Eventually, the class wrote a couple of drafts, and mine went up on his bulletin board. My mom saw it when she came for parent conference. My original audience was Mr. Hall, but after I talked to him I changed the audience to my friend Barbara. I'm glad my mom saw it."

Gaining a sense of audience and having a personal stake in the outcome of a piece improved Vanessa's narrative writing. Would it do the same for her essays?

Real-World Writing: Providing an Actual Audience for Student Writers

Before we finish Vanessa's story, let's consider how teachers can infuse writing assignments with a sense of real purpose and help students to consider the needs of an audience of readers as they write.

First, with any important assignment, teachers should always consider the possibility of *providing actual readers*. When you think about it, schools teem with potential readers. Besides the peers of students in the classroom, readers of a piece might include students in other grades, parents, other teachers, or administrators. Audiences beyond the school walls can also be important. Knowing the audience from the start of the writing process can motivate and engage student writers as well as encourage them to produce more polished results. Consider the following possibilities for reaching readers:

- **Bulletin boards.** Post student work and change the displayed pieces regularly, both in the classroom and in public areas of the school.

FEEDBACK

CHALLENGE AND SUCCESS

RELEVANCE

How Do the CCSS Frame Narrative Writing?

A great deal has been written and said about the place of narrative writing in the CCSS, largely by those who feel the narrative is slighted in the standards while expository writing receives fuller attention. On the one hand, both Anchor Standard for Writing 3 and the specific version of the standard for every grade level emphasize narrative writing explicitly:

> Write narratives to develop real or imagined experiences or events using effective technique, well-chosen details, and well-structured event sequences. (W.3)

At the same time, however, many critics point out that the majority of the standards focus on conventions and expectations that could only reasonably apply to persuasive and analytical essays. Appendix C of the CCSS, which includes sample writing by students, exacerbates this impression by including only one narrative sample for Grades 6–8, and none at the high school level.

Narrative writing is, of course, extremely valuable for students. In particular, it's important to students whose cultural background emphasizes storytelling, sometimes in nonlinear fashion or in a particular style. Harnessing the power of such instincts goes beyond common sense; it's crucial to engaging students and to helping them develop voice.

An overly methodical approach to teaching to the standards might find some schools dramatically reducing the amount of narrative writing students undertake, but reason should tell us that many of the other standards, from the six anchor language standards to the three writing standards related to production and distribution to any standard related to audience and purpose, will be more easily reached by students who care about their work and who forge the personal connections to words that short stories, poetry, and personal reflections can encourage.

- **Online sites.** While you'll want to be careful about how much information about your students is displayed online, there are sites that welcome student contributions as well as free sites that allow you to create a class webpage, a class blog, or interactive pages that offer ways to share work with the online community.

TECHNOLOGY USE

- **Online pen pals.** Find another school and trade written work with students at the same grade level. Have students email or post positive comments about one another's pieces.

- **The school library.** At a school where Barry taught, teachers annually collected student work, created a bound book, and put it in the school library and catalog. Each year, students would check out books of work from previous classes and peruse them as they prepared their own written pieces that would eventually appear in these anthologies. Students would also return to the library in later years to reread their own work in print.

- **Wikis, Glogster pages, flipbooks, or other online pages for other grades.** Besides physical books in the library, your students can post their written work with the clear intention of having other grade levels—younger or older students—read what they've written. Consider using a wiki to create a shared classroom narrative, for instance, with each student adding one page to the story. Or collect short pieces and make an online flipbook—a virtual book with pages that actually turn—using one of the many free sites that offer to create such documents for you.

- **Local businesses.** Parents in your community—those with an office waiting room, a shared bulletin board in a break room, or any other display area—might relish the thought of displaying student work for their employees, customers, or colleagues.

- **Parent reader panels.** Similarly, with only a few interested and motivated parents, you can create a panel of readers who will gather at the school and read and respond to work in a positive manner, offering a sentence or two of encouragement to each writer in your class. Such an effort saves the teacher some grading time and encourages adolescent writers at the same time.

- **Student contests.** The goal of encouraging students to enter contests should not be the extrinsic reward of winning, most of the time. Rather, contests offer a chance to revise and reshape work with a particular purpose in mind and sometimes encourage students to write and read differently. And, of course, if one of your students does happen to win a writing contest, the self-confidence about writing that accompanies such a reward is invaluable to promoting self-efficacy and future effort.

- **Time-capsule writing.** Make students their own audience by telling them you will save the pieces they write and deliver them at the end of the year or even when they have moved up a grade level or more. You can even have them write letters to include in sealed envelopes for later delivery.

With any of the above options or with similar activities, don't forget the value of allowing students of any age to add illustrations or visuals to their writing in a variety of ways. Studying informational text with a class can lead to rich discussions about the power of pairing images and text in deliberate ways.

Classroom Writing: What to Do When an Actual Audience Isn't Available

When a real audience isn't readily available (and we admit that sometimes it takes a lot of time for a teacher to connect every student with a real audience when what you really want is for students to be writing constantly), we need to consider how to create the sense of an audience and purpose in the classroom. For such assignments, consider ways in which you and your students can agree that, while the actual audience might be limited to the teacher or peer readers in the class, the writing process includes considering potential readers at each step. For instance:

- **Use photographs of readers to create the feeling of audience.** One teacher we know posts photos of an entire panel of readers—using photographs her class found online—on the wall. There's the grammar stickler (an elderly, scowling woman), the weekend reader (a younger woman with a pleasant smile), the college professor (with glasses, tie, and an expression that says he cares about research and content), and the eighth-grade boy (just looking for a good read), for instance. With each assignment, this teacher and her students must consider each reader, what he or she wants out of the reading experience, and how the writer can provide it.

MULTIPLE
LEARNING
METHODS

- **Plan or write on the same topic for a variety of audiences.** As a part of revision, have students consider a brand-new audience for the pieces they write—and create rubrics that take the specific audience into account. What if, after creating the outline for a traditional analytical essay, students then produced a "frequently asked questions" page for a website, a script for a documentary, or a letter to the editor on the same topic?

- **Use structural clues and features as part of writing.** Remarkably few students are asked to include the pieces of informational text they learn about in class when they write, including headings, graphics, or bulleted lists like the one you're reading now. Yet these features are important both to how nonfiction is organized and to how an audience responds to it. Think of ways to include such features in writing assignments and discuss their effects on readers with students.

SCAFFOLDING

- **Strategize with vocabulary and syntax.** If your students are writing newspaper articles, one-sentence paragraphs might be appropriate; if they're writing personal essays, longer paragraphs and sentences might appeal to an audience more. Before they begin to write a piece, try making a list or an anchor chart with your class. What types of paragraphs, sentences, verbs, adjectives, or punctuation are likely to engage readers of this particular piece?

Each of the above ideas is meant to engage all student writers in thinking about purpose and audience. For struggling or reluctant learners, however, such reflection is particularly critical. That's because consideration of audience points out what we sometimes forget too easily—that writing is about communication; it's a two-way street. Both writer and audience must be interested for it to work. Struggling writers turn off when writing is purposeless; Vanessa's writing actually became worse when she tried to write for her teacher alone. As you think about the above strategies, therefore, you may hone in on some key points about getting disengaged learners to write at all. In particular, struggling learners need to write

MULTIPLE
LEARNING
METHODS

- in multiple genres and styles—not just the same essays over and over;

- both nonfiction and fiction;

- numerous short pieces rather than infrequent longer pieces;

- in a collaborative manner;

- with chances to make errors early on and correct them through revision (rather than being punished for mechanical errors in every first draft);

CHALLENGE AND
SUCCESS

- for audiences they trust and care about;

RELEVANCE

- using technology where it excites and engages students without slowing down the writing process;

- with opportunities for initial success; and

- in ways that allow them to practice both their own, natural voices and the conventions of standard English.

The Writing Process and Expository Assignments: Vanessa's Story

As a summative writing and research paper in his class, Mr. Hall had each student interview a family member or teacher about a key historical event from his or her lifetime. The students then had to write both about the background of the event and a description of the interview.

AUTHENTIC
ASSESSMENT

RELEVANCE AND
INQUIRY

For some students, the assignment brought on disaster. Despite a carefully constructed assignment description and rubric, many 10th graders floundered without the expected structure of a five-paragraph essay. Some more or less fabricated their interviews, many conducted shoddy research, and several didn't complete the assignment at all. Others loved the assignment and put their all into it—the whole experience was pretty much par for the course, as Mr. Hall saw it, for a sophomore English class in April.

Here's Vanessa's introduction to the paper:

Even though my uncle was young during the Viet Nam war, his life was still affected by it and he still remembers important moments to this day. Viet Nam was a life changing not only to America itself, but also the citizens and families within it. When I zeroed in on a person who was directly affected by the war instead of just reading about what happened it made me realize that no matter how young or old you are, if you are involved in an event like Viet Nam it will shape who you are in that moment and make you who you the person you turn out to be.

"It didn't get an A," Vanessa said of the assignment. "But it did get a B. I made some errors, even in the final draft. But I worked pretty hard on that paper—I really did the research in the library and online, unlike most of my friends. Partly that was because I knew my uncle would see it and partly because I wanted Mr. Hall to like it."

RELEVANCE

What changed for Vanessa? We can safely point to several aspects of the assignment that enabled her to move from tortured prose to natural, if not elegant, expression:

RELEVANCE

FEEDBACK

AUTONOMY

CHALLENGE AND SUCCESS

- Awareness of audience and purpose
- Multiple drafts with real feedback from her teacher and peers
- Choice in her subject matter
- Inspiration from a teacher who valued her voice in all writing—and demonstrated it
- A transformation in her vision of herself—from a self-portrait as a nonwriter to confidence in her own abilities

Final Thoughts

If we were to place Vanessa's accomplishment within the scope of the skills suggested by the "note on range and content in student writing" that accompanies the Grade 6–12 writing standards, we might be tempted toward disappointment. Vanessa had not yet accomplished much of what the note suggests she needed: choosing format deliberately,

HOW TO Replicate Mr. Hall's Lesson

- Have students write daily to suggested prompts or those of their own choosing without worrying about conventions. Create a level of comfort with the act of producing words. Include visual prompts (such as maps or pictures created by the students) as well as verbal prompts.

- Ask students to address their writing to a specific person or audience—even if it's fictional.

- After each student has accrued a number of fast-writes, conference with each one to suggest revisions or ideas for extension (don't focus on grammar or spelling at this time).

- Have students write at least one more—and preferably more—drafts of the piece, using peer editing, conferencing, teacher feedback, or reading aloud to encourage them to continue revision.

- When possible, provide an actual audience for the final product. At the very least, provide a *simulated* audience for the product.

- Help students transfer learning to other tasks by making audience, purpose, and voice part of the objective for all writing assignments, including non-narrative writing.

producing complex and nuanced writing, producing high-quality first drafts under a tight deadline. At the same time, however, she had made enormous progress toward other requirements in the note, such as the ability to revisit and make improvements to a piece or to evaluate sources carefully.

The real mark of Vanessa's success—and Mr. Hall's—had little to do with these lofty goals. One could see at the end of 10th grade that Vanessa had changed as a writer because she cared about writing and expression. The writing process helped her express herself, but the culture of writing in Mr. Hall's classroom, like the culture of reading in Mrs. Randolph's, made the difference. Vanessa wanted to succeed in her final paper not just for the grade but for herself.

Audience, purpose, and *context* are more than buzzwords in literacy. They lie at the heart of why students—why anyone, for that matter—read and write at all.

4 How to Go Deeper
Creating Analytical Thinkers

Students are engaged and open-minded—but discerning— readers and listeners. They work diligently to understand precisely what an author or speaker is saying, but they also question an author's or speaker's assumptions and premises and assess the veracity of claims and the soundness of reasoning.

—Description of College- and Career-Ready Students, CCSS Introduction

Ms. Anita Hodges's eighth-grade social studies students studied with disgust the enlarged photograph of a flea projected on the whiteboard. "Yuck—look at its nasty mouth," Haley said. "No wonder it makes dogs itch when it bites them."

"What do you really know about fleas?" Ms. Hodges asked her students. "Choose someone as the recorder in your group and write down everything you know about these insects." It didn't take long for the groups to discover that they knew that fleas made both animals and humans itch, that they caused the bubonic plague, and that they are really hard to exterminate once you get a good case of them in your yard or carpet.

ACTIVE LEARNING

INQUIRY

"Now, beside each fact write down how you know it is a fact."

Most of the students' knowledge came from personal experience, but when it came to the bubonic plague, they began to guess about how they came to have that information. One student said it was from an earlier teacher, another said she had read it "somewhere," and several agreed that it was something everyone just knows.

"What if I told you there had been some doubt about that fact until fairly recently?" Ms. Hodges asked. Most of the students responded in a way that let her know they had some curiosity about her statement and were willing to entertain the idea that maybe they had been wrong about their understanding of the cause of the bubonic plague.

Ms. Hodges watched Gerome and Darius closely. They acted bored, but she knew that it was more than that; they were totally and completely disinterested. The boys were students of above-average intelligence who were good friends, and they did what was required to get a better-than-passing grade, usually a C but sometimes a D. They rarely became involved in class discussions, kept to themselves, answered direct questions politely but passively, and rarely volunteered information or asked questions. They had active lives outside of class, but openly disdained school. Ms. Hodges knew they played some sort of musical instruments in a garage band, and this talent made them popular among students who were intimately connected to their earbuds, which was just about every student in the school. Ms. Hodges guessed that they didn't really care if the bubonic plague was caused by fleas or Godzilla, and, more discouragingly, she thought there was little she could do to pique their interest about this or any other issue in class.

Gerome and Darius are clearly struggling learners but, like Lorenzo in Chapter 3, not because of inability. These boys are capable of learning most anything they choose to learn, but they struggle with "school" learning because they see no value in it, and, what's more, they aren't going to go to any trouble to find relevance. The only thing that matters to them is music and their closed society of friends. Sometimes called "aliterate," such students have the ability to read but choose not to. Ms. Hodges knows that by the time these boys become seniors, with the Common Core State Standards (CCSS) firmly implemented, they won't be able to skate by the way they have done during most of middle school. If she and the other teachers on her team can't help them hone their intellectual curiosity, their chances of graduating will be slim.

A Case of Aliteracy: The Bubonic Plague

Ms. Hodges brought her concerns about Darius and Gerome to her professional learning community (PLC) team—a group of eighth-grade English, science, and math teachers who taught a common group of students and often created interdisciplinary units such as the one on the bubonic plague. "I know I can't reach every student with every topic," Ms. Hodges said, "but these two boys as well as several other students I can name are at real risk of falling behind if they don't learn some basic literacy and research skills before they get to high school." She sighed deeply. "How can I help them become independent when their only goal is finding a way to do the bare minimum and absolutely nothing more?" There is little more frustrating than this scenario, especially for a teacher who is trying to shift her practice toward inquiry-based learning. Ms. Hodges, along with her team, looks forward to teaching this unit each year because most students find it interesting and are enthusiastic about the class activities. To watch capable students such as Darius and Gerome refuse to even give the project a chance is simply maddening.

In this chapter we tackle the challenge that Darius and Gerome pose to even the best teachers because students who *"can* but *won't"* take energy, determination, and the patience of a saint. We follow Ms. Hodges and her team as they find a way to engage Darius and Gerome, and then we turn to Ms. Garcia, who found herself with an entire class of "can but won't" high school students who had perfected strategies for getting by with the least amount of effort.

A Change of Focus: Creating Skeptical Readers

After Ms. Hodges expressed her concerns to her team of teachers, they talked about how they might engage students who were, at best, dispassionate learners. They began by looking over the online articles they had carefully selected for the unit, thinking about which ones might appeal to Darius and Gerome.

Students who have the ability to read but choose not to are called "aliterate."

- "First Case of Bubonic Plague in 2011 Appears in New Mexico" from *Time: Heath and Family*

- "The Black Death of 1348 to 1350" from the History Learning Site

- "All Bites Are Off—Fleas Did Spread Plague" from the *Worcester News*

- "Bubonic Plague Case: Fleas Almost Kill 7-Year Old" from WebProNews

- "The Church's Involvement in Bubonic Plague" from a high school project

- "Bubonic Plague" from About.com: Rare Diseases

- "Bubonic Plague Traced to Ancient Egypt" from *National Geographic News*

- "Boccaccio: The Onset of the Black Death," a primary document from Fordham University

The original plan had been to place students in groups with instructions to read the articles, summarize them, and jigsaw the information for the rest of the class as an initial background-building activity in Ms. Hodges's class. Brian Sylvester, the science teacher, would then facilitate a research project based on the articles after students had brainstormed questions, and Shelly Boris, the English teacher, would head up the writing of the research project.

COLLABORATION

INQUIRY

With their new focus on engaging students such as Gerome and Darius, the teachers began to think about deepening their instruction from simply building background to helping students become skeptical readers. Perhaps, they reasoned, if the class were given the opportunity to question the material in the articles as well as read them for information, it might tap into ownership—and thus engagement.

INQUIRY

They agreed to modify the assignment: After students summarized their articles, they would also analyze them for accuracy of information, authenticity of source, and reasonableness of claims.

Ms. Hodges, however, was still concerned that the revised assignment was not enough to engage Darius and Gerome. After all, if the boys weren't responding to an up-close photo of a flea that grossed out their peers, they most likely would not respond with interest to a mere article—even if they were given the opportunity to question what they were reading.

Group Evaluation of a News Article

Title of Article: _____

Source: _____

Write the name of the group member who will take each role below.

Facilitator: _____

Scribe: _____

Recorder: _____

Reporter: _____

Instructions: Each group member will read the article silently. When everyone is finished, the facilitator will lead a discussion based on the questions below. The scribe will take notes about each question as it is being discussed. Everyone in the group will then work together to create an answer to each question, which the recorder will write on chart paper. The reporter will share the results of the group's analysis with the rest of the class. You may include illustrations in your chart.

1. Write a new headline and subhead for this article.

2. Briefly summarize the article as if you were telling someone you know about the article.

3. Decide if the source is reliable. How did you come to your conclusion?

4. Find one statement in the article that you might question because of its accuracy or reasonableness. Write it on your chart and be prepared to explain why you chose this statement.

5. What did the writer leave out that you think he or she should have included?

6. Which statement in the article seems most accurate or reasonable to you? Why?

7. Write three questions you would like to ask the author.

8. What one piece of information that you learned from the article would you like to share with the class?

MULTIPLE
LEARNING
METHODS

Differentiated Instruction Through Multiple Literacies

"What about YouTube?" Mr. Sylvester asked. "Maybe we can find something that will appeal to kids who won't engage in traditional print."

It didn't take long to find a poem about the bubonic plague on YouTube. It portrayed a series of illustrations that went along with rhyming facts about the plague. Ms. Hodges decided that Gerome and Darius, along with two other less-than-enthusiastic students, would work together in a group with the assignment of substantiating and expanding the facts in the video by reviewing the articles or looking up additional information online.

COLLABORATION

ACTIVE LEARNING

RELEVANCE

As Ms. Hodges expected, the next day in class most students were eager to read the article they had been assigned with their team to find out more about how fleas had caused such catastrophic illness. She was dismayed, however, when Darius told her that the video was lame because it had no music. "Who wants to watch a video with some old guy reading a poem—especially without music?"

AUTONOMY

"Well, why don't you create your own, then, if you think you can do a better job than 'some old guy'?" she responded.

"Can we?" Gerome asked. She noticed a flicker of interest on his part although Darius and the other students in the group slumped further down in their chairs as if sliding out of view might get them out of this altogether. Ms. Hodges knew she couldn't let this group do something "fun" while the rest of the class analyzed a news article; she felt she had almost crossed that line already by giving them a video instead of print. Thinking fast, she threw out a challenge. "You can create a music video to show to the class if you each read a different article and share the information with everyone else in your group. You will then choose one article and answer the questions on your article evaluation handout. You can create a video if you make sure that all of your facts are accurate." Ms. Hodges had, in effect, created a more challenging assignment for this group.

AUTHENTIC
ASSESSMENT

TECHNOLOGY USE

CHALLENGE AND
SUCCESS

While Darius and the other two boys still outwardly maintained a "who cares" attitude, they each read and discussed a different article with their group and, doing most of the work at home, produced a clever video—with great music. Not surprisingly, once other groups discovered that Darius and friends were creating a video from an article, they too wanted that option. Ms. Hodges allowed any group who also would do most of the work outside of class to produce a video, PowerPoint, or multimedia project for extra credit. Six of the eight groups took advantage of the opportunity.

TECHNOLOGY USE

MULTIPLE LEARNING METHODS

Once the students in Darius's group had taken the initial step of participating in the project, they tentatively joined the class community that Ms. Hodges had worked hard to establish and, in spite of their tendency to condescension, engaged in other activities. And why wouldn't they? Their video had been enthusiastically received by their peers, and other teachers on the team also complimented their work. Ms. Hodges's challenge, of course, was to continue to engage Darius and his group without allowing them to create music for every assignment.

AUTONOMY

CHALLENGE AND SUCCESS

A Project in Progress

When Ms. Hodges reported back to her PLC what had happened with Darius's group and how other students were motivated to create projects beyond the original assignment, she and her team decided that the following year they would include in the assignment the creation of a multimedia project that students would share with other classes. This element would also more thoroughly address Anchor Standards for Speaking and Listening 4 and 5.

Ms. Hodges, who often used History.com videos with her class, suggested that in the future they might use a few of the many videos from

TECHNOLOGY USE

Anchor Standards Speaking and Listening 4 and 5

Present information, findings, and supporting evidence such that listeners can follow the line of reasoning and the organization, development, and style are appropriate to task, purpose, and audience. (SL.4)

Make strategic use of digital media and visual displays of data to express information and enhance understanding of presentations. (SL.5)

that site about the bubonic plague with students and have them compare the articles to the videos. Ms. Boris began to jot down questions that students might address after viewing the videos to help them with comparison and contrast skills, noting that such an assignment would scaffold students' abilities to analyze how two texts address similar themes.

INQUIRY

- What facts in the article were omitted from the video?

- Why do you think the filmmaker omitted those facts? Would you have included them? Why?

- What new information was presented in the video that was not in the article?

- How did the visual aspects of the film compare to the visuals you "saw" in your mind while reading the article?

The transition from traditional textbook-driven instruction to active, inquiry-based learning takes time, collaboration, and flexibility, but the benefits outweigh the additional effort for teachers as well as for students. For example, teachers in dynamic professional teams report greater work satisfaction, higher morale, and powerful learning that transfers directly to the classroom (Southwest Educational Development Laboratory, 1997).

Deepening Understanding Through Critical Literacy

Education in the past was about *not* questioning—accepting everything in textbooks and from teachers' lectures as facts—and if a student ever doubted, he quickly put that instinct away because the "facts," true or not, would be on the next test, and passing the test was all that mattered. Today, as the introduction to the CCSS shows, the meaning of learning has changed, and so have our practices. Students who assume some ownership over the text—and according to Louise Rosenblatt (1995) we all do that as readers who bring our own experiences to the text—have a better chance of reading closely, making decisions about what information is valid and important, and questioning the "veracity of claims" and "soundness of reason." What's more, teaching students to read skeptically creates citizens who are better able to cut through political jargon, commercial sales, and wholesale propaganda.

HOW TO Integrate Reading, Writing, Speaking, and Listening in Interdisciplinary Units

- Begin now to build text sets that span content areas for units that will be taught later in the year.

  o Look for print-centric text in various genres: fiction, nonfiction, graphic novels, plays, poetry.

  o Peruse websites—or have students peruse them—and evaluate their usefulness for the unit.

  o Seek out primary documents from sites such as the Library of Congress (http://memory.loc.gov/ammem/index.html).

  o Look for YouTube and other online videos on the subject of study.

  o Clip articles from newspapers or magazines related to the topic. Store them in a folder until your PLC has time to look through them. Or, have students in groups look through the articles and decide if they should be included in the study.

  o Collect artifacts that could be used as physical displays to enhance the study. Put a notice in your school's newsletter asking parents or businesses to loan items for the duration of the unit.

- Incorporate a speaking/listening component in each unit where students share what they have learned or created. Consider using such presentations as performance assessments graded by a panel of teachers involved in teaching the unit.

- Teach students how to ask pertinent, thoughtful questions and allow them to question their peers after their presentations.

- Have students keep learning logs throughout the unit as a way of documenting their ongoing learning; this is especially useful for interdisciplinary units where the information gained in one class can be adapted or used in another.

- Encourage students to conduct interviews to expand knowledge. For example, students in several classes can come together for a Skype session with a professional on the topic.

- Use interdisciplinary units to teach students how literacy skills on the same topic can differ in specific disciplines:

  o Science—reading for facts, organizing information, and writing reports accurately and concisely.

  o Social studies—reading to compare accounts, analyzing perspectives, and writing persuasively.

  o English—reading to understand themes through various genres, participating in student-led discussions, and writing analytically or creatively.

> Education in the past was about *not* questioning—accepting everything in textbooks and from teachers' lectures as facts. Today, as the introduction to the CCSS shows, the meaning of learning has changed, and so have our practices.

The CCSS open the door for addressing what is known as critical literacy, the idea that texts have multiple meanings told from multiple perspectives, while sometimes silencing others' points of view (Luke & Freebody, 1997). Speaking and Listening Standard 8.2 for Grade 8 students, for example, directs teachers to help students:

> Analyze the purpose of information presented in diverse media and formats (e.g., visually, quantitatively, orally) and evaluate the motives (e.g., social, commercial, political) behind its presentation. (SL.8.2)

Reading through the lens of critical literacy means that students question authors' motives, consider bias, and also think about text in terms of social justice. For example, in the oft-taught novel *Out of the Dust* by Karen Hesse, English teachers may concentrate on characterization, conflict, theme, or poetic language. Social studies teachers may look at the novel from a historical perspective. A critical literacy approach, however, would ask students to consider the following:

- What is the author's purpose in writing this novel?
- Has the author portrayed the Dust Bowl in an accurate, unbiased manner?
- Whose values are represented in this novel?
- How might things have been different?
- What responsibility does society have for the events in the novel?

Such questions help create discerning—not just proficient—readers.

Unfortunately, textbooks are often sanitized of the type of content that will help readers develop critical literacy skills. This is one of the many reasons that we advocate for classroom libraries, supplemental texts, and web-based resources. Young adult novels and nonfiction, many of which are topping the charts on best-seller lists as well as winning prestigious awards, provide an engaging base for developing units. They also often illuminate social issues such as racism, poverty, and global interdependence. Matt de la Peña, for instance, a popular young adult novelist, writes about the struggles of biracial teens in *Mexican WhiteBoy* and kids in foster care in *Ball Don't Lie.* The topics of these novels, as well as the manner in which de la Peña approaches the subjects, create rich opportunities for critical literacy study.

In addition, as Edward Behrman points out in an article titled "Teaching About Language, Power, and Text: A Review of Classroom Practices That Support Critical Literacy," music and film also allow students to experience the way language is used for social ends and helps them understand issues related to the environment, history, economics, and politics, for example. The goal is for "teachers and students to collaborate to understand how texts work, what texts intend to do to the world, and how social relations can be critiqued and reconstructed" (Behrman, 2006, p. 491).

> MULTIPLE
> LEARNING
> METHODS

A Novel Approach to Critical Literacy

In their ongoing attempt to engage their aliterate and struggling students, Ms. Hodges and her team decided to use a compelling young adult novel to incorporate critical literacy into their curriculum. They chose Eliot Schrefer's *Endangered* (2012), a novel about a young girl, Sophie, who chooses to save a bonobo rather than ensure her own safety. Set in the Congo during a bloody revolution, Sophie must make difficult choices and face unspeakable horrors as she makes a journey toward refuge. The team felt the novel would be interesting to students and encourage them to think more deeply and critically than they had in the past. Students would read the book in their English class with Ms. Boris while Ms. Hodges, their social studies teacher, and Mr. Sylvester, their science teacher, would lead students in discussions of content-area topics addressed in the novel. They worked together to formulate questions that reflected a critical literacy approach in each discipline.

> MULTIPLE
> LEARNING
> METHODS
>
> INQUIRY

English

- Sophie, the main character, demonstrated several times in the novel that she valued the bonobo's life as much as she did her own. She said, "Though I knew there was human suffering out there, it wasn't like there was a tragedy scale where some things outranked others, or that care given to a bonobo meant less left for people" (p. 173). What would you say to Sophie regarding her statement—or to the author, who appears to be speaking through Sophie?

- Based on the events in *Endangered*, what is the value of life in the Congo—both animal and human?

- In trying to save one bonobo, Sophie inadvertently caused the death of others. Defend Sophie's position and the position taken by the bonobo refuge in the Congo. What would you have done if you were in Sophie's place? Why?

- Identify several places in the novel where Sophie made critical decisions that altered her future. For each situation, discuss the pros and cons of her actions. Evaluate those actions in terms of bravery and practicality.

Social Studies

- What conditions in a country could create a revolution where people kill without conscience?

- The author gives the reader little perspective from the point of view of the revolutionaries, except when the young soldier, Bouain, justifies his violent actions by saying, "No person has protected me" (p. 203). What does this one short sentence say about Bouain's decision to become a revolutionary? What other information might the author have provided? Why do you think he didn't provide more information about the revolutionaries?

- How do oppositional movements such as the one in the Congo compare to those in richer countries, such as Occupy Wall Street? Why are they different?

- How does the author use the revolution as a backdrop to his narrative? How does his choice of setting influence your perspective of the Congo? Is his social portrayal of the Congo accurate? What has the author left out that may have changed how you viewed the Congo?

Science

- Bonobos are closest to humans in terms of their DNA than any other mammal. Should more protection be afforded to such animals than to those more distant from humans?

- Is it better to leave animals in the wild, even though their life spans may be shorter, or to protect them in zoos? What about endangered animals?

- Make a list of each event in the novel that has some scientific basis and analyze each in terms of accuracy. For example, Sophie said that bonobos "saw only behavior and not reasons" (p. 215). Is that true?

- Research the environmental conditions in the Congo. Is the author's portrayal of these conditions accurate?

One of the advantages of reading novels with an eye toward critical literacy is that students soon discover that there are rarely definitive answers. As such, they learn to develop the skills to think through texts by wrestling with questions and evaluating perspectives. They become aware of the decisions an author makes as he crafts a novel and come to understand that such crafting has everything to do with their response to characters, events, and conflicts. In short, critical readers become more than observers watching a plot unfold; they grow into participants who *experience* the act of reading in an active and personal way.

Reading the World Through Critical Literacy

Ms. Hodges and her team found that their students, even Darius and Gerome, responded favorably when the teachers set a purpose for reading, such as having students take a critical stance rather than assigning reading because it was next in the unit. In keeping with their interdisciplinary focus, they decided to foster the reading of informational text by incorporating a current events article each week. One week Mr. Sylvester would provide an article related to science, and the next week Ms. Hodges would provide an article related to social studies; Ms. Boris would help students critically analyze the articles each week. Their goal was to help students become discerning readers by looking at all aspects of the text: author's bias and purpose, language that may influence the reader, and perspectives that may or may not be included. Although they had focused on these skills with the novel *Endangered,* they wanted students to transfer those skills to nonfiction.

> One of the advantages of reading novels with an eye toward critical literacy is that students soon discover that there are rarely definitive answers. As such, they learn to develop the skills to think through texts by wrestling with questions and evaluating perspectives.

RELEVANCE

CHALLENGE AND SUCCESS

BOOKS

Young Adult Novels Useful for Teaching Critical Literacy and Encouraging Deep Thinking

The Chocolate War by Robert Cormier

This classic novel has been taught in English classes for many years, but its central theme, the price one pays for daring to disturb the universe, is at the core of critical literacy. Jerry Renault's refusal to sell chocolates during a school fund-raiser will not let readers off the hook as they think about what they would have done in a similar situation.

Copper Sun by Sharon Draper

The tragedy of slavery begins for Amari in her African village when strangers arrive who destroy her home and then force her onto a boat bound for the Carolinas. The story continues as Amari becomes a slave for a young boy. Readers are forced to consider the real costs of slavery and how such an ugly past affects everyone in America—even today.

Double Helix by Nancy Werlin

In this action-packed novel, Werlin raises ethical questions about genetic engineering and gives her readers much to ponder about their own futures. Eli, the 18-year-old main character, is excited about his new job at Transgenics Lab, but he soon discovers the shocking truth about experiments performed by the geneticist in charge of the lab.

Jumped by Rita Williams-Garcia

This novel highlights the phenomenon of mean girls in a high school society that does not address the often disastrous fallout of gossip, slights, secrets, and a total lack of compassion—even among friends who should know better.

Lions of Little Rock by Kristin Levine

Set in Little Rock, Arkansas, in 1958, this novel uses the tumultuous integration wars as a backdrop for friendship and courage. Students will find themselves asking what they would have done had they been there—and what they would do if such events ever happened again.

Never Fall Down by Patricia McCormick

Based on a true story about a young Cambodian boy who is separated from his family and sent to a labor camp run by the Khmer Rouge, this novel offers a stark and compelling look at the horrors that came to be known as the Killing Fields.

Shine by Lauren Myracle

At the center of this mystery is a vicious hate crime directed toward Cat's best friend, a 16-year-old who happens to be gay. While the plot will keep readers engaged, the underlying issues of poverty, bullying, drugs, and homophobia will provide a deeper look at issues that are familiar to all too many teenagers.

The Sledding Hill by Chris Crutcher

It's all about censorship, and Crutcher doesn't let up for a minute. Readers will find this quirky, clever novel fun to read on one level and yet serious in its attempt to present an argument against censorship. At the very least, such a timely tale will force readers to consider the meaning of freedom in an academic context.

Smashed by Lisa Luedeke

Katie, a gifted athlete, has taken care of herself for many years, but just as she has it all within her grasp, she makes some fateful decisions. This emotionally charged and thoughtfully crafted novel brings to the forefront societal issues such as alcohol abuse, sexual assault, bullying, and parental responsibilities. Students will love the book; teachers will find much in it to prompt deep discussions.

Ms. Hodges had seen something on national news that she couldn't get out of her mind, and she approached the team about using the news piece with their classes. They knew that the topic might be troubling for some students—and might even provoke a reaction from parents. After much discussion, they decided that their goal of making reading meaningful and relevant to students required that they bring in content that may, at times, be disturbing. The print story came from the cover of the *New York Post*, December 5, 2012. The article reported that a man had been pushed onto the subway tracks and subsequently hit by the train. The issue in question was a photograph taken of the man moments before he died as he was trying to climb out of the track pit. There had been much discussion in the media about whether or not the *New York Post* should have run the photo and why the photographer didn't help the man instead of taking his picture.

Visual Literacy With a Critical Twist

INQUIRY

Ms. Hodges showed the photograph to her students without any associated text. She began the discussion by asking them what they saw.

There was a rumble of guesses before Sabon raised her hand and said, "The guy's climbing out of the tracks. He'd better hurry . . . that train is on him, dude."

"Why do you think he was on the tracks to begin with?" Ms. Hodges asked.

"Maybe he jumped . . . or fell?" Kisha offered.

"Why would he jump and then try to get out?" Matt questioned.

"Maybe he changed his mind," Kisha said.

"He probably dropped something important—like a briefcase full of money," someone offered from the back of the room.

"Who do you think took the picture?" Ms. Hodges asked.

There was some discussion about who might have taken the photograph, especially since there didn't seem to be anyone on the platform.

"What do you think the photographer was thinking as he took the picture?" Ms. Hodges asked. The room got quiet for a moment.

What If Parents Object to Content in Supplemental Materials?

While there is no surefire way to prevent a challenge to *any* supplemental material (including young adult novels), there are some steps that schools and districts can take to minimize the risk of a full-blown censorship incident.

1. Make sure the faculty understands intellectual freedom and the harms inherent in censorship by discussing these topics each year at a faculty meeting or in-service session. *Keep Them Reading: An Anti-Censorship Handbook for Educators* (2012) coauthored by ReLeah and Gloria Pipkin offers comprehensive information on this topic.

2. Send a letter to parents at the beginning of the year explaining that research and the CCSS support wide and varied reading across all genres. As such, classroom libraries are encouraged in every discipline, and students are expected to read from a variety of sources. Emphasize that teachers will offer an alternative selection if any reading material is offensive to students or parents. Plainly state that you honor family standards.

3. Make sure your district has a strong policy on challenged materials and that you are familiar with its provisions. Follow the steps in the policy if a challenge occurs.

4. If a parent objects to something you have assigned in the classroom, first ask if the parents have filled out the proper forms to make the challenge. If so, meet with the parent (and student as well if appropriate) with an administrator present. Explain your teaching objectives and show why this particular text supports the CCSS and the learning goals you have for students. Offer an alternative selection for this student only, not for the entire class.

5. Go online to NCTE's Anti-Censorship Center (http://www .ncte.org/action/anti-censorship) and use the resources there to help you prepare for future challenges.

6. Ask your media specialist to forward to you reviews and awards for books that you use in whole-class study, in literature circles, or for small group inquiry projects. Keep these on hand to show to anyone who challenges your selection.

"I think it was someone with an iPhone and he just snapped the picture before he really thought about it. That's how it is today—everyone taking pictures," Jannel said.

In English class, the lesson continued as Ms. Boris provided an online discussion of the controversy from *USA Today*: "Should *NY Post* Have Printed Photo of Man About to Die?" (2012). In the article, the photographer said he saw that the man had been pushed onto the tracks but couldn't get to him in time and just began taking pictures, hoping that his flash would alert the driver of the subway train.

Few of the students bought his version of events, however. Ms. Boris pointedly asked Darius what he thought. He looked at her like he had been waiting for her to ask so he could shed some light on the issue. "You all think you would have just rushed up there and pulled that guy out? You would have been too scared to do that—he could have pulled you in too. The dude with the camera probably just used what he had in his hands and took a picture. Now everyone is crucifying him."

"But should the paper have run the photograph? Wasn't it enough to report that a man had been pushed onto the tracks and died?" Ms. Boris asked.

Socratic Circles: A Format for Speaking and Listening

MULTIPLE LEARNING METHODS

ACTIVE LEARNING

Instead of allowing the students to continue to engage in an open discussion, Ms. Hodges organized a Socratic circle where half of the students sat in an inner circle and the other half sat in an outer circle. The inner circle discussed first whether the man with a camera should have taken the photo and then whether the paper should have run the picture. The outer circle, silent during the first discussion, offered feedback and then moved into the inner circle where the students discussed the next prompt Ms. Hodges provided to get the discussion started. The students continued to rotate into inner and outer circles as Ms. Hodges offered new prompts:

FEEDBACK

INQUIRY

- A female news reporter said that if the victim had been a woman, the *Post* would not have run the photograph. Do you think that is true? Why would it have mattered? If you believe it is true, what does it say about our society?

- What perspective do you think the victim's family has on this issue?

- Where does a newspaper draw the line between using photos to sell papers and being sensitive to those in the photos?

When Ms. Hodges felt the discussion had been exhausted, she asked students to choose one of the following assignments and organize their thoughts in writing.

- Compose a letter to the editor of the *New York Post* expressing your opinion about whether or not you think the *Post* should have run the photograph on the cover—or at all.

AUTONOMY

- Write to the cameraman (Mr. Abassi) expressing your views—politely and maturely—about his decision to take the picture.

Ms. Hodges noticed that Darius got to work right away and shared his letter with Gerome when he finished—behaviors of engagement that she could hardly believe. In his rough draft, Darius found his voice almost immediately and expressed himself clearly.

Dear Mr. Abassi,

I read your article in the New York Post and I see where you're coming from. You didn't expect to see nobody get hit by the train, you didn't plan to be there to see it, and you didn't push him. You knew you couldn't get to him in time and I think you were pretty smart to think of using your camera to flash the driver. If the driver stopped because of your flash and the guy hadn't been run over, you would be a hero instead of a villain. So don't let all those people who weren't even there dump on you. I've never been in a situation like that but if I ever am I probably would do the same thing—if I could even think that fast.

VOICES FROM THE FIELD

Matt Copeland on Socratic Circles

Matt Copeland, author of *Socratic Circles* (2005), speaks for many teachers when he says,

> *I have witnessed students who never expressed much interest in or placed value on interpreting literature suddenly finding meaning and relevance in the process. Several of my students who described themselves as "noncollege bound" found that, for the first time in their schooling careers, interpreting literature and other text was something that was not handed down to them from experts, but a living breathing process that was created spontaneously through intellectual discourse.* (p. 14)

It took some deliberate planning and thoughtful revision of lessons for Ms. Hodges and her team to engage Darius and Gerome in class activities, but they were successful. It's worth noting at this point that just because we have a new set of standards that demand that students read more challenging text or engage in speaking and listening does not mean that our aliterate or struggling students will suddenly demonstrate rigor, persistence, or interest. It will take a concerted effort with colleagues in professional learning teams who are given the support, flexibility, and time to "collaborate, design curriculum and instruction, and learn from one another" (Darling-Hammond, 2010, p. 261) to engage our most resistant learners.

A Critical Look at Close Reading

"My students *are* practicing 'close reading,'" Ms. Yvette Garcia, a 10th-grade English teacher, insisted at a recent workshop on the subject. "They read the text closely to find the answer to the question. Once they find it and write it down, they go back to the text to 'read closely' and find the answer to the next question. If I ask them what the answer means, they shrug their shoulders. Even in literature circle groups, they really only want to answer the questions on their discussion guide sheets, not talk about what they've been reading. Close reading isn't the problem as I see it; going *beyond* close reading is the problem."

Ah . . . semantics.

There has been quite a bit of spirited discussion about this term recently. As one teacher joked, "Maybe close reading just means moving your face closer to the text." Another defined close reading as simply "rereading until you get it." Beers and Probst in their book *Notice and Note: Strategies for Close Reading* (2013) insist that close reading means "We bring the text and the reader *close* together. To ignore either element of the transaction, to deny the presence of the reader or neglect the contribution of the text, is to make reading impossible" (p. 36). The National Council of Teachers of English position statement on reading addresses close reading as well. According to the NCTE, close reading means "searching for hidden meanings, positioning the text as the only reality to be considered, and focusing on formal features." The council cautions, however, that "close reading" is often condemned for "conceptualizing the text as a closed world, for limiting student access and for emphasizing form over content" (Beatty-Martinez, 2013, p. 2).

However you choose to define it, one thing we know for certain is that reading a text "closely" for the purpose of answering low-level comprehension questions is antithetical to the very notion of reading. Lest we get carried away by definitions—and the term "close reading" itself—we might remember that the purpose of all reading is to make meaning; plenty of students can decode text and answer questions without comprehending, inferring, or making any sort of connection to what they are reading. We have concerns that our obsession with "close" reading could return us to the days of students scouring the text for answers without analyzing, synthesizing, or applying what they are reading—important 21st century skills.

In an article titled "Closing in on Close Reading" Nancy Boyles (2012–2013) points out that the organization Student Achievement Partners (until recently led by David Coleman, a lead author of the CCSS) offers a series of questions posted on its website as an example of teaching close reading of the novel *Because of Winn-Dixie* by Kate DiCamillo. She said, "Entirely missing from this question set is anything related to craft and structure (Standards 4–6) and integration of knowledge and ideas

> Just because we have a new set of standards that demand that students read more challenging text or engage in speaking and listening does not mean that our aliterate or struggling students will suddenly demonstrate rigor, persistence, or interest.

HOW TO Develop Critical Literacy

Reading

- Show students news reports from two different sources. Have them discuss the following questions about each report.

  o Whose views are represented?

  o Whose views are left out?

  o What do the reporters want you to do?

  o In what way, if any, is the report manipulative or sensational?

  o How would various people, such as those from different political parties, ethnicities, or genders, respond to each report?

- Have students read a young adult novel through a questioning stance:

  o Why did the author choose this topic?

  o What is the author's message? How do the characters illuminate that message?

  o Is the information in the novel based on true events? If so, how accurate is the information? Has the author provided a fair balance of perspectives?

  o How many perspectives are offered in the novel? Is each equally compelling?

  o Does the author try to manipulate your emotions to make a point? In contrast, do you feel emotion because the narrative, descriptions, and writing are compelling?

- Provide books about social injustices for literature circles with a culminating project that asks students to define and attempt to solve the injustice addressed in the text.

Writing

- After reading a text about a social issue, ask students to write from the perspectives of those whose voices have been silenced.

- Provide current articles about events in the local community and have students write letters to the editor of the local paper or create a wiki or blog about the issue.

- Use political cartoons, music lyrics, illustrations, or paintings that represent a social issue as prompts and have students free-write about them. Place these drafts in their writing folders to revise, edit, and publish later.

- Show students how song lyrics often address social themes, and have them create a song/video/multimedia presentation about such issues.

- Examine both sides of a hot-button issue, such as the Trayvon Martin case, through online articles or videos of news reports. Allow students to take one side of an issue and write as if they were making an argument to change the law.

Speaking and Listening

- Use Socratic circles, panel discussions, and forums to explore complex issues that have no clear-cut answers such as penal reform, immigration, or the legalization of drugs.

- Have students choose parts in novels that address social issues and then write and perform skits or Reader's Theaters.

- Utilize the engaging "mock trial" format as a way for students to ferret out facets of issues through "courtroom" questioning and arguments.

- Allow students to use their own writing, perhaps from journals or previous essays, as the basis for a debate.

- Show students videos of TED speakers and have them analyze the content of the speech and then respond to the speaker.

(Standards 7–9)" (Boyles, 2012–2013, pp. 39–40). It is easy to see her point when looking at only a few of the questions:

- How did the Herman W. Block Memorial Library get its name?

- What were Opal's feelings when she realized how Miss Franny felt?

- Opal and Miss Franny have three very important things in common. What are these? (Student Achievement Partners, n.d.)

While such questions may force students to return to the text, they will hardly create "discerning readers," a term used in the introduction to the standards that we like very much. Reading with discernment implies that readers are independent and self-regulated, that they read differently according to their purpose, and that they understand what the author literally says while also understanding what she *means*.

Close Reading Through Thoughtful Questions

Ms. Garcia wanted to find a way to undo students' ingrained "just find the answers" habits—and tap into some sort of intrinsic motivation for their learning. This seemed to her an impossible task, however, because each year more and more of her students, many of whom were from low socioeconomic environments, were simply jumping—less enthusiastically than the word implies—through the hoops she set up for them. Often, she left school feeling like she had failed at her most important task: motivating students to care about their own learning.

While Ms. Garcia tried hard to find engaging texts for her students, the assignments she created often didn't take into account practices necessary for engagement. For example, she had her whole class read Jay Asher's popular *Thirteen Reasons Why,* but she offered students no choice in the decision, nor did she allow much collaboration during reading. Furthermore, when she examined her assignments in light of engagement, she realized

Common Core and Common Sense: The Standards and the Achievement Gap

Much of the attention on education in recent years has focused on American achievement gaps: between poor and wealthy students, between minorities and white students, and between our nation's learners and those in the rest of the world. The CCSS have been at the center of the achievement gap debate since their inception. Are higher standards the key to raising achievement for low-income and minority students, or do they present practical impossibilities for students who are already several grade levels behind? Do the standards help teachers raise the level of rigor for all students so that they can pass state tests, or do they place such a burden on teachers that they can barely keep their heads above water, resulting in scores that may plummet?

No matter what stance you take, we suspect that the standards create greater despair and doubt in teachers of higher grades who feel that students are further from mastery with less time to close the gap. We suggest, however, that the standards offer a means to hope for the best for our students while maintaining our focus on improvement students can accomplish. Many of the teacher resources pertaining to the Common Core we've seen feature pictures of roads, paths, and travel, suggesting that teachers face a journey as they implement the standards. That may be true, but we prefer to see the standards as a map for the journey *students* undergo. And if students cannot reach the goals of the CCSS, it does not mean that they are forever marked. We have an obligation to give these students the best we have and to expect from them the best they can give. Most importantly, we must not impose standards in place of learning or lofty expectations in place of reality. Not all will reach the same destination using the same route or the same timeline, but our job is to help each learner, at every grade level, continue the journey. Like every map, the CCSS are an important guide—but not the *only* guide—to help us lead students further; we see them as a set of reference points, not a picture of the destination only.

that she was asking the same types of questions she had asked for years. "In looking back, I see that my major goal was to find out if my students had read the book," Ms. Garcia said.

ACTIVE LEARNING

Working with another English teacher, Ms. Garcia rewrote her questions with a new goal in mind: "I want my students to *think,* not just read."

Collaborative Close Reading

Ms. Garcia faced significant problems with engagement in her third-period class. It was a large class, and many of the kids made it clear that they thought English was boring and irrelevant. Not only did her students seem indifferent to what they were reading; they had real difficulties comprehending the text, a problem that understandably made them care even less. Ms. Garcia decided to incorporate peer interaction with the next text the students were to read, *Rosa Parks: My Story.*

SCAFFOLDING

ACTIVE LEARNING

After building background on Rosa Parks, with whom most of the students were familiar, she had students number off and move into groups based on like numbers. At first there was a lot of activity, scraping of chair legs, and loud laughter. Ms. Garcia realized that it was uncomfortable for her to release the control that desks in rows afforded, but she was determined to try what was, for her, a new approach. When everyone gathered in groups, she asked them to choose a facilitator, which led to another round of what sounded like bedlam. "You have one minute to choose your facilitator!" she called out.

COLLABORATION

She then asked students to read the text independently and mark any place that confused them. There were a few questions, such as "Do we mark whole sentences? What if we think we know what it means but we're not sure?" She reassured students that *they* were in control of this process and to follow their own instincts—there were no right or wrong "markings." She also asked them to circle words they may not know or words that Parks may have used in a new or different way. Everyone began reading—or, she feared, pretending to read—silently, pen and sticky notes in hand.

DIFFERENTIATION

AUTONOMY

> *The next stop was the Empire Theater, and some whites got on. They filled up the white seats, and one man was left standing. The driver looked back and noticed the man standing. Then he looked back at us. He said, "Let me have those front seats," because they were the front seats of the black section. Didn't anybody move. We just sat right*

Ms. Garcia's Questions for *Thirteen Reasons Why*

Thirteen Reasons Why is about a girl who decides to commit suicide and leaves cassette tapes for 13 people who, she says, contributed to her reason to end her life.

1. Does it seem reasonable that Hannah would commit suicide based on her 13 reasons? Why or why not?

Ms. Garcia's comment: "Students have to read the book to answer this question, but they also have to *use* what they are reading to formulate an answer."

AUTONOMY

2. Clay said Hannah exhibited all the signs of impending suicide. Was he right?

Ms. Garcia's comment: "Students have to read the text but also go outside the text and do some research to make an informed response. They also must use their judgment based on what they've read."

ACTIVE LEARNING

3. Write five questions you want to ask Hannah.

Ms. Garcia's comment: "I'll know from their questions whether or not they read the book, and I'll also be able to assess the depth of their understanding."

INQUIRY

4. If Hannah decided to list only 12 reasons, which one should she have left out? Why?

Ms. Garcia's comment: "I'm asking students to read closely, evaluate the content, and make a decision. If they support their answer, they can't get it wrong. This question builds self-efficacy for readers, especially those who are struggling."

CHALLENGE AND SUCCESS

5. Do you feel that the author dealt with this sensitive issue in a reasonable way? Give several examples from the text to support your opinion.

Ms. Garcia's comment: "Here I am making them go directly back into the text and question the author. They must read closely to do this."

MULTIPLE LEARNING METHODS

where we were, the four of us. Then he spoke a second time: "Y'all better make it light on yourselves and let me have those seats."

The man in the window seat next to me stood up, and I moved to let him pass by me, and then I looked across the aisle and saw that the two women were also standing. I moved over to the window seat. I couldn't see how standing up was going to "make it light" for me. The more we gave in and complied, the worse they treated us.

I thought back to the time when I used to sit up all night and didn't sleep, and my grandfather would have his gun right by the fireplace or if he had his one-horse wagon going anywhere, he always had his gun in the back of the wagon. People always say that I didn't give up my seat because I was tired, but that isn't true. I was not tired physically, or no more tired than I usually was at the end of a working day. I was not old, although some people have an image of me being old then. I was forty-two. No, the only tired I was, was tired of giving in. (Parks, 1992, p. 115)

COLLABORATION ▶

When students finished reading, Ms. Garcia asked them to share what they had marked with others in their group. She gave the groups 10 minutes for discussion as she walked around the room, listening in but rarely making comments. She was surprised that few students were off-task, although the noise level was louder than she would have preferred. She then brought the groups together for a whole-class discussion.

At the beginning of the year, Ms. Garcia had difficulty getting these students to talk during discussions—at least about the topic of study. If she asked a question, they often clammed up as if answering a teacher's question were breaking some sort of code. Because Ms. Garcia genuinely cared for her students and spoke to them individually about their lives outside of class, she eventually gained their trust, but she was surprised at how quickly this trust could disappear, especially if she pushed too hard.

Ms. Garcia was pleased at how well the group work had gone, but she wasn't convinced that students would then participate in the more academic part of the lesson. In the past she might have asked factual questions of students to check on their reading progress, but in this case she decided to just jump in with an open-ended question and see what happened.

What About Trust?

"At the heart of establishing trust between student and teacher is the relationship. First, there has to be one, and second, it has to be mutually established. Establishing a trusting relationship begins on day one when students enter the classroom for the first time. The physical layout of the classroom can speak volumes. Tables often say to students, I value what you have to offer one another, not just what I have to offer you. While kidney-shaped tables appear wonderful for holding small groups, the teacher's seat is in a leadership position, and discourse is directed from teacher to student rather than student to student. Round tables establish a feeling of mutual trust and support where discourse is shared. And while desks are still the most abundant classroom furniture, their placement can be either a barrier or an opening to establishing relationships.

"Just like the physical layout, opportunities for the teacher to get to know students, as well as students to know their teacher, must be intentional. Therefore, it is imperative that teachers plan instruction in ways that allow for this to happen. For example, giving each student a journal at the beginning of the year and building in time for students to write about themselves is invaluable. Even my most reluctant students will fill pages with writing about themselves. Academic content can be infused into the writing assignments simply by asking students to make connections to their own lives. For example, students in my class were asked to share something about their hero before beginning a unit on the civil rights movement. I learned about not only who made them feel important but also why. It moved me to discover one of my toughest male students adored his grandmother because she always remembered to make him his favorite cookies for his birthday.

"My written response to their writing provides them with an opportunity to become more familiar with me as well. Together, we have bonded over rooting for the same football team, enjoying similar movies, sharing a love for animals, and experiencing similar fears and losses. Once that happens, trust and mutual respect occur, and there are no more 'bad' kids.

"Below is an entry from one of my students' journals:

> *I don't know why you ask us all these questions but I'm glad you do. At first, I thought this teacher sure is nosy but then I realized you care about me not just my grades. That makes me want to work harder and now my mom is happy."*

—Susan Kelly, high school
teacher, Orlando, Florida

Ms. Garcia: I heard some of you say you haven't heard the phrase "light on yourself" before and you tried to figure out what it means. What did you come up with?

Conner: We know it means "easy on yourself" but that's a weird way of saying it.

Zeke: We think it's weird because at the beginning of the paragraph she was talking about whites. And then the driver said, "Make it light on yourself" like "light" is always the best thing—kind of like being white. You get what I'm sayin'?

Devon: We get it, but what's important is that the driver was really threatening her.

FEEDBACK ▶ **Ms. Garcia:** Still, that was an interesting observation, Zeke. I hadn't thought about the word in that way. Some of you said you didn't know at first what the word "complied" meant, but everyone understands that word now, right?

At first no one responded but when she waited, several students nodded their heads.

Ms. Garcia: If you didn't know it meant "to agree to do something" you wouldn't know what was happening—the meaning of one word makes all the difference. Which word is more important to know, "light" the way the driver used it or "complied"?

Jacob: Light!

Devon: You're just saying that, Jacob. "Complied" is more important.

Ms. Garcia: Why?

Devon: Cuz that's why she didn't give up her seat. The more they gave in to the whites, the worse it was for them, the more the whites would expect them to give in.

FEEDBACK ▶ **Ms. Garcia:** As I was listening in on your group discussions, most of you said you didn't know why Rosa Parks told the story of her grandfather. That was a point of confusion, right? Let's read that whole paragraph again. Do you see any line that might help you understand why the story of her grandfather was important?

After students reread, Shekela said, "I think I get it. Her grandfather had to carry a gun to protect himself because of the prejudice against him. She was sick of it."

Many students agreed with Shekela, but they also had questions: Could blacks carry guns back then? What if her grandfather had threatened a white person with it? Why did she sit up all night and not sleep?

Ms. Garcia asked each group of students to come up with one question they had about that short passage. After five minutes, the facilitators shared their group's questions. Ms. Garcia pointed out that they had to make inferences or go to other sources to find answers to their questions since there was no additional information in the text.

INQUIRY

COLLABORATION

Finally, Ms. Garcia addressed the writer's craft, asking students if they could hear Parks's voice in her writing.

Ms. Garcia: Which lines are "loudest" with her voice?

Shabon: "The only tired I was, was tired of giving in." You go, girl!

Ms. Garcia still struggles with wanting to control what goes on in her class; after all, that's the way she was taught and the way she has been teaching for years. She also still feels pressured to "get things done" before the end-of-year test. With the help of a colleague, however, she is trying new practices and seeing increased motivation on the part of her students and less resistance to her lessons.

She is also learning that close, critical reading doesn't mean that students should labor over every word or even every sentence of a text—missing the forest for the trees—but means that they understand what an author is saying and why he or she is saying it. As they read more often and more widely—fiction, nonfiction, poetry, websites, short blurbs, and long pieces—they will begin to know when they should slow

HOW TO Replicate Ms. Garcia's Lesson on Close Reading

- Choose a short text (or part of a longer text) that has some ambiguity. Build background knowledge if necessary (see Chapter 3).

- Place students in groups of four.

- Have students read the passage independently.

- Instruct students to circle any words they don't know and underline any part of the passage that is confusing—or write on sticky notes.

- Have students discuss in their groups what they have marked and work together to figure out the meaning. Encourage them to reread passages with which they have difficulty.

- Lead a whole-class discussion as you correct misconceptions and show students how to untangle the text rather than leading them toward the "correct answer."

down and reread and when such intense effort may not be necessary. Ms. Garcia's desire for her students is that they assume responsibility for their learning and come to know that, in the end, they must make decisions about *how* they read—and this process differs for each student and with each text.

MULTIPLE LEARNING METHODS

Final Thoughts

What we have found to be crucial in our work with struggling and aliterate students is that they will never become independent, capable, *discerning* readers if they believe that literacy is a painful, irrelevant process. They must come to see reading, writing, speaking, and listening as tools for personal and political empowerment, tools that define and strengthen their own positions and identities. Once that happens, they will be willing to take a step, however tentative, toward engaging in all that literacy has to offer.

5 Why Evidence Matters

From Text to Talk to Argument

Students cite specific evidence when offering an oral or written interpretation of a text. They use relevant evidence when supporting their own points in writing and speaking, making their reasoning clear to the reader or listener, and they constructively evaluate others' use of evidence.

—Description of College- and Career-Ready Students, CCSS Introduction

The unit is "The American Dream Through the Eyes of the Disenfranchised," and Amanda Swartzlander's eighth-grade students have been reading all sorts of texts in an effort to understand the facets of this complicated topic. Listed on the whiteboard of her blended social studies/English language arts class are the titles of books students have been reading.

Revolutionary Suicide by Huey P. Newton

Coming of Age in Mississippi by Anne Moody

The Autobiography of Malcolm X

The Jungle by Upton Sinclair

The Grapes of Wrath by John Steinbeck

The Absolutely True Diary of a Part-Time Indian by Sherman Alexie

Persepolis: The Story of a Childhood by Marjane Satrapi

"They read more than just books," Ms. Swartzlander said. "They also read articles and primary documents; they've really been immersed in the study of immigration for the past several weeks." Today, they are going to use what they have learned to participate in a Paideia seminar based on "The New Colossus," the famous poem written by Emma Lazarus, which appears on the base of the Statue of Liberty.

Discussions of short texts, such as poems, work in classrooms of both struggling and advanced readers because they offer a chance to look closely and deeply at evidence—to talk while drawing on specific words and phrases as proof, to read and write with evidence as a guide, and to explore larger projects grounded in research as well as fiction. The idea that learning should be grounded in evidential reasoning is one reinforced constantly throughout the Common Core State Standards (CCSS)—the word *evidence* itself appears numerous times. Indeed, the introduction to the standards proposes that evidence shapes student thinking not just about academic issues but about ethical and civic life itself, that it "is essential to both private deliberation and responsible citizenship in a democratic republic" (p. 3).

> The idea that learning should be grounded in evidential reasoning is one reinforced constantly throughout the CCSS—the word *evidence* itself appears numerous times.

In this chapter, therefore, we explore unique ways to have students collect and think about—and through—evidence. First, we take you into a Paideia seminar with eighth-grade students that follows their discussion of "The New Colossus" from the page to their own talk and writing. Then, we explore how an interdisciplinary inquiry project threads evidential research and reasoning through every aspect of the students' learning, from their initial reading to a final presentation.

Paideia Seminars: A Focus on Evidence

Paideia seminars represent a refinement of what other teachers may know as Socratic seminars, a student-centered discussion approach that good teachers have been using in one way or another as far back as ancient Greece. Paideia seminars in particular have become increasingly popular across the country, especially with the implementation of the CCSS and their focus on evidence, speaking and listening as core skills, and the need for students to engage texts actively and independently. When we began thinking about using evidence in authentic and meaningful ways, we immediately thought of the Paideia seminar and began investigating schools that used this activity as a regular part of instruction. Our search led us to the city where the National Paideia Center is housed, Asheville, North Carolina. There we spent time in a middle school where the Paideia approach infuses all instruction.

Terry Roberts and Laura Billings, authors of *Teaching Critical Thinking: Using Seminars for 21st Century Literacy* (2011), explain the Paideia seminar concept: It is "a collaborative, intellectual dialogue facilitated with open-ended questions about a text" (p. 9). The purpose of the seminar is to allow students to grapple with the "ambiguity of the text and the force of others' points of view" so that students "come to grips with the ideas and values in the text, the concepts that lie at the heart of the curriculum," by thinking and speaking for themselves rather than paraphrasing the thoughts of the teacher. All of this comes through a flow of language that helps students consider multiple, even contradictory points of view (Roberts & Billings, 2011, p. 10). Again, keep in mind that while the Paideia approach offers very useful specific guidelines for teachers in directing student talk, the underlying philosophy behind these seminars—a philosophy that allows teachers to meet many of the standards in a single class—integrates the same values that many language arts teachers have always held dear, including critical thinking, inquiry, and attention to the nuances of language.

> ACTIVE LEARNING
>
> COLLABORATION
>
> AUTONOMY

Melissa Hedt, literacy coach at Asheville Middle School, explains that the school's major focus this year is on citing evidence from text, and she believes the Paideia seminar is specifically designed for helping students develop this skill. "Students express their own ideas and build upon the ideas of others," she says, "but they know that they will be challenged to support everything they say with evidence from the text."

In Ms. Swartzlander's class, students are not given the poem ahead of time but prepare for the seminar by moving their chairs into a wide circle and folding a stiff sheet of white paper into a name tent. On the side of the tent facing the students, they write individual goals, such as

VOICES FROM THE
CLASSROOM

Paideia Seminar Effective in All Grades

Asheville Middle School principal Cynthia Sellinger has used Paideia seminars in all grade levels for many years and finds them effective in helping even the youngest students delve deeply into texts and become active learners.

> *"The Paideia seminar is an exciting way for all levels of readers to engage in complex text with multiple levels of meaning. Teachers at the elementary school for example, use seminars with students as young as kindergarteners. Even in kindergarten, a teacher can read a book to the children and pose an opening question as well as core questions to get them thinking and talking. Children learn how to engage in dialogue, and the final assessment involves having them act out the events in the book, like a theater production.*
>
> *"Of course, you need to provide lots of modeling and lots of support, but even small children absolutely can do it. With first graders we looked at the Pledge of Allegiance, talked about the vocabulary, and then discussed what it meant. Kids can be taught at a very young age to engage in a full literacy cycle and use the text while forming and adjusting their own ideas. If little kids can do it, our middle and high schoolers can be completely successful at participating in a seminar."*

"Don't dominate the conversation," "Take notes," "Speak at least three times," or "Ask questions." One student's goal is a bit more specific: "Try not to be sarcastic." Ms. Hedt will facilitate the seminar, and she reminds students of their group goal, "Refer to the text," which is posted at the front of the room. She then reviews the basics:

ACTIVE LEARNING

INQUIRY

- No need to raise hands; just wait until a speaker is finished before you begin talking.
- Take notes so you can refer back to what someone has said.
- Ask questions.
- Speak from uncertainty.

- Don't engage in side conversations.

- Be respectful to each other at all times.

- Remember this is a formal discussion, so address each other by name and make sure your posture, facial expressions, and body language reflect the formal setting.

COLLABORATION

Focusing on Evidence While Reading

Ms. Hedt initiates the process by having students engage in "pretalk" through a simple, open-ended question: "Why do people immigrate?" It doesn't take long for the dialogue to begin.

SCAFFOLDING

INQUIRY

Antonio:	People thought they would have better lives in another country. They really didn't know what it would be like, though.
Pixie:	When they came to America, they thought they were moving to the land of milk and honey, a place where the streets were paved in gold. But it was not that way at all.
Ms. Hedt:	Do you believe immigrants were able to achieve what they thought they would achieve?
Raleigh:	It was hard to fit into America if you were an immigrant. That's true even now.

After several students have spoken, Ms. Hedt asks them to turn over the handout on their desks and number the lines of the poem for easier reference. She then reads the poem aloud.

The New Colossus

Not like the brazen giant of Greek fame,

With conquering limbs astride from land to land;

Here at our sea-washed, sunset gates shall stand

A mighty woman with a torch, whose flame

Is the imprisoned lightning, and her name

Mother of Exiles. From her beacon-hand

Glows world-wide welcome; her mild eyes command

The air-bridged harbor that twin cities frame.

"Keep ancient lands, your storied pomp!" cries she

With silent lips. "Give me your tired, your poor,

Your huddled masses yearning to breathe free,

The wretched refuse of your teeming shore.

Send these, the homeless, tempest-tost to me,

I lift my lamp beside the golden door!"

—Emma Lazarus

"What words in the poem do we want to clarify?" Ms. Hedt asks.

Students offer words such as *brazen, teeming,* and *pomp,* and supply the number of the line where the word appears. Ms. Hedt then initiates a discussion of each word by asking questions rather than providing definitions. "Read line 1 again, 'brazen giant.' What do you think brazen means?"

INQUIRY

"Obvious?" one student asks.

"In what way obvious?" Ms. Hedt prompts.

"Like not subtle," he responds.

Ms. Hedt continues. "How about 'teeming' in line 13?"

Suddenly Pixie calls out, "Wait! I know what *teeming* means! Abundance."

"What do you think Lazarus means by 'teeming shore?'" Ms. Hedt counters.

"Well in line 12, it says 'huddled masses,' so 'teeming shores' might mean there are a lot of people, an abundance of people in the old country," another student reasons.

AUTONOMY

After the brief focus on vocabulary, Ms. Hedt tells the group it's time to read the text again. "Who wants to read?" she asks. Students raise their hands, waiting to be called on. "You don't need to raise your hands," Ms. Hedt reminds them. Daniel says, "I'll read," and, without waiting for permission, begins.

Why Use a Sonnet?

While Ms. Hedt does not specifically use the term with her class, you may notice that Emma Lazarus's poem is a sonnet. In Chapter 6, you'll also find a short exercise Barry used to teach sonnets through technology.

Is it important that eighth-grade students encounter sonnets? On the one hand, the intent of teaching the poem for its content is ultimately a richer and more rewarding experience, especially for struggling learners, than memorizing a rhyme scheme or counting out meter. On the other, Ms. Hedt here manages to expose students to a complex text in an accessible manner. Sonnets are mentioned only once in the English language arts standards

Analyze how a drama's or poem's form or structure (e.g., soliloquy, sonnet) contributes to its meaning. (RL.7.5)

Since both ReLeah and Barry still find discussions of poetic form fascinating but also challenging, we don't necessarily think students will master an understanding of how this form (or any other complex literary structure) underscores meaning by the end of seventh grade. We believe students should be exposed to such poems, interspersed among numerous free-verse poems and a variety of other readings, throughout their schooling. Occasionally these poems should be introduced with the intention of teaching structure explicitly, but even more often as a means of providing rewarding experiences with literature that engages and excites ideas.

When the second reading is complete, Ms. Hedt tells the group to think of another title for the poem. "We'll go around the circle so that everyone can share his or her title," she says. It is the only time each student is required to speak. "There's no hurry. Think about it. Remember if we understand the text completely, it's probably too easy."

ACTIVE LEARNING

The students sit in silence a few minutes while everyone jots down a new title. Ms. Hedt begins with the student on her right.

Sayres:	"Mother of Exiles."
Emily:	"Hope."
Josh:	I'm not sure.
Ms. Hedt:	Do you want us to come back to you?
Josh:	Yes.
Baylee:	"The Welcome Woman."
Nathan:	"Gatekeeper of the Land of Renewal."
Alex:	"The Golden Door."
Collin:	"American Propaganda."

The students continue until everyone has shared a title.

Ms. Hedt:	Would anyone like to explain his or her title?
Collin:	Most Americans don't welcome immigrants, yet the poem on the Statue of Liberty is like an advertisement to get them to move here.

A few other students offer explanations, and, after a pause, Ms. Hedt moves to another question. "What is the tone of the poem? Remember to use evidence."

Logan:	Hopeful.
Ms. Hedt:	Evidence?
Logan:	She is reaching out to the "tired and poor" in line 10 and the "huddled masses" in line 11.
Baylee:	I agree with Logan. Look at line 13: "homeless, tempest-tost."
Raleigh:	Line number 7 is motherly. I think the tone is welcoming.
Jillian:	I think it is more serious, kind of like "This is just how it is."

You can probably already see the value of such a discussion—it promotes inquiry, critical thinking, and close reading. You may also be thinking that Ms. Hedt's class sounds too good to be true, but the students at Asheville Middle School are not from a privileged background, nor is this an honors class.

Students in a Nashville school that was termed "failing" by the state of Tennessee also participated in a Paideia seminar. The teacher of this class of struggling students pointed out how much she loved the method, not just because it engaged her kids but also because it required less prep time, it worked with any subject, and, in her words, "it meets all 10 reading standards, six of the writing standards, and four of the six speaking and listening standards. All in about 15 minutes."

What's even more impressive are the responses of the Nashville students shortly after the seminar:

- "Better than just listening to the teacher talk"
- "Gave me ideas for my writing"
- "I could see everyone in the class"
- "No one acted goofy—for once we were serious"
- "Felt like a real discussion"
- "We didn't talk over each other"

And, regarding the CCSS? Both of our example classes handily met the first reading standard for eighth-grade literature:

Cite the textual evidence that most strongly supports an analysis of what the text says explicitly as well as inferences drawn from the text. (RL.8.1)

We often think of citation as something that occurs when students write; through discussion, however, students might learn not only to cite specific lines, but to analyze and internalize meaning as they do so.

Focusing on Evidence While Speaking and Listening

Back in Ms. Hedt's classroom, the discussion continues, with students beginning to talk to each other instead of only to Ms. Hedt. There is

> The teacher of this class of struggling students pointed out how much she loved the method, not just because it engaged her kids but also because it required less prep time and it worked with any subject.

COLLABORATION

AUTHENTIC
ASSESSMENT

FEEDBACK

rarely a silent moment; sometimes two students start to talk at the same time, but one stops as if on cue and lets the other continue. Ms. Hedt, who is keeping a seminar map, often returns to a student who has allowed someone else to speak and asks him what he has to say. Several students are clearly more comfortable talking than others, and soon Ms. Hedt reads off a list of names of students who haven't yet spoken. "I want to hear from everyone, so if you've spoken several times, give others a chance to talk."

"The New Colossus" Seminar Map

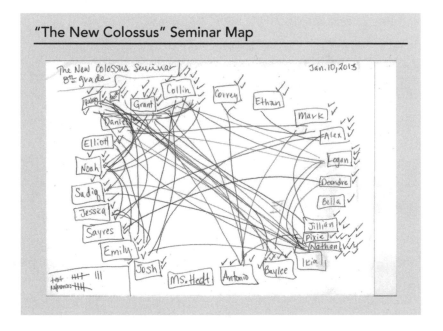

Then Antonio asks, "Why is this a poem?" and Ms. Hedt waits for someone to respond.

Ms. Hedt: What is a poem?

Logan: A short text explaining what you want to say.

Antonio: But isn't this just their opinion?

Pixie: The immigrants' or the authors'?

Antonio: Can poems just be based on opinions?

Ms. Hedt lets the question hang in the air and, when no one responds, says they will talk more about the definition of poetry later. For now, she urges them to return to the text. "Why is the New Colossus a woman?"

"Women are more welcoming," someone offers.

Grant:	I agree. More inviting.
Ms. Hedt:	What about the title?
Raleigh:	It's intimidating. Colossus is something big.
Nathan:	Not really intimidating. It's like a friendly giant will take you in.
Daniel:	The New Colossus is at odds with how America wanted to be seen. America wanted to seem welcoming like immigrants were being given a new chance to start their lives over, but it was intimidating and large. The immigrants would end up working in huge cities and factories, especially compared to the small villages in Europe that they came from.
Ms. Hedt:	Will you write that down, Daniel? And write the word "juxtaposition," because I want to talk about that later.

Ms. Hedt:	Why is this poem titled "The New Colossus"?
Grant:	A new country, but big.
Ms. Hedt:	Who is the New Colossus welcoming?
Elliott:	People from places like Ireland who were in a bad way.
Ms. Hedt:	What does the text say about those people?
Elliott:	They were poor.
Pixie:	The poem is welcoming the poor because they will work for little.
Noah:	I agree that it welcomes Europeans. The golden door is a door into America for immigrants.
Ms. Hedt:	What is the golden door?

Donte: Streets paved with gold, like in the Bible.

Ms. Hedt: Why the golden door?

Donte: That means it doesn't get any better than this.

Jessica: Riches are expressed as gold.

Nathan: I have a question. Wasn't Lady Liberty a gift from France?

Collin: That says to me that the poem is a false thing. We didn't build the statue so it wasn't our lady welcoming people in.

Raleigh: You are very disillusioned about America, Collin.

Ms. Hedt glances pointedly at Raleigh but says nothing.

In the last part of the seminar, in response to a question from Ms. Swartzlander, the students talk about how the poem was written in English but most immigrants couldn't read English, so it didn't really matter what was written on the base of the statue. When Ms. Hedt asks what they think might have been a better inscription, Jessica suggests, "Something simple, like 'hello' or 'welcome,'" and then adds that it should have been written in several languages. Many other students agree.

Here, again, it's easy to see how closely Ms. Hedt's students adhere to elements of the CCSS; for instance, compare the discussion we just described to this criteria in the first speaking and listening standard:

> Come to discussions prepared, having read or researched material under study; explicitly draw on that preparation by referring to evidence on the topic, text, or issue to probe and reflect on ideas under discussion. (SL.8.1a)

Remember that Ms. Hedt, here, is drawing on reading—preparation—that students completed earlier, but provides this poem as a means of introducing big ideas. Her students had no problem making that connection.

Focusing on Evidence While Writing

AUTHENTIC
ASSESSMENT

The activity ends with a quick-write where students respond to three questions:

1. What does the poem say about the American Dream?

2. What are your own ideas about the American Dream?

3. What did you hear someone else say that made you think?

In looking at the students' writing later, we found a wide variety of responses, but it was clear that every student did listen and engage in thinking. Amazingly, each student also provided evidence from the text in one or more of his or her responses, such as these:

- Your circumstances shouldn't suffocate your opportunities. This poem shows the glorified version of the American Dream. In it Lady Liberty says, "Give me your tired, give me your poor" which exudes a sense of kindness and acceptance, but people who immigrate don't get what they expect.

- The American Dream as reflected in this poem is a free land where everybody has a place, a dichotomy to the "huddled masses."

- This poem gives possibility to the American dream and the statue symbolizes that. The poem calls out to the poor, the suffering, and the homeless. People immigrate to America because they think they will be able to find a job easily and get lots of money to help them and their family. Instead, they are ripped off and scammed, people treat them poorly, and sometimes they get deported.

- It says that the American dream was to be rich and to prosper because it talks about how much Americans prosper, for example: "I lift my torch beside the golden door" which suggests that America is the land of gold.

Again, these student comments demonstrate just how relevant such discussions can be in meeting the CCSS, including this writing standard:

Draw evidence from literary or informational texts to support analysis, reflection, and research. (W.8.9)

Focusing on Evidence Through Self-Reflection

FEEDBACK

ACTIVE LEARNING

AUTHENTIC
ASSESSMENT

After students finish writing, Ms. Hedt thanks them for their insights and respect toward each other. She then asks students how they would rate themselves on their common goal, "Refer to the text," using a 1–5 scale, 5 being the best. "Hold up fingers to show your evaluation," she instructs. Most students hold up four fingers. "So we agree; we were about a 4? What about your personal goals? On the back of your name cards, write a number between 1 and 5 regarding how you think you did with your personal goals."

Raleigh, whose goal had been "Try not to be sarcastic," gives herself a 4. She writes, "I wasn't sarcastic. I talked a lot, but I don't believe I overwhelmed the conversation with my opinions." Jillian, on the other hand, gives herself a 2 for her personal goal, "Speak from uncertainty," because "I didn't put myself out there."

Ms. Hedt tells us that this self-reflective piece is one of the most important parts of the seminar because students learn how to evaluate their goals and think about their own learning. These types of goals, called mastery goals, are different from performance goals, the goals most often present in schools. Daniel Pink, author of *Drive* (2011), explains the difference: "Getting an A in French class is a performance goal; being able to speak French is a learning goal" (pp. 121–122). When students set mastery goals, they see the task as relevant and meaningful rather than something they do for an extrinsic reward. As an added bonus, mastery goals also tap into engagement.

When the seminar was over, we asked students if they demonstrated this level of respect toward each other in all of their classes. "Heck, no!" one student called out, and others laughed, but Ms. Swartzlander told us that their respectful behavior and thoughtful dialogue did, indeed, transfer to other classes. "Teachers say that when they have a class discussion, students really listen and use words related to dialogue, such as 'piggybacking' on what someone else has said."

"These seminars also put into practice what we try to teach students about listening to and respecting the views of others," Ms. Hedt added.

Paideia Seminars and Struggling Students

We know that Paideia seminars and similar activities often give advanced students a chance to shine, but how do students who struggle respond to this approach? According to Roberts and Billings (2011), "understanding" occurs when students engage in "intellectual striving or focused, structured thinking. When engaged in a seminar, the individual participant is witness both to the thinking process of other individuals and to the collective thinking process of the group. Both of these can serve as educative models for increasingly clear, coherent, sophisticated thinking" (p. 10).

Asheville Middle School Students Reflecting on Their Goals in a Paideia Seminar

What's more, "With struggling students, the seminars allow us to demystify text. It becomes less intimidating to them," Ms. Hedt noted.

Ms. Swartzlander said that students who have difficulty with typical school tasks often aren't given enough time in class to think through an issue or hear others' views, so it may be hard for them to clarify their own responses. "The seminar sparks thinking, and students know that there is no right answer, so it gives them the freedom to experiment with their own ideas." She also noted that students grow in maturity as well as in skills. "Students practice expressing themselves but also learn how to hold onto their thoughts and listen to others."

AUTONOMY

While we observed that some students were more reluctant to speak than others, it was clear to us that every student was engaged. In fact, the entire seminar was a good example of Brian Cambourne's Conditions of Learning, where engagement is the bull's-eye in the learning process.

One condition in particular, "approximation," was particularly evident during the seminar, especially for students who had experienced years of discouragement or even failure in school-related tasks. Cambourne (1995) explains that when learners "approximate" learning, they feel

VOICES FROM THE
FIELD

Roberts and Billings on the Advantages of Paideia Seminars

After several years of consistent seminar experience, it is not unusual for a group of participants to exhibit individually and collectively many of the following attributes (Roberts & Billings, 2011):

- Dialogue that is more nearly balanced in terms of the talkative and the quiet participants

- Dialogue in which more participants look at the person speaking and rarely talk while another is speaking

- Participants yielding to another as a way of sharing talk time

- Participants paraphrasing the comments of others

- Participants making clear and accurate statements, using appropriate pace, volume, vocabulary, and grammar

- Participants offering relevant and detailed comments in terms of sequence, purpose, and point of view

- Participants referring regularly to the text or another relevant source

- Participants considering another point of view while acknowledging their own bias

- Participants asking authentic questions

- Participants taking notes either on the text or on the comments of others

CHALLENGE AND SUCCESS

safe to take risks and make mistakes. During the seminar, every student's comment was valued. Such reinforcement helps struggling students believe that they have something worthwhile to contribute, and that very belief will contribute to success. Research on self-efficacy, students' belief in their ability to accomplish a task, creates a determination to succeed and, in fact, becomes a factor in that success (Guthrie, 2008). Paideia seminars and other authentic forums that encourage students to wrestle with learning in a safe and supportive environment go a long way not only toward meeting the CCSS, but also toward engaging even the most disinterested student.

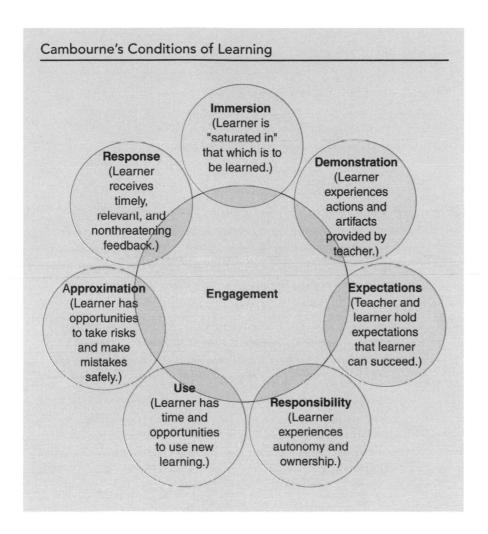

Cambourne's Conditions of Learning

Immersion (Learner is "saturated in" that which is to be learned.)

Response (Learner receives timely, relevant, and nonthreatening feedback.)

Demonstration (Learner experiences actions and artifacts provided by teacher.)

Approximation (Learner has opportunities to take risks and make mistakes safely.)

Engagement

Expectations (Teacher and learner hold expectations that learner can succeed.)

Use (Learner has time and opportunities to use new learning.)

Responsibility (Learner experiences autonomy and ownership.)

What to Do When Students Struggle

While we hope we have convinced you to at least try a seminar in your class, you may not find that every student will be successful every time. When Ms. Hedt and Ms. Swartzlander read all of the responses from their students, they were especially interested in one from a girl we'll call Dana, a quiet student who kept her eyes down during much of the activity. She had given herself a 1 out of 5 on her personal goal "Speak at least three times." She wrote, "I really didn't have anything to say, and also the poem really didn't make sense to me."

HOW TO Hold Discussions in Large Classes

If you counted the students included on Ms. Hedt's seminar map, you probably noticed that her class, by some standards, is small or medium sized—around 24 students. Some teachers balk at holding discussions because their class sizes are larger, increasing to perhaps 35 or 40 students. The reality of such class sizes requires many teachers to be flexible and creative in their discussion methods. For large classes, consider these discussion tips:

- Use an inner circle and an outer circle. Only students in the inner circle may speak, but every 5 to 10 minutes students should switch from one circle to the other. To keep the students in the outer circle attentive, have them take notes as they listen.

- For a more specific version of the inner/outer circle strategy, assign each student in the outer circle to a particular student in the inner circle (and keep the pairings when the circles switch). The outside student can write down positive comments about the points made by the student who is speaking and share these at the end of class.

- Hold discussions with half of your class while the other students work quietly on a worthwhile task, such as gathering evidence from a text to use in their own discussion. Change discussion prompts so that students do not just repeat what they've overheard earlier.

- Employ a think/pair/share strategy in which students work in pairs for one minute, then discuss for five minutes with one partner speaking and the other recording. Repeat the process so each partner has an opportunity to speak or record.

DIFFERENTIATION

Ms. Hedt and Ms. Swartzlander talked about how they would help Dana and decided that they would meet with her individually to discuss the poem and try to find out if she had trouble with the literal comprehension of the poem or with its deeper meaning. "We will also go through other reading response work samples from this student (journal entries, comprehension questions, assessments) to look for trends in her understanding of text or trends in the types of text with which she struggles. We may need to do more work with this type of poetry in a historical context, and we probably will, not only with her but with the entire class," Ms. Hedt said.

SCAFFOLDING

AUTHENTIC ASSESSMENT

"We will also make sure that the next Paideia seminar is successful for Dana by talking with her about her participation and helping her prepare for the next discussion," Ms. Swartzlander added. "I can make sure she comprehends the next seminar text even before it is given to the group. I might even give her one of the seminar questions and work with her to draft a response she could bring with her to the seminar."

CHALLENGE AND SUCCESS

DIFFERENTIATION AND SCAFFOLDING

We found it interesting that a simple self-reflection turned into a formative assessment that allowed teachers to pinpoint which students were having difficulty and then take specific action to make sure they were successful the next time around.

AUTHENTIC ASSESSMENT

Problem- and Project-Based Learning: *Using* Evidence

Considering the culture of Asheville Middle School, it was no surprise to find that the eighth-grade teachers were involved in an interdisciplinary project that would include at least one Paideia seminar and conclude with a "Future Fair." The meeting was led by science teacher Jeff Dewhirst, who was organizing a project regarding the depletion of fossil fuels. His idea was that every student in the eighth grade would complete

ACTIVE LEARNING

What If a Student Doesn't Understand the Seminar Text?

1. Analyze why the student had difficulty by helping her define her problems with the text.

2. Look for trends in the student's other work that may indicate a specific problem, such as decoding, vocabulary, or background knowledge.

3. Provide extra practice with a different, similar text.

4. Scaffold understanding for the next seminar by providing the text to the student and going over it with her.

5. Give her one of the seminar questions and help her prepare a response.

DIFFERENTIATION

SCAFFOLDING

CHALLENGE AND SUCCESS

a project and every teacher in the eighth grade would be responsible for facilitating some aspect of the project. He noted at the beginning of the planning meeting that the initiative would address four Common Core State Standards specifically and touch on many more as well:

> Conduct short as well as more sustained research projects based on focused questions, demonstrating understanding of the subject under investigation. (W.7)

> Gather relevant information from multiple print and digital sources, assess the credibility and accuracy of each source, and integrate the information while avoiding plagiarism. (W.8)

> Delineate and evaluate the argument and specific claims in a text, including the validity of the reasoning as well as the relevance and sufficiency of the evidence. (R.8)

> Analyze how two or more texts address similar themes or topics in order to build knowledge or to compare the approaches the authors take. (R.9)

In our experience with this type of problem- or project-based learning, we have found that most projects can be crafted to address virtually every standard in the CCSS, leading us to become more certain than ever that collaborative, inquiry-based activities are a key component to CCSS success. Furthermore, teachers report that such projects have a positive effect on struggling learners as they increase engagement, encourage deeper thinking, and often result in higher test scores. A significant advantage of such projects is that they offer multiple means of drawing on *evidence* from across disciplines to undergird student thinking—from research to text-based questioning to scientific or mathematical reasoning.

AUTONOMY

MULTIPLE
LEARNING
METHODS

John Barrell, author of *Problem-Based Learning: An Inquiry Approach* (2007), found that disengaged or struggling students "become far more interested and involved because we are presenting them with opportunities to make choices, take more ownership of their own learning, and to express themselves in different fashions." (p. 9). He also contends that when students engage in problem-based learning, they are better able to make judgments based on well-researched evidence.

Defining the Problem: A Key to Engagement

If you think about it, we probably don't use the word "problem" enough in education—at least, not in the context of teaching and learning (obviously, we're not talking here about discussions of poorly behaved students that take place in the teacher's lounge!). Math and science teachers present their students with problems, but how often in language arts or social studies do we think of starting a lesson with a problem? Yet the value of such an approach is clear—a problem is a mystery, an unknown that demands thought and creativity in the pursuit of a solution.

INQUIRY

The problem for the project we describe in the following section, as outlined by Mr. Dewhirst, involved alternative energy sources for the future. "Sustainability is the major theme," he said as he went over several learning goals related to the project.

- Students will understand which energy resources are fossil fuels and how they are created.

- Students will understand the implications of the depletion of nonrenewable energy resources.

- Students will evaluate renewable energy sources.

- Students will examine challenges in developing renewable energy sources.

MULTIPLE LEARNING METHODS

Note that each of these goals demands more than a lecture approach—there's a difference between students who *know about* energy resources and those who *understand* energy resources. Reaching understanding means active thinking, and that thinking would require individual research, reading, and gathering of evidence. What's more, the problem presented here has clear links to many areas of teaching—Mr. Dewhirst envisioned a learning experience in which each discipline would be responsible for a specific area of learning during this two-week project.

Science: Providing Content Knowledge

Since this project was based in science, teachers in the science department took the lead and discussed their responsibilities to provide content knowledge, make sure students had a conceptual understanding of key vocabulary, and guide student research.

VOICES FROM THE
CLASSROOM

How to Scaffold Inquiry Projects

"In teaching Terry Trueman's Stuck in Neutral to two groups of resistant senior students, I stumbled on an inquiry-based project. We had just finished reading the novel together in class, and I wanted to challenge students to think about the payoffs of reading. I simply wrote a question on the whiteboard: 'What is the point of completing a task?' I was shocked at what resulted over the span of the next 45 minutes. The essence of the group's collective response to my question was as follows: 'We complete tasks in order to make progress—to grow.' Thinking they were on to something, I challenged them further. 'In what ways do we grow as a result of completing tasks?' And then I was shocked again. 'We grow most by helping others grow,' a student chimed in. And that was the start of an inquiry-based task.

"Our discussion continued with two driving questions: (1) What life lessons exist within Trueman's novel? (2) In what ways can we share those lessons with others to help them grow? Their responses included:

- Love
- Empathy
- Bullying
- Relationships
- Death
- Divorce
- Cognitive disabilities
- Self-esteem
- Interpersonal communication

"Will science head up the seminars—and when will they be conducted, at the beginning or the end of the unit?" Ms. Hedt asked.

"Maybe both," Mr. Dewhirst said. "The first one might introduce students to the subject, and the last one would be more in-depth because they would know more about the topic by then."

SCAFFOLDING

"We came up with questions for each of the categories. For example, regarding 'divorce' the questions included:

- *How often does divorce happen today?*

- *What is the history of divorce in the United States?*

- *How do U.S. divorce rates compare to divorce rates around the world?*

- *How does divorce affect people (especially children of divorced parents)?*

"These responses and questions became the basis of our inquiry-based task. As the project gained momentum, so did my students' needs. I created a number of graphic organizers to help them as they began the project.

"In the end, this project was one of the best choices I have made in over 13 years in the secondary classroom. The trick is that it wasn't my creation. The project literally took shape as my students and I discussed our purpose for reading a novel. The project was their idea. The 'guts' of the project belonged to them, giving the students a real sense of ownership and purpose.

"Ultimately, I enjoyed watching my 'resistant' students willingly and energetically engage a variety of authentic audiences in discussions about topics of their creation. One group made a presentation to other teachers about the importance of interpersonal relationships; three different groups presented to three different groups of freshmen about the importance of fostering/maintaining positive self-esteem, the negative causes and outcomes of bullying, and the importance of giving and receiving love. In each instance, I can honestly say my students were accomplishing their original purpose for completing a task—growing personally by helping others grow."

—Nick Yeager, English teacher, Barrington, Illinois

"It will be difficult to find texts that the students can wrestle with because most articles on this topic are not objective; they advocate for one side or another. That may be a huge challenge," another science teacher noted. The technology teacher suggested that they consider infographs where students examine data and draw their own conclusions. She also agreed to help teachers find online articles that weren't biased.

MULTIPLE LEARNING METHODS

TECHNOLOGY USE

HOW TO Teach Students to Conceptualize Vocabulary

As we discuss in Chapter 8, vocabulary study means much more than providing a list of words for every unit or project. When Mr. Dewhirst at Asheville Middle School says he wants students to "conceptualize" vocabulary, he means that the wants them to understand the multiple facets of meaning represented by the words or terms, to internalize how such vocabulary is used by experts, and to be able to use important words as vehicles for conceptualizing and formulating ideas. Mr. Dewhirst wants students to make key words a permanent part of their vocabulary banks—to own the meanings.

Science teachers will use the following principles of vocabulary study to help their students conceptualize words related to sustainability:

1. Preteach vocabulary with "friendly" definitions, and point out how words provide foundational, background information.

2. Use words in context multiple ways, multiple times.

3. Make key words the cornerstones of student discussions.

4. Provide graphic organizers that will allow students to explore relationships among words that are important to understanding sustainability.

5. Provide texts that use words in clear and understandable ways.

6. Create flexible lessons and assessments that allow each student to work toward mastery of all terms rather than taking a single quiz and moving on.

"But this would be a chance for us to teach students how to determine the validity of articles and credibility of sources," Mr. Dewhirst pointed out. The group agreed that students should be given infographs as well as various articles that were both objective and one-sided.

RELEVANCE

All teachers expressed enthusiasm about having students engage in research that would be meaningful to them rather than having them go through a traditional research-paper process for some artificial end.

Language Arts/Social Studies: Engaging in Writing and Reading

In the blended language arts/social studies classes, teachers would help students write an essay based on their research. "It should be an argumentative essay," Ms. Swartzlander noted. "Our kids need to work on defending their positions and citing evidence to support their arguments. This will be a perfect opportunity for them to practice those skills." She pointed out that two standards would guide their instruction:

> Write arguments to support claims in an analysis of substantive topics or texts, using valid reasoning and relevant and sufficient evidence. (W.1)

> Draw evidence from literary or informational texts to support analysis, reflection, and research. (W.9)

The writing assignment needed to dovetail with the research the students would be doing on fossil fuels and renewable resources in science, so after a bit of discussion everyone agreed on a simple prompt: *Explain why the renewable resource you chose will most likely replace fossil fuels in the future.*

Although students would be reading informational text on the topic in science, teachers wanted them to read fiction as well as nonfiction so they could:

> Determine central ideas or themes of a text and analyze their development; summarize the key supporting details and ideas. (R.2)

> Analyze how and why individuals, events, and ideas develop and interact over the course of a text. (R.3)

They began brainstorming titles of books that would fit into the unit, especially dystopian novels because they would challenge students to think about the problems of the future.

"I like the idea of including series instead of single books," the reading teacher noted. "This may encourage students to get hooked and read several books instead of just the 'required' one."

AUTHENTIC ASSESSMENT

INQUIRY

SCAFFOLDING

HOW TO Start a Writing Assignment With Evidence

The first reading standard emphasizes that students should "cite specific textual evidence when writing or speaking to support conclusions drawn from the text" (R.1). It's a reasonable expectation and one that many

teachers work toward daily in their classes, but we'd also suggest that this standard could be turned on its head. What if we instead proposed that students should draw conclusions from the text based on specific textual evidence developed while writing or speaking?

Photograph by Creatas

To imagine this approach in the classroom, think of how you might teach a poem, novel, or passage of informational text from this starting point:

- First, have students read the text, circling or highlighting what they believe might be key words or phrases throughout the passage.

Several teachers also mentioned Jeanne DuPrau's novel *The City of Ember,* a story about a futuristic world where electricity and fire have been lost. They wanted a novel for students who may not be reading on grade level, but they were concerned that this novel might be too "easy"—and that students might only watch the movie and not read the book. They decided to continue looking for other novels at various reading levels and report back at their next meeting.

DIFFERENTIATION

"We also should include nonfiction," an English teacher noted as he clicked through websites.

MULTIPLE LEARNING METHODS

"How about having kids look up the websites of environmental groups and determine which ones seem most legitimate? They could start by evaluating their mission statements," someone else suggested.

- Through discussion, explore these words or phrases, developing connections, questions, and themes of the text drawn from this evidence.

- Have students work alone or in pairs to turn one of these connections or themes into a statement about the overall meaning of the text (a thesis statement).

- Share these thesis statements as a group or with other pairs and refine them.

- Organize the original words and phrases students circled or highlighted—as well as others that are relevant—into groups that address aspects of the thesis.

- Use this material to craft an essay, technology-based product, or an oral presentation.

This is essentially the approach that Ms. Swartzlander's students took in understanding "The New Colossus." Look back at their conversation and you'll notice that attention to the simple word "teeming" led to a deeper understanding of the themes of the poem, an understanding that could easily have led to a writing assignment about the concept of abundance. Ms. Swartzlander's students could move in that direction not only through a teacher-presented theme, but through a simple moment of noticing the evidence itself and following it with a thoughtful conclusion.

"Or Chief Seattle's Letter to All the People. It has that famous line about the earth not belonging to man but man belonging to the earth."

The discussion continued until they agreed that their next step would be to individually create a list of texts and then meet to decide on the final choices.

Math: The Nuts and Bolts

While English teachers were creating lists of texts, the math teachers said they were willing to participate, but they didn't seem very sure about their role in the project. "We can't really give up two weeks of class time for this," they reasoned. Mr. Dewhirst reassured them that they didn't need to spend every minute of class on this project but that

BOOKS

Dystopian Novels for an Inquiry Unit on Creating a Sustainable Future

Ashfall and *Ashen Winter* (series) by Mike Mullin

When Yellowstone's supervolcano erupts, Alex's town is suddenly plunged into darkness. The ash that covers everything forces Alex to leave in search of his family, who was away when the disaster occurred. The second book in the series, *Ashen Winter*, follows Alex as he continues his journey for his family and his own survival.

Birthmarked (trilogy) by Caragh O'Brien

This series, beginning with the novel *Birthmarked*, explores genetic engineering, birth defects, and environmental issues such as water rights in the story of a teenage midwife who must deliver every 10th baby to a protected enclave for unknown reasons.

Divergent (Book 1) and *Insurgent* (Book 2) by Veronica Roth

In the dystopian world Roth has created, society is divided into working "factions," and all 16-year-olds must select the faction where they will spend the rest of their lives. Civil war creates a bleak background for universal themes such as love, loyalty, and the inevitable corruption of politics in the second book.

The House of the Scorpion by Nancy Farmer

Raised in a tiny country between the United States and the former nation of Mexico, Matteo, the main character of this novel, discovers that he is actually a clone of the country's leader, El Patrón. Embedded in this fast-paced story are deft questions about human rights, science, and our environmental future.

Life as We Knew It (series) by Susan Beth Pfeffer

When an asteroid hits the moon, the world suffers unimaginable environmental catastrophes from tsunamis to earthquakes. The plot centers on a family in Pennsylvania whose members try to find a way to survive. The following two books in the series, *The Dead and the Gone* and *This World We Live In,* explore the courage and determination it takes to live when everything that was once normal is now gone.

The Maze Runner (series) by James Dashner

In a strange, enclosed world where 60 teen boys find themselves, they must learn to grow their own food and create their own supplies. In the two sequels that follow, *The Scorch Trials* and *The Death Cure,* the plot unfolds in a planet devastated by sun flares.

Oryx and Crake by Margaret Atwood

Not exactly a young adult novel, this story alternates between scenes of the final human to survive a deadly virus and the technology-driven world he lived in before the virus was released. Recommended for mature high school students.

Ship Breaker by Paolo Bacigalupi

Set in a futuristic world where oil is almost nonexistent, this novel provides one adventure after another as Nailer, a teenage boy, works as a scavenger on grounded oil tankers.

Son by Lois Lowry

In this final book in the series that begins with *The Giver,* readers enter a futuristic world where evil and good stage a terrifying battle.

it would enrich the experience and learning for students if math classes would take an aspect of it so that the initiative was truly interdisciplinary. "You could graph data that the students find in their research on energy," he suggested. "Or perhaps you could help students with a scale drawing, maybe a model of a futuristic vehicle or a town run on alternative energy such as solar, geothermal, or wind."

"Will kids actually build the model?" one of the math teachers asked dubiously, and a discussion ensued about how they could provide materials so that students could, indeed, create a simple model. The models could easily be designed around the specific geometric principles the teachers had been working on with students, someone pointed out, and scale drawings could involve reminders about ratios, fractions, and even some algebraic equations.

"We're always telling the kids that math is everywhere," one math teacher noted. "We want them to see math as evidence, as well. This project sounds like a good chance for us to prove that math is relevant."

"We'll bring a plan to our next meeting," one of the other math teachers said. "We'll figure out how to make math an integral part of this."

The Project Realized: Envisioning the Future Fair

The final phase of the project would be the fair itself, where students would present their findings to a real audience such as other students, local green industries, or politicians. "Is there a call to action, or will they just disseminate information?" the assistant principal asked.

"I just want them to become informed about the realities of their future, to think about solutions, and to use evidence to back up their thinking," Mr. Dewhirst replied.

Other teachers discussed how such a fair could bring opportunities for service learning or internships in the future. "Who knows? Maybe adults will learn something from these kids," someone else added.

The project would start in less than a month, so each content area was tasked with bringing more definitive plans to the next meeting. They also formed a subcommittee of teachers from various disciplines to work on the Future Fair. The teachers presented the idea to their principal, who was impressed both by the interdisciplinary nature of the project as well as by the collaborative work between the teachers in her school. Principal Sellinger, with fingers crossed, said she *thought* she might be able to find some money in the budget to defray the costs.

We recognize, as did Principal Sellinger, that teams of teachers don't always work together without friction. Yet the advantages of teachers working in community have been widely documented and credited with the impressive success of students from countries such as Finland and Singapore (Darling-Hammond, 2010). In the United States, studies have confirmed that when teachers collaborate on projects such as the one at Asheville Middle School, the advantages include

- increased student achievement,
- increased student learning gains,
- increased teacher-student respect, and
- increased student self-efficacy (McLaughlin & Talbert, 2006).

These advantages can be accrued by any school willing to devote the time to collaborate and develop a problem-based project. Not all projects need to be as time-consuming as the Future Fair, either; though we encourage this sort of full-blown and exciting opportunity for student learning, we also advocate projects that take only a day or two to complete. Many districts now require that students in each grade engage in some sort of inquiry project as a way of tapping into the type of deep learning advocated by the CCSS. For individual teachers or small teams, just start with your curriculum and look at topics that will lend themselves to active learning. Don't forget to delineate the standards you will be covering should anyone doubt the benefit of this approach.

The Advantages of Project-Based Learning

William Bender, author of *Project-Based Learning* (2012), cites two significant advantages of project-based learning: (1) students' motivation and interest increase, and (2) student achievement increases. When we review our standards for motivation and engagement, we understand

> Many districts now require that students in each grade engage in some sort of inquiry project as a way of tapping into the type of deep learning advocated by the CCSS.

why these advantages are evident. Project- or problem-based learning encompasses all of the components that create engaged learning: activity, autonomy, relevance, collaboration, technology use, multiple learning methods, opportunities for challenge and success, differentiation and scaffolding, inquiry, and feedback.

Real-world projects demand research and are often based on ideas drawn from reading or discussion. School projects should be no different. Students not only need to approach learning by following a chain of evidence from start to finish; they often thrive in environments where they are asked to solve problems, to discuss with proof, and to construct creative outcomes based on factual information. Evidence is the starting place; text, talk, and argument are the vehicles, but engagement and learning are the outcomes.

Evidence is the starting place; text, talk, and argument are the vehicles, but engagement and learning are the outcomes.

Examples of Problem-Based Learning

Following are some examples of problem-based learning that we've seen in various schools and at various grade levels:

ACTIVE LEARNING

- Students studied the campaign platforms of local or state candidates and chose a candidate they wanted to support. They then created campaign literature, slogans, and debating points. The culminating event was an evening forum where students made speeches in support of their candidates. The community and media were invited to attend, and several candidates showed up to lend a hand—and gain a bit of free publicity.

TECHNOLOGY USE

- Students interviewed residents of an assisted living facility and created a book of stories about their lives, along with video clips of the interviews, which are shown on holidays in the dining hall.

MULTIPLE LEARNING METHODS

- Students created awareness about recycling in their community by creating public service announcements and a lively website. They wrote a grant for recycling bins and a large billboard, which they created with the help of art students. The final component of the project involved having students create an original product out of recycled materials.

- A community was considering investing in an incinerator as an alternative to landfills. Students researched the advantages and disadvantages of incinerators and contacted other communities that had made the move to incinerating trash. They wrote informative (and a few argumentative) essays that were published in the local newspaper prior to city officials making the final decision.

RELEVANCE

- Students in an English class who were reading picture books to a first-grade class began researching why it is so difficult to get such books published. Each student wrote a children's book and submitted it to a publishing company.

CHALLENGE AND SUCCESS

- Students in a small Appalachian community wanted to know what life was like there during the Depression. They researched old news stories and interviewed older citizens who had lived during that time, creating their own "Foxfire" book, along with primary documents such as photographs, recipes, and diary entries.

COLLABORATION

- School officials in a large high school stated that they were removing all of the drink and snack machines from the campus. Students in a science class researched the nutritive value of certain snacks and fruit-based drinks and used their data to make a presentation to school administrators. Their goal was to convince decision makers to leave the machines and replace "junk" snacks with healthier alternatives.

RELEVANCE

- A journalism class researched injuries associated with certain sports, along with an analysis of the long-term effects of such injuries. They included quotes from players, coaches, doctors, and parents. They wrote articles based on their findings, and the local newspaper printed one article a week in the sports section.

INQUIRY

Final Thoughts

We are excited about the possibilities in the CCSS that students should cite and use evidence as well as "constructively evaluate others' use of evidence." And, as we found at Asheville Middle School, incorporating evidence in learning doesn't mean that every student must participate

HOW TO Structure Problem-Based Learning

While there are various ways of conducting problem-based learning projects, most include the following components:

- **Provide an "anchor" that offers background to generate interest.** Students may be given a scenario from a novel or a movie to create interest. For the renewable resources project, for example, teachers may provide students with a scenario about a future where all fossil fuels are depleted or with a compelling piece of informational text or video to help build background knowledge.

- **Give students choice in some aspect of the project.** Allow students to choose the texts they will read, an aspect of the project they want to research, the type of writing or product they want to produce, or even the makeup of their groups.

- **Generate a problem statement or driving question.** Consider using a scenario to make the project more engaging and relevant, such as this one: "You are a scientist who has just been told that fossil fuels will run out before anyone thought possible. You are responsible for finding the most efficient alternative energy source and convincing world leaders that your choice is more advantageous than any other."

- **Provide opportunities for students to raise questions, become familiar with the problem, and explore multiple facets of the issue.** Provide plenty of time for whole-class discussion, individual

in the tired and obsolete research paper. Seminars, inquiry learning, and interdisciplinary projects, all of which require authentic research, ramp up engagement while evening the playing field between "struggling

conferences, seminars, or research activities as well as multiple texts on the topic.

- **Teach students to conduct rigorous investigation and research.** Ensure that during this process students have ample time and sufficient technology to conduct a rigorous investigation. Field trips, guest speakers, Skyped interviews, and videos are also useful for research. Students must also be taught how to evaluate the credibility of sources.

- **Help students analyze findings and draw conclusions.** Provide students with a system for organizing and analyzing their findings. Model how to draw conclusions from data and offer extra scaffolding for those needing more help.

- **Provide ongoing feedback and revision from teachers and peers.** Make time for individual conferences with students or groups where students bring their research and explain their conclusions. Provide sufficient time for groups to work together with specific instructions on how to offer feedback to each other. Consider providing whole-group feedback at the beginning of each class.

- **Engage in reflection.** At the end of every work period, have students self-reflect about their day's work in their learning logs or fill out exit cards where they can ask questions or make comments.

- **Assess in authentic ways.** Consider alternative assessments for problem-based learning such as portfolios, presentations, or performance assessments rather than traditional pen-and-paper tests.

learners" and more advanced students. In 21st century classrooms, evidence can be the dynamic hub around which all reading, writing, and discussion revolve.

6 How Using Diverse Media and Formats Can Ignite Student Learning

Students employ technology thoughtfully to enhance their reading, writing, speaking, listening, and language use. They tailor their searches online to acquire useful information efficiently, and they integrate what they learn using technology with what they learn offline. They are familiar with the strengths and limitations of various technological tools and mediums and can select and use those best suited to their communication goals.

—Description of College- and Career-Ready Students, CCSS Introduction

Deborah Jaeger, a 12th-grade teacher at a low-performing high school in Memphis, asks each of her students to deliver a formal presentation once per grading period.

Last year, these presentations included a talk about an issue raised in a book of choice using technology as a presentation tool, a low-tech poetry recitation that included performance and interpretation, and a presentation on a single literary element throughout a work of literature. "I try to choose stuff that

© Ocean/Corbis

would benefit the class to hear," Mrs. Jaeger says. "Things that I might normally teach, but that they can handle sort of teaching to each other."

The presentations generally go well, Mrs. Jaeger says, especially when she sets guidelines for student technology use. In the past, when she didn't set those guidelines, she wound up with every teacher's nightmare: class after class in which students face a screen, reading in a monotone voice from presentation slides that contain too much text, distracting visuals, and little useful content.

"PowerPoint has become my worst enemy," another high school teacher told us. "When I first saw it, I thought it would be a game-changing tool. Now I feel a little ill just thinking about how bad student presentations can be."

The Common Core State Standards (CCSS) for both reading and writing emphasize the need to instruct students in appropriate and effective uses of technology and diverse media, but nowhere, perhaps, is the importance of technology more obvious than in the speaking and listening standards. The six anchor standards included under the umbrella of speaking and listening may be easy to overlook or ignore—after all, speaking and listening skills are less likely to be tested directly on a high-stakes assessment than reading and writing skills, right?—but every language arts and content-area teacher knows how important these skills are to the full education of students. What's more, most teachers are *already meeting these standards* in their classes.

> Nowhere, perhaps, is the importance of technology more obvious than in the speaking and listening standards.

That doesn't mean, of course, that we can't meet the standards more effectively.

This chapter focuses on the use of technology and media in teaching the skills students need (a note here: We won't be pointing out uses of technology with arrows in this chapter, since the entire chapter focuses on that standard). In it, we'll explore key areas that are underscored in the description of college- and career-ready students in the introduction to the CCSS:

- Research
- Communication
- Collaboration
- Showcasing

We'll return in the second half of the chapter to Mrs. Jaeger's class of seniors and to presentation using technology and the speaking and listening standards, but first we'll explore how technology plays an important role in meeting the standards for writing and reading.

And, as with every chapter in this book, this chapter is also about more than just helping students interpret or use technological tools; it's about the core skills embodied in strong teaching and learning: critical thinking, inquiry, ownership, and motivation.

> Technology plays an important role in meeting the standards for writing and reading.

The Scope of Technology in an Inquiry-Based Classroom

Many of us find ourselves at an odd turning point in education, with technology changing the landscape underneath and in front of us as we teach. On the one hand, experts are still talking to teachers about meeting the needs of the "digital native," a phrase coined by Marc Prensky in 2001, when our youngest generation of teachers *is* made up of the very digital natives Prensky described. On the other hand, we all still know—and may *be* ourselves—teachers for whom the constant shifts and developments in educational technology, from terms such as *wiki* or *meme* to an apparently endless stream of websites and programs, seem overwhelming.

We suggest that it's better to think of technology in terms of the core skills you're trying to achieve than the specific programs or tools you're using to get there. The sites will change; the basic elements of learning won't. Before moving on to reading and writing, therefore, we offer here a brief discussion, with examples, of ways many teachers today are using technology to meet both the skills demanded by the core standards and the skills endemic to solid teaching and learning in the 21st century.

Note that we do not include the use of technology for basic management and business in the classroom. Your students may be accessing their grades or homework online, or perhaps you submit daily attendance through your computer network. These uses of technology support the practice of education more and more, but are not essential to the core teaching and learning with which we are concerned here. Nor are we attempting to address the hardware used by teachers

> Think of technology in terms of the core skills you're trying to achieve, rather than the specific programs or tools you're using to get there.

and students; some educators with whom we've talked have limited access to technology in the classroom while others teach in environments where every student has a laptop, a smartphone, an e-reader, or an iPad.

What we focus on here, instead, are five ways in which technology supports student learning, worded in terms of what we see students and teachers around the country *do,* not what they have (you'll see that we address all four of the areas mentioned in the standards' description of college- and career-ready students):

- Technology for Research and Exploration
- Technology for Communication and Collaboration
- Technology for Flipping Learning
- Technology to Create and Innovate
- Technology to Present and Showcase

Technology for Research and Exploration

Key references in the CCSS:

> Integrate and evaluate content presented in diverse media and formats, including visually and quantitatively, as well as in words. (R.7)

> Gather relevant information from multiple print and digital sources, assess the credibility and accuracy of each source, and integrate the information while avoiding plagiarism. (W.8)

It's rare to find a student or teacher who isn't adept at performing a quick Internet search on a topic or following links from site to site out of curiosity. More advanced uses of the Internet for research and exploration, however, need to be taught. The core standards touch on many of the skills that students need in this area, including the ability to assess reliability and accuracy, to integrate material well, and to cite as needed.

How does one teach these skills? We suggest that teachers might help students in this area by doing any of the following:

- Visiting sample websites as a class or in small groups and discussing issues of authorship, citation, timeliness, accuracy, and presentation

- Conducting multiple short research projects rather than one long "term paper" in order to facilitate the kinds of immediate research required of today's learners

- Introducing students to sites that construct bibliographies and citation format online

- Discussing the various forms of information available online with students, including databases

- Introducing students to advanced search engines (such as Google Scholar) as well as advanced search forms and terms

- Allowing students to try a number of ways, both digitally and in print, of note-taking and collecting research (as opposed to adhering strictly to the old-fashioned note card system only)

- Including both digital and print source material in assignments and rubrics in order to help students discover where valuable information lies in both arenas

- Having students complete research in teams that not only share material but are jointly responsible for critically evaluating that material

- Enlisting the help of school librarians to shepherd students through tricky forms of research

COLLABORATION

DIFFERENTIATION AND SCAFFOLDING

MULTIPLE LEARNING METHODS

AUTHENTIC ASSESSMENT

COLLABORATION

Consider the goal of producing college- and career-ready students expounded by the CCSS: It's less and less clear that the one-size-fits-all, formulaic approach to research often promoted in the past by research assignments (complete with note cards, a formal outline, an advance bibliography, and a rough and final draft) represents the kinds of research and collection of information students will actually do once they leave school. Our goal in guiding students through research should be to reinforce the core values we associate with research at the best levels, including synthesis of information and appropriate attribution of and interaction with source material, and to create engagement with

> Our goal in
> guiding students
> through research
> should be to
> reinforce the core
> values we associate
> with research at
> the best levels.

the idea and process of researching—not dread at the very mention of the term.

We also want to value the unique form of exploration of ideas that technology today offers, such as the ability to surf and connect tangential ideas; to view and comprehend information not only in text but also through visuals, video, interactive sites, and other formats; and to share ideas with others as one comprehends them. It's not a bad idea, every now and then, to allow students the chance just to see what they find online (with the caveat, of course, that there is much inappropriate material online to guard against) and to explore topics in a general way.

Technology for Communication and Collaboration

Key references in the CCSS:

> Use technology, including the Internet, to produce and publish writing and to interact and collaborate with others. (W.6)

© Pop! Studio Photography/Corbis

> Prepare for and participate effectively in a range of conversations and collaborations with diverse partners, building on others' ideas and expressing their own clearly and persuasively. (SL.1)

Perhaps in no area is the gap between how students learn in school and how they function outside of school, including in workplaces, more obvious than in the realm of collaboration and working together. Put simply, schools value independent learning; the world increasingly values collaboration. We tend to bemoan the hazards and distractions caused by today's social networking sites, but there's much about the world of collaborative learning to recommend it, including increasing student motivation and interest.

Consider an assignment that Barry tried with an 11th-grade class. He partnered the students with another 11th-grade class—in a school in another city 200 miles away. Both classes read and discussed, on their own, five sonnets by a diverse group of poets ranging from Shakespeare's Sonnet 18 to modern poet Marilyn Nelson's "How I Discovered Poetry" and Billy Collins's "Sonnet," a fun poem about writing and reading sonnets. (For more on sonnets, see the discussion of Emma Lazarus's "The New Colossus" in Chapter 5.)

COLLABORATION

What happened next was unusual. Barry and the other school's teacher set up an online discussion board with five different discussion prompts. Over the course of the next week, each student in each class got online and added at least two posts to each of the five discussion threads, with the following rules:

- At least two of each student's comments had to feature original thoughts or comments about the poem or discussion question.

INQUIRY

- At least four of each student's comments had to address in three or more full sentences another student's thoughts directly (by agreeing, disagreeing, or qualifying a peer's statements).

COLLABORATION

- The rest of the comments could be quick responses to another student's ideas ("LOL," "That's a great point!" etc.).

- Extra points were given for quoting and citing evidence from the poems in original posts.

At the end of the week, students in both classes were given the weekend to review all of the comments. Then, on Monday, each teacher handed the students three of the five discussion questions—and the students chose one to respond to on paper. Students who read and participated in the online discussion were allowed to use any ideas they'd gleaned from the posts.

AUTONOMY

COLLABORATION AND SCAFFOLDING

AUTHENTIC ASSESSMENT

To make matters more interesting, Barry decided to follow this assessment up with another, more creative assessment that also involved collaboration. Instead of a traditional "test" on sonnet form, Barry's students were to compose a sonnet on their own (iambic pentameter was optional). Furthermore, Barry included these elements in his instructions and rubric:

MULTIPLE LEARNING METHODS

- Students could work alone or in pairs to complete the assignment, but regardless of the outcome or process, both students in a pair would receive the same grade.

COLLABORATION

- Students received the assignment at the end of school one day, and it was due at the end of school the next day.

- Students could use any and all resources they wished to complete the assignment, including the Internet, their notes, their peers, other teachers, or their parents.

AUTONOMY

- The sonnets had to be coherent and unified but could focus on any topic or reasonable sonnet form.

- If students were stuck or felt like they had writer's block, they could start with the first line of any of the five sonnets they'd read as a class.

- The sonnets could be turned in as a hard copy, a digital file, or even a video recording of the student delivering the poem.

Though many of Barry's students worked in pairs, one of Barry's struggling students, Mary, took an unusual approach—she communicated throughout the day with an advanced student from the school in the other city, and even emailed the other teacher after getting the address from Barry.

DIFFERENTIATION

Mary and her online partner soon found that regardless of ability, the playing field could be largely leveled by an assignment that relied not on students' ability to memorize but on their creativity, skills at synthesis, ability to ask the right questions of the right people—and diligence. In the end, Mary's partner credited her with much of their success on the assignment—though the teacher in the other city rewarded her student for the extra work she put in.

Collaborative work of this sort takes preparation and clear instructions and rubrics, and it doesn't always work as well as the example of Mary (partners may bicker, disagree, or contribute different amounts of work to projects). But not only do students become engaged when working together; they don't even have to be in the same physical location to do it. Consider the benefits technology offers:

COLLABORATION

- Students can partner on projects or discussions with peers in a different class, school, or country.

RELEVANCE

- Students can maximize online resources rather than being removed from them (in the case of the above assignment, one of Barry's students contacted a poet through a social networking site and received online guidance in composing in meter from an authority).

- Through discussion boards, wikis, transcripts, emails, or recording, a teacher can follow actual student discussion—and respond to it—even when it takes place outside of class or when numerous groups are working at the same time.

  FEEDBACK

- Using shared online documents and drop boxes, students can collaborate and share notes and drafts easily.

- Students can compensate for their own weaknesses and build on their strengths because they have the time and resources to do so—just as they often will in the world of work.

  DIFFERENTIATION AND RELEVANCE

Group work in class is generally dictated and carefully structured by teachers. In the online world, and the world of work, groups often form spontaneously to address real and immediate needs, aim to deliver solutions to community problems with community rewards, often involve tensions and disagreement, and include members who self-select as participants. As we structure assignments for today's learners, it makes sense to look for ways to introduce these elements into our assignments and classroom expectations.

Technology for Flipping Learning

Key references in the CCSS:

> Integrate and evaluate information presented in diverse media
> and formats, including visually, quantitatively, and orally. (SL.2)

Rose Anderson, a seventh-grade English teacher, started "flipping" her classroom last year. What does this look like in practice? A day or two before each class, Ms. Anderson makes screencasts for students; each screencast is a recording (made and stored on one of many free sites on the web) of what Ms. Anderson presents, draws, or writes on the screen while she narrates and teaches. The students view these screencasts before coming to class, as homework, freeing up class time for teacher-supported hands-on activities. In the screencasts, Ms. Anderson

FEEDBACK

HOW TO Write as a Class Using Wikis

If you've never used a wiki for class writing projects, you might want to consider it. Advertisement-free wikis are available at a number of sites for free, including www.wikispaces.com. A wiki works much like a standard webpage, but every user can add a new page and link to other pages (think Wikipedia).

Try this approach to writing and editing collaboratively using a free wiki— your students will love it. You can read a sample group wiki of this sort from a middle school class at www.chooseyourmyth.wikispaces.com.

Example of Wiki

- Create the wiki. You, the teacher, write a short story opener in second person. At the end of the short opener, allow the reader three choices. For instance, you might ask the reader to choose one of three doors or walk forward, left, or right. On the example site above, the story opener introduces "Mythology High School," in which each scene is set in a school classroom but is populated by a mythological creature.

- Share the wiki with your class, have every student sign into it, and then explain that you're going to write a group story in the model of *Choose Your Own Adventure* stories. These stories, popular with kids, allow the reader to make choices and, in a print version, jump to a certain page to continue the story ("If you choose to climb the stairs, turn to page 49 . . .").

- For your story, choose a single element that every new page should include in some way. Some suggestions:

  o A character or monster from Greek mythology

  o A famous writer

  o A character from your reading during that year

  o A particular location in your school or in your town or city

  o A metaphor, a simile, or another rhetorical device

- Now, have three volunteers add pages that continue the story, each beginning from one of the options you left open at the end of the introduction. Make sure the students add hyperlinks (if you don't know how to make these, one of your students will figure it out and show you) from the choice on your page to their new page. A reader will now be able to click on the choice and continue reading the story.

- Your three volunteers should each leave three choices at the end of their entries. Now you can have nine more students add their own entries on new pages.

- As your class writes, create a visual flowchart of the story to keep track. Make sure some of the story lines end quickly (happily or sadly) and others continue for some time. Each student might wind up contributing several pages to the story. You might use a spreadsheet for this purpose—or have a student in your class take charge of this step.

- Test-drive the final product (proofing and editing as you go) by having each class member read through the story multiple times, choosing different story paths each time to make sure the various options work technologically and as a narrative.

- Share the final product with other classes, teachers, or parents.

In the online world, and the world of work, groups often form spontaneously to address real and immediate needs.

might also provide links to other key sites or suggestions for delving deeper into the topic online. (The most well-known videos of this kind, those aimed largely toward mathematical subjects and hosted by Khan Academy online, are now being watched by millions of users.) Ms. Anderson tailors her videos to her classes, allowing her to teach as homework what she would have taught, in the past, in the classroom.

Imagine, for instance, that you wish to teach students to write a business letter. In the past, teachers might have demonstrated and explained the form and tone of a letter in class while students dutifully watched or took notes. Then, for homework, students would try writing their own letters.

In Ms. Anderson's class, things look different.

DIFFERENTIATION

ACTIVE LEARNING

FEEDBACK

- Students receive the information about the form and concept of the business letter online as homework the night before they come to class. They can pause, rewind, or watch the video over again as they wish (and it will still be there later, when it's time to review for a quiz or test).

- The next day, in class, the students immediately apply the information by writing a sample letter while Ms. Anderson circulates and helps those with questions. She's able to tell whether or not the students completed the homework by their understanding of the task at hand, not because of a worksheet or quiz (and she sometimes embeds certain information in her video, such as a key term or even an odd bit of information, as a way of checking whether or not students really viewed the material).

DIFFERENTIATION

- Ms. Anderson differentiates her teaching because now she has the ability to work with students at the very moment when they grapple with the hard work of *doing*. As they work through the actual task, she makes suggestions for revision or for more depth, creates partner groups for peer editing, or helps particularly struggling students simply begin the task.

Flipped learning is intimidating to many teachers because it removes control from the teacher and because it requires an initial investment of time, but today's students are more and more comfortable learning material in this way. However, it's important to distinguish between flipping and flopping: The key to success is not simply making a video for students to watch or changing the nature of homework; it's the quality of what students are doing in class—and the role the teacher takes in guiding and supporting students in that process. Flipping the classroom works when it opens up time for teachers and students to work in close contact on difficult tasks that students would otherwise struggle with alone.

Technology to Create and Innovate

Key references in the CCSS:

> Make strategic use of digital media and visual displays of data to express information and enhance understanding of presentations. (SL.5)

To be honest, the above speaking and listening anchor standard does not do justice to what we mean by creation and innovation. The standards from the K–5 strand come closer to this meaning; consider, for instance, how the Grade 4 band expresses the need for children to "make strategic use of digital media":

> Create engaging audio recordings of stories or poems that demonstrate fluid reading at an understandable pace; add visual displays when appropriate to emphasize or enhance certain facts or details. (SL.3.5)

Nowhere in the Grade 6–12 standards are students explicitly encouraged to create and innovate through the exciting and varied means available to them in an online world, such as streaming media, podcasts, website creation, or artistic invention.

However, it's equally clear in the standards that students *do* need to conceptualize, organize, and produce material in "diverse formats." It's also clear that today's teachers have harnessed technology to allow students these opportunities; one only needs to search online to find examples of student-created book trailers, music videos related to literature, Tumblr-style poster pages, websites, or Common Craft–style videos explaining key concepts of language or literary study.

> The key to flipping (not flopping) is the quality of what students are doing in class— and the role the teacher takes in guiding and supporting students in that process.

MULTIPLE
LEARNING
METHODS

Remember Ms. Anderson, the middle school teacher whose flipped classroom we described earlier? Each spring, Ms. Anderson asks her students to create a multigenre project inspired by similar projects described by Tom Romano in his book *Blending Genre, Altering Style* (2000). Ms. Anderson's project, which includes both print and digital genres, emerged as an alternative to a traditional portfolio or year-end project and emphasizes reflection, multiple perspectives, scholarship combined with creativity, and cohesiveness. In addition, students use memoir as their focus, further encouraging them to examine the lines between fiction and nonfiction and the purposes of each. Ms. Anderson introduces the project through daily writing prompts, combining technology and low-tech classroom writing to inspire students to create and innovate.

The results offer a platform for student creativity to shine; among the 10 pieces each student creates as part of the multigenre product, Ms. Anderson has seen everything from doctor's eye charts to mock newspaper articles to manuals (e.g., *A Manual Guide to Seventh Grade*) to one of last year's projects by student Sarah Tillman, one page of which is

AUTHENTIC
ASSESSMENT

pictured below; Sarah's product included a short story, a mock-FBI letter created online, emails, and online graphics and visuals.

The very existence of technology, teachers such as Ms. Anderson have found, is changing not just the products students produce—and *want* to produce—but the process by which they get there. Students compose, edit, and share differently using technology than they did in the paperbound past; such processes now more often happen simultaneously with creating rather than after the fact. Ms. Anderson's project allows students to explore and create using technology without sacrificing an emphasis on the basic skills of communication, precision, language, and audience.

Technology to Present and Showcase

Key references in the CCSS:

> Use technology, including the Internet, to produce and publish
> writing and to interact and collaborate with others. (W.6)

> Make strategic use of digital media and visual displays of
> data to express information and enhance understanding of
> presentations. (SL.5)

Example of Multigenre Memoir Element Created Online

7

The Daily News
October 14, 2012

FEDERAL BUREAU OF INVESTIGATIONS: BY NANCY ARRABELLAN

The FBI had always been strong. The FBI has always persevered. The FBI has always walked with their heads up. Recently though, the FBI has been struggling. Although we are still strong, persevering, and walking with our heads up, we are troubled. The FBI is currently unsettled by threat notes to our own Jenks and the very Director.

Everyone is aware of the recent trials we are being put through. They are completely uncalled for. As most people would know, the FBI does *not* lose things, at all. That is why we stress the importance of order and neatness. With recent threat notes from "Unknown", people have begun to question the FBI. In the note placed to the side, it says that we are missing something and "Unknown" has this item we need and want so desperately. Of course if we wanted and needed it so badly, we would not have lost it in the first place. Way to think through that one, "Unknown". If anyone has any news whatsoever about these threats, contact Noah Edwards immediately. Never forget what our emblem says, fidelity, bravery, and integrity.

These times are hard and trying; there's no point denying that. Even one of our lead agents, Noah Edwards, admits it. But Jenks and the Director are acting as relaxed as always saying there's nothing to be worried about. Jenks said to me himself one time "The FBI has dealt with many things much more vexing than these notes. We are missing nothing. His threats are empty."

Latest Note:

Dear FBI,

You may not realize it now, but you are missing something, something you need and want desperately. I have it. I'm holding it until you pay my ransom – 1 million dollars by Halloween at midnight. If my requests are not fulfilled, more things will go missing. *They* will be missed. Do not forget: 1 million dollars by midnight Halloween, or else.

Sincerely: Unknown

Integrate and evaluate content presented in diverse media and formats, including visually and quantitatively, as well as in words. (R.7)

It might not seem immediately clear from the standards related to presentation and publication of student work using technology exactly

RELEVANCE

FEEDBACK

what the goal of such sharing is. On the one hand, the standards aim at preparing students for the world of work, in which the ability to deliver a smooth, informational presentation is a valuable asset. On the other hand, they encourage sharing for the sake of learning and using the rich array of tools available to students through technology to disseminate and receive responses to their thinking and creations.

We encourage you to embrace both uses of technology and to have students create both formal presentations and portfolios or other technology-based creations that allow for creativity, reflection, and the simple sharing of material and ideas. The tools for such presentation and sharing are so varied and change so constantly that it's risky to list any specific means of student creation, but it's worth noting that PowerPoint, a program that still dominates teacher thinking about presentation, no longer stands alone in the world of Prezi, Tumblr, blogs, wikis, do-it-yourself website creation, Instagram, Facebook pages, Glogster, screencasting, and Photo Story. It's probably far more useful for teachers to concentrate on the *goals* of student creation and rely on adolescents themselves, with guidance and support, to deliver creations using a variety of tools.

AUTHENITIC
ASSESSMENT

Thus, we suggest that, over the course of a year or throughout a particular class, students should experience multiple opportunities for using technology to present and showcase, including these:

COLLABORATION

- Formal presentations to the class or others using PowerPoint, Prezi, or other software, carefully structured through rubrics to avoid monochromatic presentation and to enhance thoughtfulness and connection with an audience

INQUIRY

- Informal presentation and exploration of ideas through the use of blogs or other organically developed sites

FEEDBACK

- Using, for instance, a wiki or drop box, collection of student work with opportunities for metacognition and self-reflection on development, learning, and craft throughout a course

COLLABORATION

- Presentation of student final products (written or otherwise) by sharing with peers, parents, or a broader online community through tools such as websites, wikis, online flipbooks, or Glogster

- Integration of multiple avenues of examining, thinking about, and expressing ideas about a topic through a tool that allows the presentation of written text, video, visuals, and other formats

MULTIPLE LEARNING METHODS

If our goal is to engage and motivate students (the surest road to improving learning, as we've discussed), no transition is more likely to help us accomplish that aim than making the work adolescents produce valuable, shared, and authentic instead of cloistered and dissected. Technology offers a magnificent expanse of opportunities for students to showcase and publish, but because it also takes time to produce such pieces, many teachers balk at initiating projects of this sort. We encourage you, however, to consider the valuable learning—about both the specifics of language and the joy of creation—that arises from such experiences.

RELEVANCE

Preparing for Reading and Writing: Interpreting Material in Diverse Formats

Before we return to Mrs. Jaeger's 12th graders, let's quickly take a look at research in the ninth-grade classroom of one struggling learner. Jackson, a freshman, was preparing to compose the rough draft of a short research project assigned jointly by his English and social studies teachers. Ultimately, Jackson's teachers expected him to produce two documents as a result of his research:

- A brief paper exploring a literary document (such as a poem or speech) related to the civil rights movement of the 1960s
- A technology-based presentation exploring a social or political issue related to the same period. Jackson had chosen to research voting issues in the South.

Jackson tried about as well as most students in his class, but his comprehension of class material was limited. He performed better on rote tasks or simple assignments than on those that required synthesis, higher-order thinking, or complicated investigation. His test scores reinforced his struggles with reading comprehension—he'd barely

HOW TO Help Students Choose Research Topics

It's tempting to control research assignments tightly, because you, the teacher, probably know what students can research well and what they can't. But remember that discovering good topics—and abandoning bad ones—is part of the process of learning and research, as well. Using technology, there's no longer much reason not to let students in on the initial decision of what topic is worth pursuit.

A fifth-grade teacher we know asks students to research mysteries of the world. A 12th-grade teacher assigns each student in her class a modern poet and poem. A social studies teacher has each student research a speech delivered by a living person. Any of these topics allows room for initial exploration and autonomy on the part of students.

- Begin by discussing the overall topic and having a class brainstorm some possible specific examples together. Discuss the purpose and expectations of the project. What kind of example will make a good focus, and why?

- Discuss source material and what it means for a website or other text to be credible, reliable, and scholarly. Outline your expectations clearly (is Wikipedia an acceptable source? What about an online encyclopedia? Should usable sources be limited to those with a named author, date of publication, or sponsoring organization?).

made it into the third stanine on the previous year's reading test. So it was no surprise to his teacher, Mr. Clay Keith, when he came to class one morning armed with several pages of text he'd printed out from various websites and online encyclopedias, but also with three web sources, which, as he said to his teacher, "I'm not really sure I understand."

First, Jackson showed his teacher one page containing a chart and another with a graphic.

- Get students online and let them explore specific examples related to the topic. As they look, ask them to write down what they find and to answer these questions:

  o Why does this topic appeal to you?

  o Can you easily find at least three sources for this topic that meet the class criteria for credible and reliable sites?

  o What big questions or themes are raised by this example?

- Enlist the help of your librarian and be sure to include print sources as well as technology in your students' search.

- Show students how to collect, record, and eventually cite the sources they find online using an online service such as www.noodletools.com.

- Invite students to share their findings with the class, presenting their online resources on a projector or in groups. Allow other students to ask critical questions about the source material and topic. Conference with individual students as needed.

- Once students have explored the initial research possibilities, have them sign up for specific topics.

Not only will the extra days such research requires pay off by increasing motivation and interest (and probably cutting down on plagiarism and cheating in the research process), but you'll also be meeting more standards by encouraging both research and inquiry from the start of the research process through the end.

Chart Similar to One Found Online in Jackson's Research

African-Americans Registered to Vote			
State	Alabama	Miss.	Tennessee
1960	66,000	22,000	185,000
1966	250,000	175,000	225,000

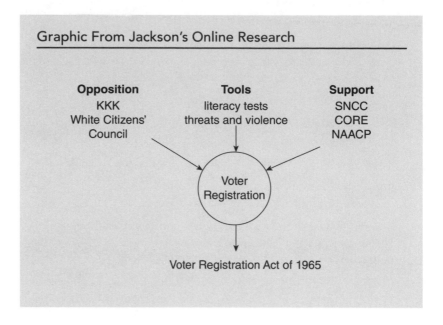

Graphic From Jackson's Online Research

Opposition	Tools	Support
KKK	literacy tests	SNCC
White Citizens'	threats and violence	CORE
Council		NAACP

Voter Registration

Voter Registration Act of 1965

The final source Jackson had was simply the URL of a video he'd found on voter registration in the civil rights movement.

"I don't know if these are OK," Jackson said to his English teacher, Mr. Keith. "What do you think?"

FEEDBACK

"Well, what do these pages tell you?" Mr. Keith asked.

"I'm not sure about the first one," Jackson answered. "I think it shows that Tennessee was way ahead of other states in voter registration. The second one just shows some of the stuff that helped the Voter Registration Act pass, right? I got the third one, but I don't know if I can use it in my paper."

Jackson was partly right, of course, though he missed the key point of the first graph—namely, that voter registration of African Americans increased greatly in all states during the 1960s—and he oversimplified the second visual. His questions, however, drove home to Mr. Keith the need for all of his students to better comprehend and evaluate the material they found in their research, particularly online. Considering the chart and graph Jackson brought to him, for instance, Mr. Keith knew that he wanted a student in Jackson's position to ask questions such as these:

INQUIRY

- Are these figures and charts accurate, reliable, and trustworthy? How can I tell?

- What key information do I gain from this material? How is this information different from what I would find written out in text?

- How do I describe and cite this information when I write about it?

- Should I—and can I—produce similar charts or visuals in what I write or present?

AUTONOMY

These questions were particularly important for this project because Jackson and his classmates were expected not simply to write a paper about their documents, but to present, using technology, on the issue they researched. In other words, Jackson needed first to understand how graphic and quantitative information was presented to him online so that he could then showcase his understanding of material to others using technology.

SCAFFOLDING

Each of the questions above, incidentally, is reflected in the CCSS. Consider, for instance, the seventh anchor standard for reading, which asks students to undertake precisely the sort of comparisons Jackson was making in the research he produced. In addition, the standards suggest that students need both to *comprehend* and to *apply* information from diverse formats, as specific standards related to Grades 9–10 demonstrate:

> Analyze various accounts of a subject told in different mediums (e.g., a person's life story in both print and multimedia), determining which details are emphasized in each account. (RI.9–10.7)

> Gather relevant information from multiple authoritative print and digital sources, using advanced searches effectively; assess the usefulness of each source in answering the research question; integrate information into the text selectively to maintain the

HOW TO Help Students Avoid Plagiarism

The CCSS explicitly address plagiarism as an important concern in the research process:

> Gather relevant information from multiple authoritative print and digital sources, using advanced searches effectively; assess the usefulness of each source in answering the research question; integrate information into the text selectively to maintain the flow of ideas, avoiding plagiarism and following a standard format for citation. (W.9–10.8)

Struggling students sometimes plagiarize on projects like Mr. Keith's because they fall behind on their work, feel they aren't capable, or simply don't understand the rules of attribution. We suggest that, for students like Jackson, more can be accomplished before the assignment begins than after the student has completed it; prevention in such cases is more desirable than punishment. We suggest planning a research assignment with these steps in mind:

- Give students ownership of their research topics and of the process they use to collect information; increasing interest and ownership will increase the likelihood that adolescents complete original work.

- Help students construct thesis statements that involve genuine research problems in class. This step will make papers more interesting to write and research and also make it harder to find prepackaged online materials.

- Discuss *why* the rules of citation and attribution are important. Help students understand not only when and how to cite, but the purpose of citation. Include a discussion of how to find and evaluate credible sources online.

- Assign research and writing in small steps. Allow time at each stage for students to work carefully, revise, get feedback, and work thoughtfully.

- Build time into the revision process for students to work on their own, in pairs, or in conferences with you to review quotes, facts, and citations in their papers.

For more detailed information regarding plagiarism, see Barry's book, *Plagiarism: Why It Happens and How to Prevent It* (2008).

flow of ideas, avoiding plagiarism and following a standard format for citation. (W.9–10.8)

What's more, throughout the CCSS, the concept that information comes to students in more than one format arises commonly. For instance, it appears in the reading standards:

Integrate and evaluate content presented in **diverse media and formats**, including visually and quantitatively, as well as in words. (R.7)

And also in the speaking and listening standards:

Integrate and evaluate information presented in **diverse media and formats**, including visually, quantitatively, and orally. (SL.2)

Mr. Keith, Jackson's teacher, realized quickly that Jackson, as well as other freshmen in his class, were attempting to "integrate information" that included more than just text. In fact, getting students to learn more about charts and graphs had always been a goal of Mr. Keith's, but when their only practice came through sidebars in the textbook, it was tough to get them interested. Now, students were bringing this material to him because they found it online, but they had trouble making sense of what they found. And why wouldn't they? To many ninth-grade students, videos online seem "authoritative," perhaps even more than most websites or, for that matter, textbooks.

> To many ninth-grade students, videos online seem "authoritative," perhaps even more than most websites or, for that matter, textbooks.

Mr. Keith knew that his assignments and rubrics needed to change to accommodate the needs of the students he was teaching.

Helping Students Apply Information From Diverse Formats

The old model was fairly simple, wasn't it? We took students to a library, showed them how to use the card catalog and perhaps a microfiche reader, and then worried about integrating the text they found into the text they wrote (OK, perhaps it was never really that simple, but you get our point). Today, in a quick online search, students are likely to come across information ranging across many media. Indeed, imagine that Jackson had thought to go to the *New York Times* website to begin his

© Pop! Studio Photography/Corbis

research and had simply typed "civil rights movement" into the search bar. On the first page of hits alone, he would have come across a variety of sources:

- An article on FBI investigations during the civil rights movement

- Blog entries on the ongoing importance of civil rights

- Ideas shared by teachers for instructing students about civil rights

- A slideshow of photographs from the 60s

- Links to other sites and resources

Students conducting research today need to be prepared to deal with information delivered in all sorts of ways. We suggest, in fact, that you *intentionally* structure short research assignments that help students make sense of information presented in a variety of formats:

MULTIPLE LEARNING METHODS

- Printed books and articles

- Historical primary sources in print or online

- Academic and formal text (journal articles, essays, criticism)

- Informal text by one individual (blogs, websites, opinion pieces)

- User-edited community sources (Wikipedia, online discussion forums, social networking pages)

- Videos and photographs

- Graphs, charts, and maps

- Visual diagrams and flowcharts

- Online sources such as podcasts and interactive sites

SCAFFOLDING

But finding such sources isn't enough. A discussion of the relative merits and uses of each source is critical, as is discussion of assignments that allow students to apply these formats in their own writing or presentations.

Again, consider Jackson. His assignment included a formal paper and a presentation using technology. We presented a simple chart Jackson found online on page 189. Here is a section of his paper dealing with this chart, after Mr. Keith helped him make sense of the information it contains:

> *Between 1960 and 1966, the number of black voters raised in many Southern states, including Alabama, Mississippi, and Tennessee (Smith). This proves that more efforts were being made to include African-Americans in elections because of groups such as the NAACP.*

Depending on the students you teach, you might praise or criticize Jackson's writing in these sentences, but his grasp of the material is accurate. More interesting, however, was how Jackson applied this information in his presentation.

The following shows a slide from the first draft of Jackson's PowerPoint.

An Initial Slide From Jackson's PowerPoint

African-American Voting Patterns, 1960-1966

- Between 1960 and 1966, the number of black voters raised in many Southern states, including Alabama, Mississippi, and Tennessee (Smith).
- This proves that more efforts were being made to include African-Americans in elections because of groups such as the NAACP.
- Black voters went from 66,000 to 250,000 in Alabama during this time.
- Black voters went from 22,000 to 175,000 in Mississippi during this time.
- Black voters went from 185,000 to 225,000 in Tennessee during this time.

As you can see, Jackson took the two sentences from his paper and statistics from the chart and created a text-heavy slide that would likely not be conducive to a strong presentation.

"What do you want your audience to get from this slide?" Mr. Keith asked Jackson.

Jackson thought a moment. "I guess that voter registration went up, and why."

"And how do you plan to explain that to the audience?"

"I'm just going to show them the slide," Jackson answered.

"OK," Mr. Keith continued. "Let's look at the rubric for the presentation and think about what you're being asked to do other than just show the slide."

FEEDBACK

FEEDBACK

ACTIVE LEARNING

Together, Jackson and Mr. Keith discussed both the content and presentation possibilities offered by the slide. Mr. Keith helped Jackson realize that the original chart actually showed the information in a better format and that it was *Jackson's* job, not the slide's, to help the audience make sense of the information. The following shows the revised slide Jackson eventually created.

Jackson's Revised Slide

African-American Voting Patterns, 1960-1966

African-Americans Registered to Vote

State	Alabama	Miss.	Tennessee
1960	66,000	22,000	185,000
1966	250,000	175,000	225,000

What caused this growth?

Who opposed this growth?

Mr. Keith's Rubric for Classroom Presentations

English/History Presentation Rubric				
Content • You clearly explain a social or political issue related to your paper topic • You use accurate and relevant information	Excellent (5 points)	Good (4 points)	Average (3 points)	Poor (2 points)
Source Material • Your source material is incorporated into your presentation in ways that support your main points • You cite your sources using MLA format • You interpret charts and graphs correctly	Excellent (5 points)	Good (4 points)	Average (3 points)	Poor (2 points)
Use of Technology • Your slides or presentation graphics are well organized and don't distract • Slides or graphics illustrate or support the points you make but don't make them for you • Slides or graphics include key information—not too much or too little	Excellent (5 points)	Good (4 points)	Average (3 points)	Poor (2 points)
Presentation Delivery • You speak to the class rather than reading off of the screen • You are organized and prepared to deliver information • You use technology as an aid for your own oral presentation	Excellent (5 points)	Good (4 points)	Average (3 points)	Poor (2 points)
Answers to Class/Teacher Questions • You are able to answer questions knowledgably based on your research	Excellent (5 points)	Good (4 points)	Average (3 points)	Poor (2 points)

CHALLENGE AND
SUCCESS

AUTHENTIC
ASSESSMENT

Note that Jackson also animated the elements of this slide so that the key questions appeared one at a time, allowing him to address each one more effectively and carefully for his audience. Using this revised presentation slide, Jackson was able to present his findings in ways that visually appealed to his audience, allowed him to take a center role in the presentation, and demonstrated and promoted his own understanding of information presented in a variety of formats.

What's more, it engaged him in his own presentation in a way his first slide would not have; by the time Jackson presented to the class, he was excited about his ability to share this information and promote understanding of it among his classmates.

But presentation, especially when technology is involved, is never as simple as having one good PowerPoint slide. Many professions our students enter in the future will require high-level skills involving technology and presentation. And, like the ability to write, these skills may be a key differentiator as they seek to demonstrate their proficiency in the workplace. That's partly why the speaking and listening standards exist; the other reason is that speaking and listening—including presenting

Jackson's Presentation and the Speaking and Listening Standards

By adapting the slides in his presentation to move away from simple repetition of information and to emphasize his own reasoning and research, Jackson clearly showed greater mastery of two important ninth-grade standards:

> Present information, findings, and supporting evidence clearly, concisely, and logically such that listeners can follow the line of reasoning and the organization, development, substance, and style are appropriate to purpose, audience, and task. (SL.9–10.4)

> Make strategic use of digital media (e.g., textual, graphical, audio, visual, and interactive elements) in presentations to enhance understanding of findings, reasoning, and evidence and to add interest. (SL.9–10.5)

findings to others—are key ways not just to share, but also to learn. To understand these standards better, let's return to Mrs. Jaeger's 12th-grade class in Memphis.

Speaking and Listening: Technology and Student Presentation

Mrs. Jaeger's 12th-grade classes functioned as a sort of last chance for most of the students she taught. Housed in a portable classroom behind the main school building, her classes were made up entirely of minority and low-income seniors, some of whom would not graduate and most of whom would not continue on to college (about a third of her students moved on to local universities or community colleges each year). At times, Mrs. Jaeger admitted, the work could be disheartening, but not always.

"Actually, there are far worse jobs in this school," she told us. "My kids may not go to college, but they like to learn. There are 10th-grade classes in the main building where teachers are literally afraid to teach because of the discipline issues or where the teachers feel all they're allowed to do is prepare for standardized tests. The seniors want to discuss—they want to be engaged. They just don't want to spend their time discussing material they don't think applies to their lives."

Mrs. Jaeger's students were, for the majority, not close to meeting the Grade 11 and 12 standards of the CCSS. In department meetings where administrators led reviews of state test scores and the standards, Mrs. Jaeger tended to tune out. As a teacher with over 20 years' experience, she felt she knew what her students needed and did not need to learn. Most of them had passed the state test at the minimal level needed for graduation. Mrs. Jaeger cared most about where these kids would land the year after high school—in the workplace, in their communities, and in life.

> Mrs. Jaeger cared most about where these kids would land the year after high school—in the workplace, in their communities, and in life.

"I would never say I have nothing left to learn as a teacher," she was hasty to add. "Some of the discussion surrounding the new standards has really made me think. Lately, I've been having the students engage in more presentation and discussion, and they love it. It's the most successful thing we do, until it's not. The bad presentations, with bad technology, wind up being a waste of everyone's time, and there are too many of them."

Preparing for Class Presentations—With or Without Technology

With Mrs. Jaeger's presentation dilemma in mind, we contacted colleagues around the country—teachers of students from fifth grade through the graduate level—and asked them what they do to prepare students to give presentations to a class. Besides the obvious measures of outlining general expectations and encouraging students not simply to read material to a class, these teachers responded with quite a bit of advice. In no particular order, here's a list (note that many of these suggestions assume that student presentations will be accompanied by slides created in PowerPoint or similar software):

AUTHENTIC ASSESSMENT

- Agree upon a rubric as a class, or in groups, for grading the presentations.

COLLABORATION

- Discuss and include peer evaluation methods.

- Set time limits (minimum and maximum).

SCAFFOLDING

- Outline the presentation format with the class in advance and/or have students create a written outline.

MULTIPLE LEARNING METHODS

- Require every slide to include a visual, a heading, and either a question, a quote, or a statistic.

- Set a maximum number of words per slide (perhaps 30).

- Outlaw complete sentences from graphic material (but not from oral material)—encourage bullet points instead of sentences, phrases instead of bullet points, and pictures instead of phrases.

- Demonstrate using graphic material to communicate, not merely adorn.

- Force students to practice orally without the slides, then add the slides back in.

ACTIVE LEARNING

- Show students a really poor PowerPoint and ask them to critique it, including distracting noise, movements, visuals, and text.

INQUIRY

- Show students examples of excellent graphics and visual slides— and discuss how visual presentation affects comprehension.

CHALLENGE AND SUCCESS

- Have students practice presentations for one another in pairs or trios before delivering to the entire class.

- Model a works cited slide.

- Discuss the effects of vocal delivery, eye contact, grammar, and confidence.

- Encourage students to consider what their audience knows and needs to know (by having them write about it and discuss it beforehand).

  SCAFFOLDING

- Treat the topic as you would a thesis statement; ask students what they'll prove, what evidence they'll use to prove it, how they'll organize the proof, and how they'll extend the argument to make interesting connections.

  AUTONOMY

- Assign topics or help students choose topics thoughtfully and with inquiry-based approaches; good presentation topics include enough ambiguity to spark critical thinking, but not so much that it's impossible to organize material.

  INQUIRY

Notice the key concepts for teaching reflected in this list: These teachers have learned that it's best not to assume students will understand the basics of a good presentation on their own; they model successful products, they help students focus on structuring content successfully, and they emphasize the need for thoughtfulness in organizing a presentation. They assume students will use technology to present, but technology is not the *point* of the presentation; it's a *tool* with which the presentation becomes more effective.

Similarly, in Mrs. Jaeger's 12th-grade classroom, modeling for students emerged as a clear necessity. Indeed, much of the preparation Mrs. Jaeger included before presentations aimed at helping students who were uncomfortable with presentations think through ways of sharing with an audience. "I always do my own sample presentation on the topic before I ask them to do one and let them critique," she told us. She also worked with students explicitly on listening skills, because "they really need the practice. Many are so used to saying whatever they want and then tuning out what everyone else says. We mime what a good listener does, what she asks, how she sits, everything. We also do the same for someone who is not listening. I grade them on listening and watch them about as much as the presenter. They need to know how to be taken seriously. I think it's

SCAFFOLDING

MULTIPLE LEARNING METHODS

a detriment that even at the end of high school, they don't always know how they come across in front of an audience, and word choice, the right voice and tone for the situation, and tactics for the beginning and end are things that are still tough for them."

ACTIVE LEARNING

Mrs. Jaeger's willingness to put her own self-confidence to the test and to allow students to critique her not only showed them what it takes to present; it showed them that every presentation will have room for improvement. It also allowed her to model how one receives feedback, and it engaged students in the entire activity more fully.

Presentation and Struggling Learners

Presentations involving technology were a primary way Mrs. Jaeger tried to get students engaged and interested in texts, especially challenging literary texts. Recalling a recent set of class presentations, Mrs. Jaeger told us about a student named Maleka who'd remained stubbornly disengaged all year. Maleka was a popular and socially successful student, but she just didn't seem to care about school and rarely studied. As the first grading period drew to a close, Maleka was in serious danger of failing.

AUTONOMY AND DIFFERENTIATION

INQUIRY

Mrs. Jaeger set aside the last three class days of the grading period for student presentations—each student had read a book of choice during the quarter, and each was to offer a five-minute presentation on a key social, political, or historical question raised by the novel or nonfiction text he or she read (early in the school year, Mrs. Jaeger had provided a list of possible choices to guide students). The book Maleka read was *The Adoration of Jenna Fox* by Mary Pearson, a near-future story that deals with the issue of cloning.

"To be truthful," Mrs. Jaeger told us, "I can't be certain that Maleka read the whole book. She said she read it, and she might have—it's a high-interest read, and many 12th-grade girls love it. But I didn't do a separate reading quiz on each novel each student read; I wanted them to read these books without that weight hanging over them, and it would have been too much for me to make separate quizzes for every novel."

DIFFERENTIATION AND ACTIVE LEARNING

Mrs. Jaeger *did* have students keep a reading log and, three times during the reading, write a brief reflection about a paragraph in response to

How I Use Technology

"I teach 18- to 24-year-old males who either are in custody or have recently been released from custody; my job is to help them obtain their GED (which will be aligned with the CCSS next year). Luckily, I have a small class with computers for everyone. I use computers like elementary teachers use centers; I'll set up different games and activities on computers, and they'll play for 10 minutes, then rotate—I use PowerPoints, Khan Academy videos, and YouTube for this.

"Right now we're making graphs and charts (circle, bar, line, others in Word) on the computer. This is a big GED skill, and they have trouble figuring out how to interpret graphs. I give each student a newspaper article and ask them to make a graph based on info in the article. When they finish, we rotate to each computer to see if they can figure out the different graphs. They also vote on the best. They have to explain why they voted as they did; my students aren't crazy about formal presentations but do well with this kind of informal discussion and sharing.

"Overall, the best way I've found to engage and motivate my students is to break learning into small steps and vary the activities and assignments as much as possible. In one class period, we'll watch a video, find some examples in the newspaper, move from table to table completing problems, play Jeopardy, and make posters. We don't spend several days on one topic because they get bored, but we will come back to each topic several times. They like moving around, games, learning new things on the computer (anything involving technology works better than print), short practice sessions, writing on the board, anything timed, stories that make the work seem relevant, hands-on activities—and all lessons that involve food."

—Chaney Cruze,
GED instructor, Nashville, Tennessee

the book, to which she responded in turn. Maleka's reflections showed that she found the novel interesting, but they were typically short and underdeveloped. Mrs. Jaeger worried that her presentation would show the same lack of interest and depth as much of her other work.

AUTHENTIC ASSESSMENT

FEEDBACK

BOOKS

Books That Inspire Meaningful Presentations

Beyond Courage: The Untold Story of Jewish Resistance During the Holocaust by Doreen Rappaport

Rappaport's meticulously researched accounts of Jews all over Europe who dared to resist the Nazis during World War II will give readers a new definition of courage. The narratives are supported by an extensive bibliography and often chilling photographs.

Chew on This: Everything You Don't Want to Know About Fast Food by Charles Wilson and Eric Schlosser

Readers learn more than they want to know about the fast-food industry while reading this intriguing book. With the debate in New York City regarding the size of food and drink items that can be sold, this topic is timely and will make students think twice about their food choices.

One Crazy Summer by Rita Williams-Garcia

Who were the Black Panthers, and what role did they play in the civil rights movement? This novel, set in Oakland, California, during 1968, takes readers into the revolutionary workings of this radical ethnic group, all seen through the eyes of two young girls on a summer visit with their mother.

The Fault in Our Stars by John Green

Green's story about two teens stricken with cancer is insightful, funny, and, ultimately, heartbreaking. While learning about the realities of this devastating illness, readers are ironically enjoying a magical love story.

Before those three days of presentation, however, Mrs. Jaeger worked with the students to create a rubric based on the six speaking and listening anchor standards and the specific 12th-grade versions of those standards. Of particular interest in this case were two standards that relate specifically to technology.

The 9/11 Report: A Graphic Adaptation by Sid Jacobson and Ernie Colon

This graphic novel allows access to the Final Report of the National Commission on Terrorist Attacks Upon the United States in an accurate and understandable manner.

Photo by Brady: A Picture of the Civil War by Jennifer Armstrong

This photo essay of places, people, and events of the U.S. Civil War is enhanced with a comprehensive narrative. Brady's famous photographs are haunting yet mesmerizing. A feature titled "Photos Not Taken" allows readers to imagine what scenes Brady might have captured had he been there.

Stiff: The Curious Lives of Human Cadavers by Mary Roach

For older students interested in forensic science, this book will spark as many questions as it answers as readers take a bizarre journey through the eyes of those who deal with human cadavers. Though not a quick or an easy read, it is filled with incredible stories and written in an engaging (often hilarious) style.

Zeitoun by Dave Eggers

Set in August 2005 before, during, and after Hurricane Katrina, this true account of a resident who decides to remain in New Orleans after sending his family to safety will rivet readers from beginning to end. The Syrian-born Zeitoun rescues people in his canoe after the storm but is soon accused of being a member of al-Qaeda. What follows will foster troubling questions with few answers.

The first of these two key standards emphasizes the need for *comprehension* of material presented in a variety of formats, including digital content:

> Integrate multiple sources of information presented in diverse formats and media (e.g., visually, quantitatively, orally) in order

to make informed decisions and solve problems, evaluating the credibility and accuracy of each source and noting any discrepancies among the data. (SL.11–12.2)

The second key standard emphasizes the need for thoughtful use of technology to *share and showcase* student perspectives and products:

Make strategic use of digital media (e.g., textual, graphical, audio, visual, and interactive elements) in presentations to enhance understanding of findings, reasoning, and evidence and to add interest. (SL.11–12.5)

Like Mrs. Jaeger's students, in structuring any rubric for presentations using technology, we might keep this message of the standards in mind: We must be both careful consumers and careful users of what is available online and through software.

FEEDBACK

COLLABORATION

AUTHENTIC ASSESSMENT

Mrs. Jaeger had students present in the school computer lab rather than her own classroom, which had no projector. As each student presented, the rest of the class evaluated the presentation using an online version of the rubric they'd created. Mrs. Jaeger loaded the rubric into an online survey site so that each audience member could just click a button and rank the presenters on a scale of 1 to 5 for each of the elements on the rubric. At the end of the class, Mrs. Jaeger could then download the averages from the class evaluations and use them as part of her grading mechanism (in addition to her own observations).

"I learned that trick in a workshop," she said, "and it works wonders. Not only do the students stay engaged and focused on the presentations; they do a pretty good job of evaluation and learn what works and what doesn't work."

Mrs. Jaeger was pleased with results overall, especially when she gathered comments at the end of the three days from her classes. They were "all talking about how grown-up everyone seemed," she said, "and many thought it was cool to see their classmates in a new light. One commented that she enjoyed seeing her classmates 'say smart things that made me think more about the novel.' Another said, 'I never knew everyone could do this so well!' They agreed that watching what people presented was amazing, so I guess those Common Core areas of focus worked for most."

Preparation for these students, Mrs. Jaeger agreed, was particularly important—they needed to be set up for success, not expected simply to achieve it on their own, without support. For presentations, preparation often resembles formal writing; the same note-taking skills, outlining process, and organizational thinking apply. Students might use webbing or hierarchical note-taking to shape ideas, and they might develop a speech or presentation much as they develop a written essay, though audience and purpose might change the tone or wording of such a speech. There is a difference, however: Most student writing is assessed by the teacher, and often by the teacher alone. Student presentations and speeches in the classroom are, by their very nature, assessed by everyone in the room either formally or informally. Mrs. Jaeger harnessed that characteristic of presentations to help the whole class become more engaged in the process. What could have been three days of excruciating PowerPoints turned into a continuous learning process for her classes.

> CHALLENGE AND SUCCESS
>
> AUTONOMY
>
> SCAFFOLDING
>
> MULTIPLE LEARNING METHODS
>
> FEEDBACK

Maleka's Presentation

What about Maleka's presentation?

"What I can say," Mrs. Jaeger told us, "is that she saved her grade with the presentation she gave. She did everything on the rubric, including how she organized the information and how she spoke. Her classmates recognized that, too. But I wasn't sure what turned Maleka on to this book when she hadn't been interested in other material we'd read."

Because Mrs. Jaeger later assigned each student to write a reflection on the process of creating and delivering the presentation, we were able to read Maleka's own answer to the question we'd most wish to ask her: What was it about the project that motivated her? Was it the reading? The chance to share in a format other than formal writing? The quality of the student-created rubric? The fact that she was being evaluated by her peers?

> FEEDBACK

Here's Maleka's answer:

> *I liked this project because I liked the book and topic, but mostly, I got really into the presentation format I used. It was an online software called Prezi that I saw someone use in [another] class. Once I started playing with it at home, I just couldn't stop, and it made it really easy to condense the information I found online and put it in a cool format that I could present. I'll definitely be using Prezi again next time we present!*

HOW TO Replicate Mrs. Jaeger's Assignments

In Maleka's case, technology itself provided the spark for more engagement. However, lest it seem like Maleka's self-reflection contradicts our earlier statement that technology should serve as the means, not the end, of student presentations, keep in mind that Maleka's effective use of new presentation software was possible because of how Mrs. Jaeger structured her assignment. Below are key elements of that assignment that might help guide the development of your own lesson:

1. Offer students a chance to choose a novel and/or topic and thus to become more engaged with the presentation topic.

2. Embed elements of critical thinking and inquiry into the project by extending the presentation topics to current events and issues (and thus aligning your teaching both with the second anchor standard for speaking and listening and also the same standard within each specific grade).

3. Involve all students in the class with each presentation through a student-generated rubric and evaluation system.

4. Model successful presentations for students.

5. Reward the effective use of technology only when it supports effective presentation strategies as a whole.

6. Include self-reflective writing so that both students and teacher can evaluate what went right and what went wrong.

Final Thoughts

Like much of the material in the CCSS, references to technology and diverse formats of information offer teachers a goal—*what* students should be able to do—without much detail about the journey—*how* students should reach their goals. In Appendix B, which offers sample tasks for students related to exemplar texts, there is no mention of technology or digital tasks or assignments for students, for instance. What *is* mentioned? The ability of students to compare and contrast, to research, to comprehend, to present, and to discuss. All of these core skills might be accessed and promoted through technology and the many areas of exploration it offers. Throughout this chapter, we've tried to demonstrate that the use of various media in teaching is not ancillary to the work language arts and content-area teachers have always done but *integral* to it; you don't have to teach your subject *and* technology, but you can gain a lot from teaching your subject *through* technology, emphasizing the core skills and concepts most important to learning in every subject and using the exciting tools available in a 21st century classroom to motivate and engage students even more fully.

> You don't have to teach your subject *and* technology, but you can gain a lot from teaching your subject *through* technology.

7 Why a Culture of Reading Is Critical— and How to Create One

> *Students appreciate that the twenty-first-century classroom and workplace are settings in which people from often widely divergent cultures and who represent diverse experiences and perspectives must learn and work together. Students actively seek to understand other perspectives and cultures through reading and listening, and they are able to communicate effectively with people of varied backgrounds. They evaluate other points of view critically and constructively. Through reading great classic and contemporary works of literature representative of a variety of periods, cultures, and worldviews, students can vicariously inhabit worlds and have experiences much different than their own.*
>
> *—Description of College- and Career-Ready Students, CCSS Introduction*

Anita Hernandez, a 10th-grade English and reading teacher, believes there is no problem that reading won't solve. Her classroom walls look like they are held up by bookshelves filled to overflowing with hundreds of books. In her spacious room, pods of desks are arranged in the center with cozy reading spaces tucked into corners. With the implementation of the Common Core State Standards (CCSS), her principal has pushed back on her methods a bit, even while

admitting that the test scores and attendance records of Ms. Hernandez's students, including the ones who struggle, are higher than those of other students of equal ability.

"These kids don't read—they devour books," Ms. Hernandez laughed. "My toughest task is to move them outside of their comfort zone and get them reading books of various genres and topics. They tend to get stuck reading only their favorite authors or themes. I mean, how much dystopian fiction can one person read?"

FEEDBACK

Before 10th grade, many of her students have not read a book for pleasure in years, and the reading surveys that she administers at the beginning of the year often reveal a negative perception of reading. It takes a lot of time and many booktalks for Ms. Hernandez to lure these kids into the texts that she knows will transform them. Once she can talk them into reading a few good books and they begin to share titles, they start to exemplify a description they would find very uncool: "bookworms."

Ms. Hernandez's principal, Susan Flowers, admits that she wants kids to read and appreciates the way Ms. Hernandez engages even the most reluctant student with her enthusiasm for and vast knowledge of books that hook kids. Her concern is that students must learn to read "complex text"; face more challenging, scholarly tasks; and analyze informational text. "It's not enough to just have kids reading, even reading a lot," she said. "With the CCSS, they must do more."

A Culture of Reading: How It Supports the CCSS

It's true that the CCSS demand more than the popular "drop everything and read" practice, where everyone in the school grabs a book and settles in for a quick read. With that approach, there is no instruction, there is often no monitoring, and in many classes, except English, there may be little commitment on the part of teachers or students. Independent reading, a practice where students read books of their own choosing with guidance and feedback from their teacher, however, is a critical scaffold for the challenging texts with which Ms. Flowers ultimately

FEEDBACK

wants students to engage. Struggling learners must become comfortable with the *act* of reading in order to understand how to use reading for academic purposes. For students who do not view themselves as readers, this step is absolutely critical.

SCAFFOLDING

The National Assessment of Educational Progress (NAEP) reported that in 2011 most students in Grades 4, 8, and 12 had reading scores that showed no measurable difference from their scores in 2009, and only about a third of students were deemed "proficient." Where does that leave students such as those in Ms. Hernandez's reading class? Remember our research about struggling learners in Chapter 1? Given greater access to books, struggling readers will often read more (Krashen, 2009). And reading more is the first step toward helping students tackle challenging text because, as with every other activity, practice leads to proficiency.

CHALLENGE AND SUCCESS

For those who doubt that extensive reading supports other Common Core goals, let's take a look at research from a variety of sources.

Wide and frequent reading

- increases vocabulary (Graves, 2009; Nagy, 2003);

- develops fluency and knowledge of text structures as well as helping readers construct meaning with more challenging text (Ivey & Fisher, 2006);

- increases students' scores on standardized tests (R. Anderson, Wilson, & Fielding (1998);

- builds academic background knowledge (Marzano, 2004); and

- improves writing, spelling, and grammar (Krashen, 2004).

While we are not proponents of programs that promise to deliver "Common Core results," we were happy to see that the *Revised Publishers' Criteria for the Common Core State Standards* is encouraging teachers to provide students with opportunities for regular, independent reading of texts based on their interest:

Students need access to a wide range of materials on a variety of topics and genres both in their classrooms and in their school libraries to ensure that they have opportunities to independently

HOW TO Incorporate
Independent Reading Into Your Curriculum

Independent reading can be incorporated into any discipline without taking time away from the topic of study. Following are tips to help you get started.

1. Begin collecting books for your classroom library in your content area. Many grants are available for just this purpose, and often principals will find money for books if you ask. Look in used-book stores for good titles to add to your permanent collection, and ask your librarian to put together a box of books on your current topic of study.

2. Allow students to choose their own texts. If you find that students are not reading or that they are consistently choosing books that are below their reading levels, have a conference with them and suggest other titles or try to determine why they are not reading.

3. While students are reading, walk around the room and quietly ask questions of individual students, such as "What's going on now in your book?" or even "Are you getting into this book?" If you prefer, you may call students up to your desk and discuss their reading with them.

4. Give participation grades only. You may want to have students write in their learning logs after reading or have them briefly discuss what they are reading with a partner or the entire class, but avoid placing grades on their efforts.

5. Read aloud each day to students (even for five minutes) using books from your discipline, especially those that may be above most students' silent reading level. Research indicates that reading aloud not only encourages students to read more but also increases their vocabulary (Padak, Newton, Padak, & Rasinski, 2008).

6. Have each student keep a reading log with the books he or she has read over the course of the year and, if you wish, the time it took to read each book. As students see the titles pile up and reading times shift, their feelings of self-efficacy as readers will increase.

7. Read books along with your students or read in advance books that match their interests so that you can make strong recommendations and give effective booktalks. Cheryl L. Wozniak (2011) describes students who listen to booktalks as "engaged and want[ing] to know more about the books" (p. 18).

How I Get Kids Reading

"Inevitably, when I meet my students for the first time each year during Open House, they tell me how much they dislike reading. If their mom or dad is with them, they usually follow their child's statement with 'He liked reading as a child, but he doesn't read anymore.' My unspoken response is 'No one has put the right book in your hands; no one has shared good literature with you,' and I think sadly to myself that no one has helped this child stay connected to the printed word. This lack of enthusiasm hinders the potential of a young adult's path to lifelong learning.

"I get my students reading by doing booktalks, giving time for independent silent reading (usually the same time and duration each day), reading novels as a whole class, modeling my habits as a reader, and having a well-stocked, current classroom library. I also have a secret weapon. Behind my desk sits a small, white bookshelf that houses books that are on my to-read list. Right now it includes Cheryl Rainfeld's Scars and Living Dead Girl by Elizabeth Scott. It also includes books that disappear and I have to replace often—anything by Ellen Hopkins, Todd Strasser, or Paul Volponi. It also contains books that I have used for read-alouds like Susan Kuklin's No Choirboy or Greg Neri's graphic novel Yummy: The Last Days of a Southside Shorty and banned books like The Earth, My Butt, and Other Big Round Things by Carolyn Mackler. There are books I want to keep an eye on, like Sapphire's Push, a graphic, raw, somewhat controversial read about a young girl who suffered abuse as a young child. This book and many others like it need the proper audience and monitoring. Kids know they are welcome to read anything in my room, and they also know the white bookshelf behind my desk holds the 'really good ones.'"

—Pam Ayers, high school
English/reading teacher, Port Charlotte, Florida

read broadly and widely to build their knowledge, experience, and joy in reading. (Coleman & Pimentel, 2012, p. 4)

Solid research and statements regarding the importance of reading from the authors of the CCSS provide strong support for teachers such as Ms. Hernandez who know that getting their students to read is crucial for their long-term success.

The Workshop Approach: Does It Meet the Standards?

Troubled by her principal's comment that "reading was not enough," Ms. Hernandez went back through the CCSS and analyzed each standard in light of her curriculum. She was encouraged to find that her students were, indeed, meeting almost all of the standards, and she had evidence through their writers' notebooks, portfolios, presentations, and other assessments. In addition, she felt that her student-centered approach was creating independent, self-regulated learners far more quickly than in classes where students were spending the period taking notes from lectures. Just because her teaching wasn't unit-based or textbook-driven did not mean that she wasn't challenging her students or meeting the standards.

Ms. Hernandez took a copy of her daily schedule to Ms. Flowers and invited her to drop in and see for herself how a workshop-based classroom could be just as rigorous as a more traditional approach.

Ms. Flowers did visit Ms. Hernandez's classroom the following week and spent time talking to students during independent reading.

"What are you reading?" she asked Maria, a pretty, shy girl with long dark hair and wide brown eyes.

"*Hate List,*" Maria responded.

"You like it?"

"Yeah."

> Just because Ms. Hernandez's teaching wasn't unit-based or textbook-driven did not mean that she wasn't challenging her students or meeting the standards.

Ms. Hernandez came up behind Maria and asked her to tell Ms. Flowers what she had said earlier in class about politicians needing to read the book. Maria looked doubtful, as if the principal might somehow betray her to authorities. She finally said, "Well, if politicians would read this book instead of just talking about why kids are shooting other kids in schools, maybe they would have a clue and could really do something to stop it. I said I thought we should send this book to Congress."

"What does the author suggest as the reason kids do such horrible things?" Ms. Flowers asked, clearly trying to see if Maria would give a text-based answer. Ms. Hernandez held her breath.

"It's all about bullying. I mean, the author doesn't just come out and say that. You can figure that out, though, because she talks about how all the kids hated Nick. But just because he did something horrible doesn't mean *he* was all bad. Maybe all that hate made him go off because he couldn't take it anymore—or maybe hate can make someone crazy. It's not easy to understand; even his girlfriend didn't know what he was thinking, and she really loved him."

Ms. Flowers nodded, but she appeared less than impressed with Maria's interpretation of the novel. "Well, it's a very complicated issue with no simple solutions, and I admire the author for taking it on. Maybe you can read some news articles about recent shootings and see if you can find some more clues as to why this type of horrible thing happens—especially in schools."

"Yeah," Maria replied.

Ms. Hernandez knew that the visit had affirmed to her principal that she was an engaged, caring teacher, but she wasn't sure Ms. Flowers was convinced that she had made "the shift" to the more rigorous tasks demanded by the CCSS, a faculty-wide goal. She thought about Maria's response to Ms. Flowers and felt certain that Maria had, indeed, exhibited the "capacities of the literate individual," as outlined in the CCSS introduction, especially because she was beginning to "evaluate other points of view critically and constructively."

The following day Ms. Hernandez went into Ms. Flowers's office and pointed out the seven components of a literate individual from the CCSS introduction. "Maybe this last one, 'Students come to understand other perspectives and culture,' is one of the most important. I was thinking about Maria's answer yesterday. She is giving the issue of school shootings serious thought, as are others in her group. They have been evaluating the author's message and thinking through it, trying to understand the characters' perspectives. That may seem like a low-level achievement, but for students who haven't read much of anything before this year, it is really amazing.

> Ms. Hernandez knew that the visit had affirmed to her principal that she was an engaged, caring teacher, but she wasn't sure Ms. Flowers was convinced that she had made "the shift" to the more rigorous tasks demanded by the CCSS.

Reading/Writing Workshop: Typical Schedules for 90- and 50-Minute Blocks

Reading/Writing Workshop: Typical Schedule for 90-Minute Block	

Readers' reports and booktalks
 	
• Examples of activities
  o Booktalks by teacher or student
  o Passages from books shared by students
	5 minutes

Independent reading and individual student conference
 	
• Examples of teacher instruction during conferences
  o Checking on students' reading choices and encouraging them to move into more challenging texts
  o Reviewing or teaching reading strategies appropriate to text
  o Helping students monitor comprehension or self-reflect
	20 minutes

Whole-class lesson
 	
• Examples of instruction
  o Use of mentor texts for writing instruction
  o Analysis of short, complex text
  o Review of reading strategies
  o Grammar/usage lessons
  o Discussion of whole-class novel, poetry, nonfiction, or short story
	15 minutes

Individual/partner/group work or whole-class presentations
 	
• Examples of activities
  o Writing
  o Research for essay or project
  o Reading related to essay or project
  o Presentation of project
  o Small-group work in literature circle or inquiry group
  o Reading of whole-class novel
	45 minutes

End of class
 	
• Examples of activities
  o Short, wrap-up discussion
  o Exit slips
  o Student questions
  o Sharing of notebook entries
	5 minutes

Reading/Writing Workshop: Typical Schedule for 50-Minute Block	
Readers' reports and booktalks	5 minutes
• Examples of activities	
o Booktalks by teacher or student	
o Passages from books shared by students	
Independent reading and individual student conference	12 minutes
• Examples of teacher instruction during conferences	
o Checking on students' reading choices and encouraging them to move into more challenging texts	
o Reviewing or teaching reading strategies appropriate to text	
o Helping students monitor comprehension or self-reflect	
Whole-class lesson	10 minutes
• Examples of instruction	
o Use of mentor texts for writing instruction	
o Analysis of short, complex text	
o Review of reading strategies	
o Grammar/usage lessons	
o Discussion of whole-class novel, poetry, nonfiction, or short story	
Individual/partner/group work or whole-class presentations	20 minutes
• Examples of activities	
o Writing	
o Research for essay or project	
o Reading related to essay or project	
o Presentation of project	
o Small-group work in literature circle or inquiry group	
o Reading of whole-class novel	
End of class	3 minutes
• Examples of activities	
o Short, wrap-up discussion	
o Exit slips	
o Student questions	
o Sharing of notebook entries	

"So, I was thinking that I could work on 'making the shift' by concentrating on this aspect of the Common Core. I promise that with this one component, I will be meeting almost all of the other standards." She sat back in her chair, as if taking a break before embarking on the next round of persuasion.

"OK," Ms. Flowers said. "Keep the workshop approach; I don't doubt your abilities or the power of reading. The assessment will tell the story—as always."

Understanding Perspectives: A Piece of the Portrait

We like to think that the authors of the CCSS painted the last brushstrokes of the portrait of a literate student (see the description of college- and career-ready students at the beginning of this chapter) because they knew that, without it, the picture would never be complete. Students who *only* learn to analyze informational text, conduct research, or evaluate arguments will be denied an important aspect of their education.

As you know, the standards call for students to read increasingly more informational text in secondary grades, and we appreciate this focus on reading in all disciplines. When the standards first appeared, there was some confusion because many of us thought this emphasis on nonfiction meant that nonfiction was replacing literature in English classes. Thankfully, this misconception has been addressed by the authors of the standards, and we now understand that literature is still a mainstay in all language arts classes. This is an important distinction because literature is one of the few ways that students are able to understand other perspectives or cultures and, as the authors state in the introduction, "vicariously inhabit worlds and have experiences much different than their own."

In the multicultural world that our students inhabit, there is little place for a single perspective or them-versus-us approach. While values such as tolerance and respect for those who are different are essential for the future well-being of our world, such attributes are difficult to teach. We know one of the best ways for students to develop accurate

> Students who *only* learn to analyze informational text, conduct research, or evaluate arguments will be denied an important aspect of their education.

Common Core and Common Sense: Does Independent Reading Support Close Reading of Challenging Text?

It seems that common sense has taken a back seat for many years regarding reading instruction. First, there were those who criticized independent reading because the National Reading Panel did not explicitly endorse it; then, there were those who insisted that independent reading took time away from "real" reading instruction (the most nonsensical idea we've ever heard); and now there are those who say that inherent in the CCSS are statements that discourage independent reading of personal-choice books in favor of reading only those texts that are challenging and complex. If ever there was a case of the emperor having no clothes, these arguments exemplify it.

There *is* research that shows the value of independent reading, of course, as we have presented in this chapter, but any measure of common sense (or simple observation) reveals that kids who read more become better readers. It doesn't take a research panel to tell us that the more you do something, the better you become at it, and becoming a better reader means that your comprehension skills increase—which supports your ability to read more challenging text.

Every English teacher has a story of a student who was a poor reader until he found the right book. ReLeah likes to tell the story of a student she once had with a major attitude who often (and loudly) announced that no one could make her read. During independent reading time, she had to read or sit quietly and do nothing, so one day she picked up Sharon Draper's *Tears of a Tiger* and became a convert. Years later, she told ReLeah that she never would have gone to college, and might not have even graduated from high school, had she not found that one book that transformed her from an aliterate student into, in her words, a book freak. "I can read anything," she boasted in the same loud voice she had once used to proclaim herself a nonreader.

We are so certain of the power of independent reading that we would go as far as to say that, without it, close reading of challenging text is virtually impossible.

and compassionate worldviews is by entering other worlds through literature that grips their hearts as well as their intellect.

For the remainder of this chapter we will zoom in on Ms. Hernandez's high school reading class and also visit a middle school language arts teacher. Both teachers utilize the workshop approach as a way of helping students appreciate varied perspectives while they come to love reading.

Literature Circles: Sharing Perspectives

MULTIPLE LEARNING METHODS

Ms. Hernandez decided to come up with an explicit plan for helping her students understand other cultures by placing students in literature circles with novels and nonfiction set in different countries or at critical time periods in history. Each group's final project would show the extent to which students had been successful in appreciating "widely divergent cultures" and their accompanying perspectives.

DIFFERENTIATION

Ms. Hernandez felt strongly that choice and ownership were key, especially for her reluctant learners. With the help of the media specialist, she chose several books at various interest and ability levels that would meet the goal of having students read "great classic and contemporary works of literature representative of a variety of periods, cultures, and worldviews."

Ms. Hernandez first booktalked each of the novels and asked if any student who had read one of the books would like to join her.

AUTONOMY

DIFFERENTIATION

Students then wrote their top three book choices on a card, and Ms. Hernandez organized groups based on students' choices, their reading ability, and the possible dynamics of the group.

Prereading: Setting the Stage

INQUIRY

Before the groups began reading, Ms. Hernandez wanted to make sure her students had a common understanding of vocabulary that would be used in the assignment. She gave each group three questions to discuss in their small groups:

- What is perspective?
- What is a worldview?
- What is culture?

After the groups shared their thoughts on perspective, Ms. Hernandez wanted to make their thinking concrete by referring to a novel they had read earlier in the year. "Think about when we read *To Kill a Mockingbird*. We read the story through Scout's eyes or her perspective, sometimes called a lens. How would it have been a different story if it had been written through Boo's lens?" Ms. Hernandez then gave each group a different character from the novel and asked the students to talk about how the story might have changed if it had been told from his or her perspective instead of Scout's. This was an easy task for the groups since they had discussed the novel a few months earlier and had talked about perspectives at that time.

SCAFFOLDING

COLLABORATION

"When you begin reading your book in your group, I want you to think about the perspective of the characters; that's one of our main goals with this activity. It doesn't mean that a certain perspective is right or that other perspectives aren't equally valid. It's just important to recognize point of view and know that it could change based on who is telling the story," Ms. Hernandez said.

Groups also shared their understanding of "worldview" and "culture." A couple of groups made the point that it was easier now to have a broad worldview than it was during the time *To Kill a Mockingbird* had been written. "It's because of social media; anyone can be in touch with people from all over the world if you have a smartphone or computer," Sasha said.

RELEVANCE

"And sometimes, like on music videos, you don't even have to know the language to understand what they're saying," Alden said. "Also, I think young people are more ready to accept different cultures than our parents or grandparents."

"Are you stereotyping the older generations?" Ms. Hernandez laughed.

"It's true!" Alden said.

"Don't you think that it's easier to accept people who aren't like you when you really get to know them?" Ms. Hernandez asked.

"Sure. Look at how many different cultures we have in this school," Danielle said.

"But I've been discriminated against by people who know me pretty well," Sadie pointed out. The discussion moved into stereotyping and

RELEVANCE

BOOKS

Books Representative of Various Periods, Cultures, and Worldviews

The Absolutely True Diary of a Part-Time Indian by Sherman Alexie (set on a Spokane reservation and in Reardan, Washington)

Junior, a 14-year-old Spokane Indian, thought things were bad on the reservation, but when he transfers to the "rich, white school" in a city, he finds other challenges. In this novel, sometimes funny and often heartbreaking, readers will see an unvarnished view of life on a reservation and think about important issues such as racism, poverty, community, and, most of all, identity.

The Breadwinner by Deborah Ellis (set in Kabul, Afghanistan)

Parvana's father was arrested by the Taliban, and now she and the rest of her family live in a bombed-out apartment building with no resources and little hope—until Parvana decides to disguise herself as a boy to earn money. The author researched the topic before writing the book by talking with girls and women in Afghan refugee camps.

Crossing the Wire by Will Hobbs (set in Mexico)

Fifteen-year-old Victor Flores is the only person in his family who can save them from starvation, but in order to do so he must "cross the wire" and make an illegal passage into the United States from Mexico. His trip, one that millions have attempted, is an amazing story of fortitude, courage, and desperation.

Fallen Angels or ***Sunrise Over Fallujah*** by Walter Dean Myers (set in Vietnam and Iraq, respectively)

Fallen Angels takes place during the Vietnam War in the 1960s. Perry, a Harlem teenager, volunteers for the service and is sent to the front lines where he discovers the true horrors of a war that he begins to doubt. *Sunrise Over Fallujah* explores the same themes almost 40 years later as Robin joins the U.S. Army and is deployed to Iraq.

Fire From the Rock by Sharon Draper (set in Little Rock, Arkansas)

Sylvia Patterson is one of the first black students to integrate at Central High School in Little Rock, Arkansas, in 1957. Sylvia is terrified because the overt racism in her town is ever-present. The novel contains a great deal of historical background and realistic dialogue so readers can clearly imagine this era in history.

I Am Nujood, Age 10 and Divorced by Nujood Ali, Delphine Minoui, and Linda Coverdale (set in Yemen)

This true account of Nujood Ali's marriage at 10 years of age to a man she barely knows in an isolated village is shocking and painful to read, especially at the beginning. When Nujood finally flees her husband's home, the reader cheers her on and is relieved when a well-known lawyer takes her case. Nujood's stand against child marriage is now famous and has elicited positive changes for women in many Middle Eastern countries.

Inside Out and Back Again by Thanhha Lai (set in Vietnam and Alabama)

After Hà's father is missing in action during the Vietnam War, she and the rest of her family must escape to America. There, Hà finds out what it means to be a refugee and face the cruelty of those in her new land. While this novel may at first seem simple, the poetic lines and strong, evocative images will have readers going back to the first page and starting all over again.

The Kite Runner by Khaled Hosseini (set in Afghanistan)

This classic for mature readers, the story of the friendship between a wealthy boy and the son of his father's servant, is much different from the Afghanistan seen on news reports today. Through this gripping novel, readers will come to know the culture, the land, and the universality of friendship and family.

A Long Walk to Water: Based on a True Story by Linda Sue Park (set in Sudan, Ethiopia, and Rochester, New York)

Eleven-year-old Salva runs for his life when his small village in Sudan is attacked by rebel soldiers in 1985. Having no place to go, he begins walking and continues to walk until he is rescued and sent to live with a family in New York. In 2008, Nya, a young Sudanese girl, also walks—eight hours a day to find freshwater for her family. These stories connect in a triumphant ending that readers will remember forever.

Sold by Patricia McCormick (set in India)

Thirteen-year-old Lakshmi believes she is being sent away to work as a maid in the big city but, to her horror, discovers that she has been sold into prostitution. Written in beautiful poetic vignettes, every page is filled with Lakshmi's desperate desire to escape.

Teri Lesesne on Creating Effective Booktalks

"The point of the booktalk is to sell the book. You want to tell just enough about the book to whet the appetite of the reader. Tell too much and you have ruined the book. Tell too little and you won't generate enough excitement. Some people opt to become one of the characters from the novel and speak about the book as if it were her personal story. Reading aloud a short passage from early on in the story is another approach to beginning a booktalk. Follow up the read-aloud passage by talking about the conflict or some exciting incident or the setting."

—Teri Lesesne (2010, p. 43)

DIFFERENTIATION

racism; Ms. Hernandez let the dialogue continue for several more minutes. She then reviewed what the groups had said about each of the key terms, *perspective, worldview,* and *culture,* and asked each student to fill out what she called a prereading reflection form, emphasizing that there were no right or wrong answers to the questions. She planned to have students fill out a similar form after they finished their book so she could gauge how the reading had affected their perception of the cultures represented in their books.

During Reading: Discussion and Writing

COLLABORATION

CHALLENGE AND SUCCESS

AUTHENTIC ASSESSMENT

The assignment was the same for all groups. Students had seven days to read their book. Forty minutes of class time was set aside for reading, 10 minutes for writing in notebooks, and 15 minutes for discussion with other group members. Each group had to create a schedule of pages to be read each day, and all students signed a contract stating that they would read the required number of pages per day, either in class or at home, so they could be effective contributors in their group. Students were required to write responses to what they had read each day, using prompts such as the following to help them think through the text:

- Did anything that happened in your book today surprise you? Make you sad or frustrated? Please you?

Prereading Reflection Form

Title of Book: _____

Setting: _____

1. Why did you choose this book?

2. What facts do you think you already know about the setting, characters, or themes in the book?

3. What stereotypes do you think you may have, either positive or negative, about the country or people of this book?

4. Have you ever had a desire to visit any of the places referred to in your book? Why or why not?

5. How might your own worldview color your reading of this book?

This tool is available for download at **www.corwin.com/commoncorecpr**.

Postreading Reflection Form

Title of Book: _____

Setting: _____

1. To whom would you recommend this book? Why?

2. How has your own perception of the events or people in the book changed based on your reading?

3. What more do you want to know about this topic, culture, or period?

4. Will you read other books on this subject? Why or why not?

5. Think about this book from the perspective of a different person, either another character in the book or a real person. How might the story have been different told from that perspective?

- Write down and comment on a passage that you found to be well written, confusing, or interesting.

- How are the events in the book different because they happen in a country or time period other than the United States today?

- What would like you like to say to a character in the book? To the author?

- What do you predict will happen in your reading tomorrow?

Maria's group had chosen the book *Sold*. Ms. Hernandez spent extra time with this group since two of the students were English language learners and had difficulty with some of the poetic phrases. She asked the students to read the book twice since it was a relatively quick read. For the first reading, the purpose was to get a sense of the plot and become familiar with new vocabulary. The second time students read, they were asked to concentrate on the perspective of Lakshmi, the main character. Ms. Hernandez also encouraged the group to talk about areas of the novel they found confusing.

Ms. Hernandez had facilitated literature circles many times in the past, and she felt she had finally worked out the kinks, although she was wise enough to know that in group work anything was likely to happen. This time, however, all of the groups seemed to enjoy reading their books, and their discussions were, for the most part, insightful and focused.

Postreading: Performance Assessments Bring Books to Life

Each group had to decide on a project to present to the class. The groups had two days of class time to work on their projects, and presentations began the following week, which allowed students time over the weekend to finish their projects. Ms. Hernandez also told students that they would be responsible for answering questions from the class at the conclusion of their presentation.

The group of students who read *Fallen Angels* asked if they could interview a Vietnam vet and compare his perspective to the main character's. Ms. Hernandez was pleased that the boys had tapped into their own curiosity, and she readily agreed to the project. In the end, the group videoed the interview, edited it, and showed it to the class, stopping

DIFFERENTIATION AND SCAFFOLDING

COLLABORATION

AUTONOMY

ACTIVE LEARNING

RELEVANCE

TECHNOLOGY USE

What If Students in Literature Circles Don't Complete the Reading or Are Habitually Absent?

Group assignments only work if there are enough participants to make a group and if everyone in the group is prepared to engage in a discussion. Ensure participation and success in literature circles by trying the following:

AUTONOMY

- Give students choice over the text to gain buy-in from the very beginning.

DIFFERENTIATION

CHALLENGE AND SUCCESS

- Allow some flexibility. If students have a legitimate concern, for example the book being too difficult or the group dynamics not working, allow students to change groups (and thus books) one time.

- Encourage mastery goal-setting by having students sign a contract promising that they will read the required pages per day, contact the group facilitator if they know they are going to be absent, and make up the reading for days they are not present. There should also be a sentence in the contract that states the students will participate in discussions and contribute to the final project.

DIFFERENTIATION AND FEEDBACK

- Conduct individual conferences during reading time so that you can monitor progress, encourage participation, and build self-efficacy.

AUTHENTIC ASSESSMENT

- Remove students from a group if they violate the contract and give them individual assignments.

after each question to explain how the veteran's answer was similar to or differed from the main character's.

COLLABORATION

Maria's group decided to engage in a panel discussion. These students worked together on creating questions and decided on their roles. Caitlin, an extrovert who didn't mind taking charge, was the host. Maria would take the part of Lakshmi, the girl in the novel who had been sold into prostitution. Jade would be Anita, Lakshmi's friend, who was too scared to escape. For the panel discussion, the group decided that

Literature Circle Projects for Ms. Hernandez's Students

1. **Panel Discussion.** This project will look like a talk show on television. One person in the group is the "host," and other members of the group will discuss events in the book as if they had participated in those events. The entire group is responsible for helping the host come up with good questions, and each person is responsible for contributing to the discussion.

2. **Book Trailer.** A book trailer is much like a movie trailer advertising an upcoming movie. The trailer should contain music appropriate to the setting, pictures of characters, short videos, and any other "advertising" material you deem appropriate. Go to www.booktrailersforreaders.com for information about book trailers and student-created examples. This project may take considerably more time than other projects, so pace yourselves if you choose this option.

3. **Reader's Theater.** Choose one section of the book and create a Reader's Theater. This project usually requires some rewriting of the original text or interjections from a narrator. Every group member must have a role. Costumes are not necessary, but props may enhance the performance. Make sure there is enough information presented about the book before the "theater" begins for the audience to know what is going on.

4. **Research and Reveal.** How accurate is the author in portraying the setting, culture, and/or events in the novel? Research the major topic in this book to discover "the truth." Tell the class the basic plot of the book and then reveal what you discovered when you researched the topic. You may use a PowerPoint or Prezi if this helps in your presentation.

5. **Website.** Create a website or wiki on the topic of your book.

AUTHENTIC ASSESSMENT

COLLABORATION

TECHNOLOGY USE

ACTIVE LEARNING

MULTIPLE LEARNING METHODS

INQUIRY

TECHNOLOGY USE

Anita did end up leaving with Lakshmi, although that is not how the book actually ended. Alisa would be an American woman, Ms. Smith, who took the girls into her home when they arrived in America. This character was created by the girls since the book ends just as Lakshmi is escaping.

ACTIVE LEARNING

The girls arranged their chairs in a semicircle and announced that their show was called *Eye on the World.* Catlin, as host, introduced her guests and then began the discussion.

Caitlin: How did you feel when you found out that you had been tricked and sold into prostitution?

Lakshmi: I couldn't believe it. At first I was very confused. I never liked my stepfather, but I couldn't believe that he had done something so horrible to me.

Anita: I've never been so scared in my entire life. If I could have found a way to commit suicide, I would have done it. It seemed like there was nothing to live for.

Caitlin: What did you think of America at first?

Anita: Americans seemed like silly people. They watch shows on TV where everyone laughs and no one really cares about what is happening in the world.

Lakshmi: Most of the kids just play games—either video games or sports, like soccer. I couldn't imagine a life like that, and sometimes I hate American children because it seems like they have so much. They have nothing to worry about.

Anita: I couldn't believe kids in America could just go to school and not work all the time. It's like everyone in America lived like a king. What spoiled brats!

Caitlin: Ms. Smith, when you rescued the girls from the brothel, how long did it take for them to feel safe?

Ms. Smith: They were scared to death, poor things. They jumped at every little sound and were afraid to even go to sleep. It took a very long time for them to believe that they could trust me.

Caitlin: Girls, what do you miss most about your country?

Anita: The food. I'll never get used to the strange food in America.

Lakshmi: My mother.

The class was mesmerized by the discussion, which continued for almost 15 minutes since the girls' responses became longer as they began to feel more comfortable with their roles. In the end, their classmates asked questions about the age of girls sold into prostitution, how they were treated, and whether or not most of them died of AIDS. The girls answered the questions as well as they could. Virtually every student in class wanted to read the book once they saw the presentation.

INQUIRY

In two short weeks, students in Ms. Hernandez's class had a new perspective on life outside of the present-day United States in such places as the following:

RELEVANCE

- Afghanistan under the Taliban as well as in Afghanistan over 30 years ago

- India

- Yemen

- Vietnam during the war for both Vietnamese and American soldiers

- Alabama during 1960

- An Indian reservation in Washington

- Iraq during the war

- Mexico

- Little Rock, Arkansas, during integration in 1959

Do Literature Circles Meet the Standards?

Ms. Hernandez needed to verify that this project had addressed the standards, so she ran off copies of the standards and checked off the ones that were clearly covered. Not surprisingly, she found that most students

What About Students Who Struggle With Issues Beyond Our Control?

Many students who struggle in school have issues that go far beyond their academic abilities or attitudes. Bullying, abuse, hunger, or an unstable home life, for example, may play a significant role in a student's chance for success. While it is outside the parameters of this book to offer advice regarding these challenges, we do know that students often find solace or the courage to confront their problems by reading books that mirror their struggles. Counselors often refer to this practice as bibliotherapy. Go to http://bibliotherapy.ehs.cmich.edu/index.php to find out more about how teachers, librarians, and counselors can use books to help students who suffer from a range of out-of-school traumas.

Two books stand out among those we have recently read that deal directly with issues that may be more common that we would like to admit:

> *Panic*, by Sharon Draper, takes readers into the frightening underworld of pedophiles and, at the same time, illuminates the emotional abuse girls often suffer at the hands of their boyfriends.
>
> *Skinny*, by Donna Cooner, explores the bullying associated with obesity and the main character's decision to take the drastic step of weight-loss surgery in an effort to change her life.

had participated in virtually all of the reading standards and really honed in on Anchor Standard for Reading 6:

> Assess how point of view or purpose shapes the content and style of a text. (R.6)

More particularly, the students met the Grade 9–10 version of this standard:

> Analyze a particular point of view or cultural experience reflected in a work of literature from outside the United States, drawing on a wide reading of world literature. (RL.9–10.6)

Students who chose to do research for their final project covered more of the writing standards than other students, but all students:

> Wrote routinely over extended time frames (time for research, reflection, and revision) and shorter time frames (a single sitting or a day or two) for a range of tasks, purposes, and audiences. (W.10)

What's more, all students also participated in at least four of the speaking and listening standards, and some covered even more.

What Ms. Hernandez reported to her principal, and what we also have found to be true, is that good instruction, quality texts, peer interaction, and relevant, meaningful assessments create an environment that is conducive to deep and thoughtful learning. In contrast, following each standard in a rigid, linear fashion will constrict teaching and learning and, worse, defuse the intrinsic motivation that blossoms when students take ownership of the process.

Creating a Culture of Literacy in a Middle School

When Cynthia Sellinger transferred from her job as the elementary school principal to become principal of Asheville Middle School, she brought with her a firm conviction that literacy should be foundational in every subject area, and all her teachers understand just how strongly she holds this belief. In fact, she says that establishing a culture of literacy was one of her first goals as principal. "We're all about the Common Core, but students won't grapple with complex text unless they first become successful reading at their level." Her plan was straightforward:

1. Request additional funds from the central office for classroom libraries.

2. Allow teachers to choose books for their own classroom libraries and allow students to choose their own books for independent reading.

3. Require that *every* student complete at least 30 minutes of reading at home each night.

> Good instruction, quality texts, peer interaction, and relevant, meaningful assessments create an environment that is conducive to deep and thoughtful learning.

SCAFFOLDING

AUTONOMY

HOW TO Replicate Ms. Hernandez's Lesson

1. Choose approximately 10 books on various reading levels set in a variety of countries or books with perspectives that may challenge readers' assumptions.

2. Booktalk each of the titles. Allow students to contribute to a booktalk if they have read one of the books.

3. Have students write their top three choices on a card.

4. Create groups based on students' choices, reading ability, and group dynamics.

5. Have students discuss key terms in groups, such as *perspective*, *worldview*, *culture*, and *stereotype*.

6. Provide a prereading reflection form for each student to fill out individually prior to reading and a postreading reflection form for each student after groups complete the book.

7. Have each group choose a facilitator.

8. Meet with group facilitators separately and instruct them on how to moderate discussions (i.e., by having the group ask questions, point out interesting or confusing passages, or talk about a particular scene, character, or event that stands out). You may wish to provide written tips and/or prompts for facilitators.

9. Provide basic information, such as logistics, rules of conduct in groups, and an explanation of the purpose of the project to the whole class.

10. Allow groups autonomy in deciding how many pages to read each day and how they will conduct their meetings.

11. Avoid providing "role sheets" and encourage authentic discussion.

12. Move from group to group frequently, monitoring progress and helping the discussion stay on track.

13. Require that individual students write in their notebooks after reading each day.

14. Give students a choice of projects to complete.

15. Have groups share their presentations with the entire class.

HOW TO Use the Standards as Ms. Hernandez Did

Too often, the CCSS are viewed as a checklist; teachers are expected to isolate one standard and "teach" it. Notice the difference in Ms. Hernandez's approach. While she was teaching a lesson she knew would be engaging and motivating for students, she marked **all** of the standards she was covering. Many of your lessons will cover multiple standards. We suggest keeping copies of the standards handy (once you're familiar with the standards, you can use a shortened, one-page version such as the one that appears inside the back cover of this book) and simply mark off standards as lessons progress. Save these pages for future planning and for discussion with your PLC or administrator about the effectiveness of your lessons.

4   Provide students with reading logs, which are monitored by the English language arts teachers.

5. Have science, math, and social studies teachers assign content-area articles, as well as nonfiction books, for their students to read.

6. Ask English language arts teachers to take students to the library once a week to check out a book and require that the book stays with the student at all times.

7. Institute a school-wide policy that states, "When students finish their work in any class, they bring out their book and read."

8. Create professional development with a focus on reading. For example, teachers who attended literacy workshops over the summer will present strategies to the rest of the faculty once a month.

9. Work closely with the literacy coach and provide the support, resources, and time she needs to be successful in working with teachers.

10. Ask that all teachers talk about books with students and listen when students talk about books with them.

DIFFERENTIATION AND ACTIVE LEARNING

MULTIPLE LEARNING METHODS

FEEDBACK

COLLABORATION

On the sixth-grade hall we observed students working in groups in every classroom, reading, writing, and conferring with teachers or their learning partners. In Carrie Buchanan's room, for example, students were reading various historical fiction books they had chosen based on interest.

SCAFFOLDING

AUTONOMY

Ms. Buchanan had spent a lot of time talking with students about the characteristics of historical fiction before she took them to the library to choose their books. They also had to research the time period of their books to gain background knowledge prior to reading. Ms. Buchanan's focus this week was on "emotional atmosphere," a mood created by the author that is often as important as the physical setting in the novel. "Readers pay attention not just to the place and what it looks like, but also to what it feels like," she said. Understanding the emotional atmosphere, or mood, of a text helps students understand perspective, she pointed out.

ACTIVE LEARNING

In their notebooks, students were to make a note when the emotional atmosphere changed in the text and use quotations around passages from the novel that demonstrated this change, along with the page number where the passage was found.

Thinking Tracks: Pinpointing Evidence

Jessie was reading *The Red Badge of Courage* by Stephen Crane, seemingly riveted to the pages. In her notebook, she recorded her thinking about the novel each day. Ms. Buchanan called these entries "thinking tracks," and with each entry students included a reference to the text. Jessie had used her notebook to also record questions and responses.

INQUIRY

DIFFERENTIATION AND SCAFFOLDING

While students were reading independently, Ms. Buchanan held individual conferences where she reviewed notebooks with students and talked with them about their books. "Some of the students are voracious readers who are reading way above their grade level. It's sometimes hard to find books that are challenging to them and also appropriate for their age. Those are the easy ones, though," she said.

CHALLENGE AND SUCCESS

And what about the ones who are not voracious readers? We sat in on a conference with Ms. Buchanan and Sara, a girl who was having difficulty citing evidence for her thinking in *Out of the Dust*. She had written simple sentences such as "The atmosphere is stressful because there is dust everywhere" with a page number and very little documentation from the novel. Ms. Buchanan gently prodded her.

DIFFERENTIATION

Ms. Buchanan's Sixth Grade: Choices in Historical Fiction

The Boy in the Striped Pajamas by John Boyne

Bruno's father is a Nazi, but Bruno doesn't really understand what that means. One day his entire family must move to a new town where his father will preside over a concentration camp, and Bruno discovers secrets he was never supposed to learn.

Elijah of Buxton by Christopher Paul Curtis

The main character, Elijah, lives in the Buxton settlement in Ontario in 1849. His home is unusual in that it is a refuge for former slaves. There, Elijah hears stories from slaves that change everything he understands about life.

Fever 1793 by Laurie Halse Anderson

Set in Philadelphia, this story of a young girl with a good life takes a tragic turn when horrible illness breaks out and she must deal with death at every turn. This novel is based on actual events that occurred in Philadelphia during the yellow fever epidemic.

Goddess of Yesterday by Caroline Cooney

The main character, Anaxander, is the daughter of a king during the time of Homer's "Iliad." Her adventures lead to an exciting, up-close encounter with the major players in the Trojan War.

Iron Thunder by Avi

Iron-clad ships were built during the U.S. Civil War in huge ironworks. In this novel, Tom becomes an assistant to the *Monitor*'s inventor in Brooklyn, New York, and learns everything there is to know about a ship that no one believes will actually float.

Milkweed by Jerry Spinelli

A young, orphaned Jewish boy faces cruelty as he struggles to survive in Nazi-occupied Warsaw during World War II.

New Boy by Julian Houston

As the first African American to attend a prestigious boarding school in the 1950s, Rob discovers the reality of bigotry as he experiences the early days of the civil rights movement.

(Continued)

(Continued)

Out of the Dust by Karen Hesse

This classic novel written in free verse poems tells the story of a girl whose mother dies and whose father is cold and distant. As she struggles through the devastating dust storms, she learns how to find a measure of peace.

Soldier's Heart: Being the Story of the Enlistment and Due Service of the Boy Charley Goddard in the First Minnesota Volunteers by Gary Paulsen

Charley decides he will join the Union Army and fight in the Civil War even though he is only 15. His experiences on the battlefield leave him with a broken "soldier's heart."

Under a War-Torn Sky by L. M. Elliott

Hank is an American pilot during World War II. When his plane is shot down and he escapes to France, he learns the horrors that France has endured under Nazi rule.

"Who is stressed?"

"Everybody, but mostly Billie Jo."

"How do you know she's stressed and not angry or sad?"

"I guess she's sad too."

"How do you know? What does the author say to let you know that?"

Sara looks through the pages of her book and says, "Well, on page 77 it says she spends all of her time in pain. That would make me sad."

"It would make me sad, too. For the next several pages be on the lookout for any change in the emotional atmosphere. What changes do you think you might see?"

Sara sits quietly for a minute, flipping through the pages of the book as if she might find an answer highlighted in yellow. Finally, she looks up and says, "Umm . . . fear? pain?"

FEEDBACK

"Sure. And when you see that change, be sure and jot down the clues the author gave you to let you know about that change. And don't forget the page number."

Jessie's Notebook Entries for *The Red Badge of Courage*

> 1/7/13
>
> The Red badge of courage
>
> 1. the author isn't really making a big deal about somebody dying. p.35
> 2. how could this be? Isn't the youth going to flee too? p.39
>
> —46
>
> The Red Badge of Courage   1/8/13
>
> 1. Henry feels a bit Startled, because the narrator said, "after the battle, the youth glanced back behind his shoulder. It slightly frightened him that so many lay dead, in posistions that only pain and stress could have figured on the bodies." p.50
> 2. YES! THEY WON THE BATTLE! p.56
>
> ⁶ Readers pay attention not just 1/9/13 to the place and what it looks like, but also to what it feels like.
>
> The Red Badge of courage   1/9/13
>
> 1. The overall mood in the setting is scary. I know this because the narrator says "There was the ripping sound of Musketry and the breaking crash of the artillery" on p.62
> 2. wow! how did that happen? p.73

Such differentiated instruction is how Ms. Buchanan and other English teachers at the school make sure that each student "gets it." "It takes more work with some of the students, but it's important for each of them to be able to access the text and feel that they are successful. If the book is too hard, they just give up," Ms. Buchanan said.

None of her students looked like they were ready to give up; in fact, they seemed reluctant to stop reading when Ms. Buchanan told them it was time to change activities, but they put their books away anyway and, while talking a minute to wait for others in their group, got out their writing folders.

CHALLENGE AND SUCCESS

Final Thoughts

The two classrooms we highlighted in this chapter exemplify the kind of literacy-rich environments that must become the norm if we want to reach struggling learners such as Maria and Sara. What struck us in our work with these teachers and their students is that literacy in these classrooms is not an add-on, something that is done before or after the "real lesson." It is, instead, the bedrock of all instruction.

Yes, the CCSS do require a more rigorous approach than we have seen in the past, but the authors of the standards also note that students "must read widely and deeply from among a broad range of high-quality, *increasingly* challenging literary and informational texts." For our struggling students, the only way to lead them into increasingly challenging texts is to *immerse* them in literacy, so that reading, writing, speaking, and listening become a natural part of their daily experience. Such immersion does not mean allowing them to drown in waters that are too deep; it means, instead, supporting them as they gain the skills necessary to swim on their own.

8 What Do We Do About the Language Standards?

> *Without prompting, [students] demonstrate command of standard English and acquire and use a wide-ranging vocabulary.*
>
> *—Description of College and Career-Ready Students, CCSS Introduction*

Remember Daniel?

We introduced Daniel in Chapter 1; you'll recall that he was a struggling eighth grader whom Barry taught early in his career. We shared both the challenges and the successes Daniel faced during his eighth-grade year, ending with a Holocaust-related reading project in which he became more engaged and motivated than he seemed to have been previously. Daniel's story, as a model of increased desire to read and learn, was one of modest success.

But what about Daniel's writing? What about his command of language?

To begin thinking about the role of the language standards—those devoted to usage and vocabulary—let's revisit Daniel and his writing. Recall, for instance, the first piece of writing Daniel produced for Barry in eighth grade. It was not only riddled with errors, but it was underdeveloped, included only simple sentences, and showed no awareness of style:

> *Robert Frost poem talk about two roads that meet in a forest. The poem mostly says he is standing there thinking. He don't know which road to take. Frost poem at last makes a choice. He take the road less travelled. Then he is happy with his choice.*

As an early career teacher, Barry learned an important lesson from this assignment. As we mentioned in Chapter 1, Barry's first instinct was to reach for the red pen, to correct and suggest avenues for development purely related to writing. What he came to understand over the course of the year—and of his teaching career—was that until Daniel was motivated and interested in learning, no amount of correction or practice would produce long-term changes to Daniel's written expression. For that matter, until Daniel became motivated, not much would affect his learning at all.

But what about that second step? Daniel's interest increased by the end of eighth grade, but where was the place for increased attention to writing and the conventions of standard English? Where, in fact, did he become accountable not just for thinking deeply but for communicating clearly?

In this chapter, we'll explore how the six anchor standards related to language, along with the specific standards for each grade level, might be applied in classrooms that include reluctant and disengaged learners. We'll consider what the standards do and do not ask of our students and the specific skills related to grammar and word acquisition they outline. Besides revisiting Daniel's writing, we'll also take a look at another student, Melissa, and her struggles with vocabulary. And we'll consider, as we have throughout this book, the connections between the information students learn and the way they interact with that information as they learn it—the strategies and approaches that help students to learn by increasing engagement and intensifying motivation.

What Do We Do About Grammar?

We pick up Daniel's story at the end of eighth grade. This is an excerpt from the first draft of Daniel's final essay of the year, on Elie Wiesel's *Night*:

> *One situation Eliezer is in that is related to real life situation is when*
> *he loses his belief in god and gives up. People in the world today*
> *sometime question their religious belief or lose their belief in god.*
> *"Never shall I forget those flames which consumed my faith forever,"*
> *Eliezer says. "Never shall I forget that nocturnal silence which*
> *deprived me, for all eternity, of the desire to live. Never shall I forget*
> *those moments which murdered my God and my soul and turned my*
> *dreams to dust." This quote addressed by Elie is when he lost his faith*
> *in god and took matter into his own hands. Even though he lost his*
> *faith, he didn't give up and instead he took a stand and fought hard*
> *to survive.*

It's a messy paragraph grammatically, but this essay still illustrates Daniel's growth as a reader and critical thinker. Daniel had moved from turning in the shallowest possible response to producing work that showed his ability to, for instance:

> Cite the textual evidence that most strongly supports an analysis
> of what the text says explicitly as well as inferences drawn from
> the text. (RL.8.1)

And to

> Analyze how particular lines of dialogue or incidents in a story
> or drama propel the action, reveal aspects of a character, or
> provoke a decision. (RL.8.3)

Yet Daniel's paragraph demonstrates less growth when one looks at it through the lens of the language standards. Based on this writing sample, would any experienced teacher believe, for instance, that Daniel is a student who could, as the eighth-grade standards demand, "explain the function of verbals (gerunds, participles, infinitives) in general and their function in particular sentences"? Even more to the point, if Daniel learned to explain the function of a gerund, would he be more likely to use one correctly in his next piece of writing?

Yet here's Daniel's eventual final draft of this same essay. While it's not perfect, it's closer to the mark:

One situation Eliezer found himself in that relates to a real life situation was when he lost his belief in God and gave up. People in the world today sometimes question their religious beliefs or lose their belief in God. "Never shall I forget those flames which consumed my faith forever," Eliezer says (32). "Never shall I forget that nocturnal silence which deprived me, for all eternity, of the desire to live. Never shall I forget those moments which murdered my God and my soul and turned my dreams to dust." This quote, addressed by Elie, comes when he lost his faith in God and takes the matter into his own hands. However, even though he lost his faith, he didn't give up. Instead he took a stand and fought hard to survive. He may have stopped believing in God, but not in himself. Showing persistence is a major theme of the novel.

What changed?

FEEDBACK

After a session of peer review, a round of revision activities in class, and individual work with Barry, Daniel worked to clean up his writing because he cared enough about the material to do so. There are still errors, and this revision did not happen in one fell blow—it took guidance and practice in class. But remember: Daniel chose to write about *Night* after he chose to finish reading it, based on interest he'd shown in the subject matter (the Holocaust) and his pairing of the text with a reading selection of his own choosing (the graphic novel *Maus*). The assignment was relevant and personal. Even if he didn't like writing in general, Daniel liked thinking about these works in particular.

Daniel left Barry's class at the end of eighth grade a better reader but still lagging in his progress toward the language standards; he struggled with issues of agreement, verb tenses, and punctuation, just for starters. He also left at the end of eighth grade more willing and able to revise work he cared about and to seek out assistance in correcting his use of language.

Importantly, Daniel also offered evidence that he could springboard from his personal connection to a text to a level of academic insight in which readers:

> Determine a theme or central idea of a text and analyze its development over the course of the text, including its relationship to the characters, setting, and plot; provide an objective summary of the text. (RL.8.2)

Improvement in reading and writing was a natural outcome of greater interest in and concern over the texts Daniel encountered. For many students, however, that improvement in reading and writing, even imperfect improvement such as that Daniel exhibited, lies buried beneath a lack of ownership. The lesson is plain: Practice can lead to improvement, but practice combined with the *desire* to improve is invaluable.

RELEVANCE

That's a lesson that can help us greatly as we think about how we meet the language standards.

The First Three Standards:
Approaching Grammar Unconventionally

Some teachers and administrators unfortunately see grammar as an either-or proposition: Either you're teaching the formal rules through explicit, out-of-context exercises, or you're not really teaching grammar at all. That perception can be reinforced by the types of test questions students must answer on high-stakes tests, which can lead us to believe that students need to master technical labels and checklists of rules. Obviously, there are grammar rules we all need to internalize in order to communicate effectively, but rules alone don't prompt excellent communication, and studying rules alone certainly isn't likely to engage reluctant students.

Practice can lead to improvement, but practice combined with the desire to improve is invaluable.

The proposition that grammar needs to be taught in context to matter to students is further complicated by the fact that the first three language standards do, indeed, offer a checklist of rules and conventions students need to master. Unlike other areas of the CCSS, the language standards are highly specific about *what* students need to know, so much so that some observers of the Common Core get more hung up on what's on or off the list (should ellipses be mentioned more frequently?) than on the nature of the list itself.

Yet the list, by itself, wouldn't have helped Barry reach and engage Daniel, who was at least several grade levels behind the standards in his command of conventions. According to the standards, for instance, Daniel should have encountered and moved toward mastery of subject-verb agreement by the end of third grade, yet he struggled with this area of language five grades later. Presumably, he'd received instruction and feedback about subjects and verbs during each of those five years, yet the lesson hadn't stuck. Was another year of out-of-context exercises and worksheets likely to make a sudden difference?

The First Three Anchor Standards for Language

Demonstrate command of the conventions of standard English grammar and usage when writing or speaking. (L.1)

Demonstrate command of the conventions of standard English capitalization, punctuation, and spelling when writing. (L.2)

Apply knowledge of language to understand how language functions in different contexts, to make effective choices for meaning or style, and to comprehend more fully when reading or listening. (L.3)

Daniel and Mrs. Fromm

Barry only began an approach with Daniel that, fortunately, a very good ninth-grade teacher was able to continue the next year. Because Daniel stayed in touch, Barry was lucky to be able to track his progress further and to see the changes in his writing when he started high school and encountered Mrs. Fromm, his freshman English teacher.

Mrs. Fromm had taught at the same high school, in the same classroom, for more than two decades. Her classes did not include any of the most advanced students; year after year, she taught those whose grades placed them in the "lower half" of the ninth grade (Mrs. Fromm herself hated any designation of students as "lower"). Most of her students struggled with reading—indeed, Daniel moved, in ninth grade, from being one of Barry's most severe strugglers to being a top performer in Mrs. Fromm's class. After all, unlike his peers, he had read *Night* and *Maus*—two entire books—cover to cover.

Based on this composition of classes, Mrs. Fromm developed approaches to teaching grammar that she'd learned worked well for whole classes of struggling learners. In particular, she told us that she tried to do the following (the citations and quoted terminology are ours, not hers):

- Rely on explicit grammar instruction only to introduce or reinforce concepts, but never exclusively or in isolation.

- Structure lessons that "zoom in" and "zoom out" (Anderson, 2006) by starting with the smallest units of meaning, then building context and writing assignments around those units.

  SCAFFOLDING

- Use strategies such as sentence combining and imitation of sentences in order to provoke student thinking about language, not just rote memorization of rules (Strong, 1994).

  ACTIVE LEARNING

- Reinforce grammar in the context of writing and reading as often as possible.

  RELEVANCE

- Focus on talk about language rather than terminology, and introduce terms as needed rather than in checklist form (Dean, 2011).

  SCAFFOLDING

- Vary her approach to grammar instruction by using multiple methods of instruction for every lesson (Langer, Close, Angelis, & Preller, 2000).

  MULTIPLE LEARNING METHODS

- Use collaborative exercises to help students learn together and from one another—and to increase interest (Langer et al., 2000).

  COLLABORATION

- Differentiate learning by using group work, writing assignments, and other homework to focus on rules each student needed to know rather than only those on a list.

  DIFFERENTIATION

"Now, this all sounds well and good on a list," Mrs. Fromm warned us. "But I've had principals who still demand test prep and out-of-context instruction, I've had days where I have to can the lesson because the boys in a group start a fight, and I've had times where students couldn't read well enough to understand the simplest mentor text. It would be so easy to revert to the old approach I used as a first-year teacher and just

HOW TO Teach an Implicit Grammar Lesson on Gerunds

In this chapter, we mention that few teachers would believe, based on Daniel's writing samples, that he could "explain the function of verbals" as the first eighth-grade language standard suggests. What if, in fact, we wanted to be sure Daniel understood gerunds, one form of verbals? Here are some steps we might use to guide Daniel in this understanding; note the gradual shift from explicit to implicit instruction.

- Be clear about the lesson's purpose. We'd suggest that if a student can *implement* a rule correctly, terms and definitions (such as the ability to define the word *gerund*) are less relevant. There may be times, however, when terminology is important to later understanding, and thus it is part of the goal.

- Begin with a short, explicit definition and review of rules. Have students work in pairs to sketch their own anchor charts and then make one as a class and display it prominently. This should take no more than a few minutes.

- Ask students to take out their personal-choice reading books. Have them go through the books and find two or three examples of words ending in *-ing*.

- Call on a few students to write their examples on the board. Make sure you have examples of gerunds being used as subjects, objects, direct objects, and, if possible, appositives or objects of prepositions (you do not need to use these terms with students; just ask them to read their sample sentences aloud and choose the most appropriate to write on the board). Also make sure a few examples of participles (*-ing* words used as adjectives, not nouns) and progressive verbs (e.g., "I am walking") are included.

- Have a few of your own examples from mentor texts in your classroom library ready to add if you wish.

- Once the examples are on the board, have one student circle all of the *-ing* words. Ask pairs of students to conference and eliminate examples that are not used as nouns. Return to the anchor chart as needed.

- Have student pairs or small groups discuss each of the other examples. What is different about where the gerund appears in the sentence? What common mistakes might writers make in using—or not using—gerunds? How can gerunds add to sentence variety, voice, tone, or meaning? Why do we need to understand gerunds at all? Share as a class and, if necessary, add these bigger ideas to your anchor chart.

- If you wish, use a sentence-combining exercise with a sentence from a mentor text to reinforce the contribution gerunds make to sentence variety and voice. Consider, for instance, a sentence such as this one from *Harry Potter and the Sorcerer's Stone*: "And then they heard it—a low grunting, and the shuffling footfalls of gigantic feet" (Rowling, p. 174).

- Individually or in pairs, have students write a short paragraph about a common topic (playing a sport, giving a performance, or getting to school in the morning, for instance) in which they use at least three or four *-ing* words, each placed in a sentence differently. Share and discuss the results.

- Have students look through their own longer writing pieces in their writing journals, narrative pieces, or essay drafts. Identify any *-ing* words already in place. (Note: If students use typed work on a computer, they can perform a search for these words.) Ask the students to review these words and find gerunds. How do these gerunds contribute to the style and voice of the writing? If there are none, have students choose three sentences from the piece in which they *might* add gerunds. Share and discuss possible revisions using gerunds with an emphasis on style, voice, and meaning.

- Reinforce this lesson by returning to it and using it as a focus for comments, feedback, and student self-reflection as your class writes throughout the year.

teach test items day after day. Instead, I do something else for a day, do what I can to please the bad principals (and thank the heavens for the supportive ones), and try a different approach—another from my list of what works—the next day."

RELEVANCE

It's important to note that Mrs. Fromm echoes here what we've known from research and expert writing for more than half a century: Grammar taught out of context just doesn't stick. It may even inhibit improvements in student writing. There's so much research to back this notion up that, in recent decades, researchers have just about stopped studying the teaching of grammar in and out of context only. We *know* what doesn't work. What's harder to determine is what *does*.

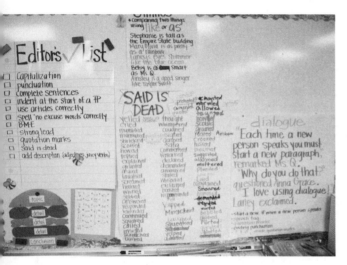

Anchor Charts to Support Editing

In that sense, calling Mrs. Fromm's approaches unconventional is misleading: Many teachers understand that we've got to balance some explanation of rules with lots of practice. In the research report *Guidelines for Teaching Middle and High School Students to Read and Write Well: Six Features of Effective Instruction* (2000), Judith Langer and her colleagues describe this approach as offering both "separated" and "simulated" instruction. They note that higher-performing schools include teachers (like Mrs. Fromm) who rely not just on *separated* instruction—the explicit teaching of a rule—and *simulated* activities—applying the concept in a limited manner such as writing a short passage or reading a short text—but also on *integrated* learning—applying the rules in an ongoing manner using students' more substantial reading and writing assignments.

MULTIPLE LEARNING METHODS

A Point of Origin: Daniel's Writing

Early in the year, Mrs. Fromm assigned Daniel to read the novel *The No. 1 Ladies' Detective Agency,* which includes a series of linked detective stories set in Botswana. Daniel completed this reading assignment in a group with three other students while others in the class read a variety of other texts.

DIFFERENTIATION

What Does the Third Language Standard Ask?

While the first two anchor standards for language clearly require students to demonstrate mastery of rules and conventions, the third standard lends itself to less precise evaluation:

> Apply knowledge of language to understand how language functions in different contexts, to make effective choices for meaning or style, and to comprehend more fully when reading or listening. (L.3)

Notice the key words—*apply, contexts, choices, comprehend.* This standard acknowledges that language is more than a set of prescriptive statutes—that it involves choice and creativity. When we look deeper, at the specific versions of this standard for each grade level, we see that students are expected to move from varying sentences *with their readers or listeners in mind* at sixth grade to write and edit work *for the discipline in which they're working* at ninth and tenth grade. On the one hand, the shift from simple audience awareness to discipline awareness makes sense; on the other, that shift unfortunately orients the standard toward academic writing more than narrative or personal writing.

Yet the fundamental purpose of this standard is important: Grammar exists not for its own sake, but for the sake of real communication with real audiences.

Rather than requiring a formal essay on the reading, Mrs. Fromm had each student write a letter to the author of the work he or she read that addressed a question about one of several thematic areas chosen by the group. Daniel chose to write about truth and lying in the story:

RELEVANCE

> *Dear Alexander McCall Smith,*
>
> *I enjoyed your book* No. 1 Ladies' Detective Agency. *I like how the detective character, Mma Ramotswe, lies when it is necessary throughout this book. For instance, when she was telling her friend Mr. J. L. B. what the plan was to get the truth out of Mr. Gotso, there*

where no if, ands, or buts about it , he is going to do it. The idea of
lying come up again throughout the novel and each time, she believes
her conscience is clear again and its okay to lie if its for a good cause.
I think this was a strong lesson for readers to learn because we always
hear about lying is wrong but its not really as easy as all that.

Your friend,
Daniel

Think back to Daniel's reluctance to engage with literature one year earlier, and this excerpt from Daniel's letter may seem like a success. Apply the language standards to it, and we might view it as presenting an immense challenge. Either way, we *should* view the paragraph as an opportunity. Daniel was interested in communicating about the book; he just needed help on the format of the communication itself.

Here's how Mrs. Fromm handled this area of instruction:

DIFFERENTIATION

- **Mrs. Fromm aimed her instruction at Daniel's specific needs.**

"I used to mark all over my students' papers and then hand them back to the entire class with some general instructions about revision," Mrs. Fromm told us. "The papers would rarely come back seriously revised—the students would make the easiest, most obvious changes and ignore the rest."

Later, Mrs. Fromm initiated a different approach. She'd choose three—and only three—elements of any piece of writing that she wanted that individual student to focus on. She'd list these three items at the top of the paper, then mark *only* those areas on the paper.

FEEDBACK

DIFFERENTIATION
AND SCAFFOLDING

"It's tough, really tough, to keep myself from marking every grammar error. Eventually, I hope to get to them all. But this way, we build gradually. More to the point, each student gets what he or she needs the most. Sometimes that's attention to the thesis statement, or the evidence, or spelling, or a specific convention. It's different for every child and every paper."

Mrs. Fromm noticed, for instance, that Daniel tended to refer to scenes from a novel or story without quoting or specifically identifying the relevance of the moment. While this offered a stark contrast to the majority of her students who tended to summarize plot too much, she felt that Daniel needed to work on clearly and concisely relating the key point of his evidence back to his main point or thesis. This was his first instruction for revision, and his alone.

- **Mrs. Fromm chose to limit the areas of focus.**

Of the three areas of revision Mrs. Fromm identified for each draft, she tried to make no more than one of them focused purely on conventions. The other two, generally, she used to aim students toward improving style, argumentation, organization, and content.

"For one thing," she said, "the other areas are ultimately more important. Grammar and usage can overwhelm students and send the wrong message—that revision is about changing mistakes, not improving communication. And I always include a peer revision session that catches some of those errors, though not as many as I'd like."

On Daniel's first draft, Mrs. Fromm instructed him to focus on what she saw as the most pressing issue—verb tense. His only job in revision, as far as grammar was concerned, was to check every verb against its subject and make sure they agreed in tense and form. Mrs. Fromm ultimately conferenced with Daniel to help him in this area.

> FEEDBACK

However, Mrs. Fromm slyly slipped in another lesson, as you'll see in Daniel's revision below. "I sort of broke my own rule," she admitted. "I didn't force him to learn the rule for the use of an apostrophe with the pronoun 'it,' but in our conference I suggested he change the word to an actual noun every time he could. When he did that, he started to see how the two uses might differ. Then I followed up later that year with apostrophe use as one of his three revision points on a different assignment. This way, he didn't have to learn this rule right away, but he did improve the immediate piece of writing."

> ACTIVE LEARNING

- **Daniel's support included a classroom rich with guidance and examples.**

At no time did Mrs. Fromm expect Daniel to learn to revise only from her notes on his paper. "Thinking students will learn only from written comments is sort of like having someone watch a video of himself trying

SCAFFOLDING

to hit a baseball and then expecting him to improve the very next time at bat," Mrs. Fromm said. "It takes more than that—it takes practice and guidance."

COLLABORATION

There were times in Mrs. Fromm's class when she paired more interested or able students with less engaged students; in this case, she grouped more advanced readers and less advanced readers. While Daniel's group read Smith's novel, for instance, another group worked on Sandra Cisneros's *House on Mango Street,* a substantially shorter and, probably, more accessible novel with some similar characteristics. That also allowed her to differentiate her approach to grammar.

DIFFERENTIATION

COLLABORATION

Mrs. Fromm could rely on Daniel's group of four students at least to attempt peer revision and editing in a serious manner. "I tried to get them to look at sentences, not rules," she told us. "I wanted them to focus on units of meaning, not constructions. But, in the meantime, I had to work with other groups on other issues, such as simply including a subject and predicate in every sentence or actually using periods."

DIFFERENTIATION AND SCAFFOLDING

At the same time, Mrs. Fromm created anchor charts, chose mentor texts, and discussed some rules with the class that included constructions with which everyone struggled. Appropriate comma use, for example, cropped up as a difficult obstacle for every learner in the class. In such cases, Mrs. Fromm posted rules for student reference and used anonymous writing by students from previous years to spark class discussion on what worked and what didn't. She always, however, focused on the meaning of writing, not just the conventions.

- **Daniel acquired a real audience for his writing.**

RELEVANCE

Since she was teaching a book by a living author, Mrs. Fromm *could* have had her students send their letters to the author of *The No. 1 Ladies' Detective Agency,* had she wished. But she had a different idea: Her class of mostly disengaged learners would probably work harder, she decided, if their letters went to someone who would be likely to respond. With that in mind, she had each student rewrite the letter for a parent, a grandparent, or another adult (for those who expressed reluctance about writing to adults in their lives, Mrs. Fromm allowed letters to other teachers in the school or, in a pinch, to her).

In Chapter 1, we discussed Daniel's mother's involvement in his education. Though she herself was not a strong reader or writer, Daniel's mother was invested in his success and thus made an excellent audience for his work. Mrs. Fromm sent a short letter home with the finished assignment asking each reader to at least sign the paper and, preferably, to compose a short response to the student.

Here is the same excerpt of Daniel's final draft, rewritten for his new audience:

> *Dear Mom,*
>
> *I recently enjoyed reading the book* No. 1 Ladies Detective Agency. *One thing I like about this book is how the detective character, Mma Ramotswe, lies when it is necessary throughout the story. For instance, when she tells her friend Mr. J.L.B. what the plan is to get the truth out of a character named Mr. Gotso, there are no if, ands, or buts about it, he is going to do what she says, even though it involves a lie. The idea of lying comes up again throughout the novel and each time, Mma Ramotswe believes her conscience is clear again and that it is okay to lie if lying is for a good cause. I think this is a strong lesson for readers to learn because we always hear about how lying is wrong but telling the truth is not really as easy as we might think.*
>
> *Your son,*
> *Daniel*

And here is Daniel's mother's response, in part:

> *Daniel,*
>
> *Thank you for sharing your ideas about this book with me. It sounds very interesting and I will try to read it as well. I look forward to discussing the truth and lies in the book with you to see whether or not I agree with you. You are a wonderful thinker and you make me proud.*
>
> *Your mother*

AUTHENTIC ASSESSMENT

VOICES FROM THE
FIELD

Thoughts About Teaching Grammar Implicitly

You don't have to take our word for it—below are the words of experts on grammar instruction as they reflect on what has changed in the teaching of language and what's important for us to remember as we engage students.

- "Traditional grammar instruction—that which isolates the teaching of grammar from language usage—is, at best, simply ineffective in changing students' language use . . . If grammar instruction doesn't work as widely practiced, why is it such a staple of the English curriculum?" (Peter Smagorinsky, Laura Wright, Sharon Murphy Augustine, Cindy O'Donnell-Allen, & Bonnie Konopak, 2007, p. 7)

- "We are learning that what we mean by grammar is bigger than identifying parts of speech or even using standard usage expectations. It's not about grammar so much as language." (Deborah Dean, 2011, p. 22)

- "Most packaged editing programs only tell part of the story: Grammar is about fixing, not creating. Grammar is lifeless sentences riddled with multitudes of mistakes that would take hours to meaningfully process." (Jeff Anderson, 2006, p. 28)

- "Students are seduced into trying writing techniques they find in the work of professionals. When the teaching of grammar is used as a way to *enable* students to use their voices more effectively, to deliver their ideas and passions with greater impact, we can reinstate it as an important means to an end." (Joan Berger, 2006, pp. 58–59)

- "Years of research have made it clear that grammar taught in isolation does not contribute to the writing skills of students. Yet, it is also clear from the various articles and books recently published that thoughtful grammar instruction can lead to better, more effective writing if it is done in the context of reading and writing, with an eye toward connecting grammar to rhetorical and stylistic effects." (Cornelia Paraskevas, 2006, p. 65)

The Importance of Engagement

Daniel's letter to his mother shows a limited but significant renewal of attention to mechanics, but only because of his interest in expression and meaning. The relevance of the assignment or guidance of a good teacher propelled his attempts at editing, but his own investment in communication fundamentally altered Daniel's relationship with language in a way no stand-alone exercise ever could.

RELEVANCE

What we learn from Daniel's example, besides specific strategies for attacking the language standards, is what we've learned from examples throughout this book: First comes the desire to learn, then engagement in class, and then specific learning through solid strategies. Other models may work for students who see the extrinsic rewards of scoring well or accomplishing a task, but are likely to fail for those who just don't care. The teacher's role, then, even in what can seem like prosaic areas such as grammar or vocabulary instruction, is first to understand students' needs, then to engage students in learning, and then to impart specific lessons through strategies that capitalize on that engagement rather than squelching it.

With that role in mind, let's turn to the second set of three standards that make up the language standards—those focused on vocabulary—and a final story of a teacher and student learning not just about words, but also about how learning itself works.

What Do We Do About Vocabulary?

Second-year teacher Mr. Noel Crawford stood in front of his class, ready to hand out the 10th vocabulary quiz of the year. Looking out at the faces of his 10th-grade students, he could almost predict how each one would do on the quiz. A few students looked over their flashcards nervously. Others were eager to get the quiz in their hands before the hasty memorization work they'd done seeped out of their brains. Still others looked completely resigned, accepting that they'd score yet another low grade on this quiz.

Among the latter group was a girl named Melissa. Melissa did well in some aspects of the class, but she had great difficulty mastering new words. They just wouldn't stick in her mind, no matter how she studied.

HOW TO Replicate Mrs. Fromm's Lessons

- Have students compose a letter to an author about a particular theme or idea in a book or reading selection.

- Choose three elements of the letter and respond to students only about those three elements. Two should be about meaning and one about grammar or usage.

- Make sure all students understand the grammar or usage rules through referring them to anchor charts, conferencing, introducing mini-lessons, or giving them time in class to make their own charts for the rule.

- Have students rewrite the letters for a new, personally accessible audience, addressing the three points from your comments as they do so.

- If the recipients of letters respond, share those responses in class and discuss the results.

Melissa and Mr. Crawford had discussed the problem, and she'd tried every trick they'd discussed: flashcards, Quizlet.com, writing her own sentences with the words. No matter what, she just couldn't apply the words correctly on Mr. Crawford's quizzes, even with a word bank. She did fairly well at matching words and definitions, but Mr. Crawford wanted his students to do more than know meanings; he wanted to see application. Therefore, he always included a series of what he considered transparent but somewhat humorous sentences that required students to fill in blanks with the various words. He remembered his own favorite high school teacher giving similar quizzes; Mr. Crawford had been the sort of student who did well on them without having to study too hard, and he always enjoyed the sentences. Yet it was here that Melissa failed to do well week after week, and Mr. Crawford was running out of suggestions for ways she could study differently.

He could tell she was giving up. This week, she'd admitted bluntly, she hadn't bothered studying much at all. Melissa's engagement in the vocabulary lessons was slipping. Worse still, the low vocabulary scores meant that she probably wouldn't make above a C for the grading period, and that was lowering her engagement in other parts of the class.

Mr. Crawford looked down at the first 10 words on his word bank with a sigh, then handed out the quiz.

Out of Context, Out of Mind

Here's the actual list of 10 words that began Mr. Crawford's quiz:

1. tranquilly
2. hove
3. presently
4. gait
5. melodious
6. personating
7. slackened
8. starboard
9. ponderously
10. pomp

Now ask yourself: How would you teach Melissa these words?

Or, to phrase the question more accurately, how would you help a student such as Melissa learn these words?

You might be thinking to yourself, "Why this list?" It's a reasonable question. Of course, students who encounter such prescribed word lists from vocabulary texts rarely encounter satisfying rationales for their existence or how they were grouped together. At best, there's sometimes the explanation that words may appear on standardized tests such as the SAT (the implication being that we learn words in order to prove, later on, that we've learned words). But simply memorizing lists of SAT words and their definitions is unlikely to help or appeal to most students, and especially disengaged, struggling 10th graders, if they don't understand how words work in the first place or feel a need to comprehend them.

Take the eighth word, for instance—*starboard*. Is this a valuable word for a 10th-grade student to learn? Perhaps. To us, it's a fascinating word, conjuring romantic images of navigation and the sea. We're interested in the fact that its etymology has nothing to do with stars; the first syllable derives from the Old English word *steor*, the name for a paddle or rudder, because early Germanic cultures placed the rudder on the right side of a ship. And if Melissa were to uncover that information because she was interested in the term itself, it's true that she might latch onto and remember it.

But a student who sees the word on a class list, who has no interest in boats, and who is just forced to memorize the term and its definition could probably care less whether she memorizes *starboard* or *stepladder.*

So how would you get reluctant students to learn this list? Flashcards? A quiz? Playing bingo with the definitions as clues and the words on a card?

Any of these strategies might help some students memorize the list for a quiz (if they cared about making a good grade in the first place), but are they likely to help students really learn to apply and use the words later on? Such strategies had failed Melissa again and again. More importantly, are these techniques likely to instill in 10th-grade students (much less already reluctant students) the ability to acquire and use, as the introduction to the standards suggests, a wide-ranging vocabulary *without prompting?*

"I just didn't know how to help Melissa, or other students in her scenario," Mr. Crawford later admitted. "It actually took me a long time to consider that maybe the problem wasn't with the students, but was with my expectations and the way I was approaching vocabulary in the first place."

Creating the Word-Rich Classroom

Fully one half of the language anchor standards—three out of six—fall under the umbrella of vocabulary acquisition and use. Vocabulary is, in fact, not only a constant concern for any language arts teacher; it's a vital area of focus for any teacher striving to embrace the core standards. But vocabulary also presents a particularly tricky area of instruction, especially in preparing struggling learners or, for instance, for English language learners. After all, students learn far more words from reading and casual encounters than they ever learn from explicit instruction, and those words form the foundation for learning more words, so students who don't read or who fall behind in school have even more trouble catching up later on.

> The standards suggest that true learning about language involves not just acquiring a memorized list of terms and meanings but instilling in students the skills to learn and apply new word meanings on their own.

The Second Three Language Standards

Determine or clarify the meaning of unknown and multiple-meaning words and phrases by using context clues, analyzing meaningful word parts, and consulting general and specialized reference materials, as appropriate. (L.4)

Demonstrate understanding of figurative language, word relationships, and nuances in word meanings. (L.5)

Acquire and use accurately a range of general academic and domain-specific words and phrases sufficient for reading, writing, speaking, and listening at the college and career readiness level; demonstrate independence in gathering vocabulary knowledge when considering a word or phrase important to comprehension or expression. (L.6)

Note that the standards for language call for students to do more than remember words. They suggest that students be able to determine word meanings, to understand the nuance of meanings, and to apply vocabulary in reading and writing. And here, again, in Anchor Standard for Language 6, we encounter an emphasis on the idea that students should demonstrate *independence* as they gather knowledge of words. Clearly, the standards suggest that true learning about language involves not just acquiring a memorized list of terms and meanings but instilling in students the skills to learn and apply new word meanings on their own.

But consider some of the factors we know from research about how struggling learners, especially poor readers, learn (and don't learn) vocabulary:

- There are strong links between vocabulary knowledge, reading comprehension, and academic success (Baumann, Edwards, Boland, Olejnik, & Kame'enui, 2003).

- Most vocabulary development occurs indirectly through exposure to language rather than through direct classroom instruction; students need to encounter words in the real world and in context in order to learn them (Miller & Gildea, 1987; Nagy & Anderson, 1984; Sternberg, 1985, 1987).

- Struggling readers require more exposures to learn a word than proficient readers—sometimes many more (Beck, McKeown, & Kucan, 2002).

- Children in poverty hear far fewer words over time than do those in higher economic categories—the differences are significant and hard to erase over time (Hart & Risley, 2003).

- If the goal is deep understanding and ability to use words, the use of the words in context, combined with some degree of explicit instruction, is probably the best method of instruction (Baumann et al., 2003; McKeown, Beck, Omanson, & Pople, 1985; Stahl & Fairbanks, 1986).

- Despite all we know about how students learn words, there has been very little change over the years in the way teachers actually approach vocabulary instruction (Blachowicz, Fisher, Ogle, & Watts-Taffe, 2006).

We know that students, especially struggling students, have difficulty learning new words from rote exercises such as weekly word lists and quizzes, yet most teachers continue to teach vocabulary in precisely this rote fashion.

To sum up, the lesson is similar to those we've learned about grammar: We know that students, especially struggling students, have difficulty learning new words from rote exercises such as weekly word lists and quizzes, *yet most teachers, just like Mr. Crawford, continue to teach vocabulary in precisely this rote fashion.*

Changing the Game: Rethinking How We Help Students Learn Words

Depending on how you look at it, the news is both good and bad: As with the first three language standards, Anchor Standards for Language 4–6 don't tell you precisely *how* to help students learn vocabulary in a rich and meaningful way, but they do provide a fairly useful road map for the skills students need to acquire in order to be word-wise. Here is the first anchor standard focusing on vocabulary for 10th grade, for instance:

Determine or clarify the meaning of unknown and multiple-meaning words and phrases based on *grades 9–10 reading and content*, choosing flexibly from a range of strategies (L.9–10.4).

Active Study

VOICES FROM THE
CLASSROOM

"In our eighth-grade class, we have two word walls. The first is for subject-specific words like simile *or* thesis. *In another part of the room, we have a word wall that's just for compound words with more than one Latin or Greek root. When students encounter a word like this—*neurology, *for instance—they write it on the wall themselves. Then every now and then in class we take all of the roots and write them on the board and try to make up our own words with three or four roots smashed together. What's a* neurophototopia? *Or an* antibibliophobe? *It's fun, but it also gets the students working with cognates and roots."*

—Beth Rice, middle school
teacher, Little Rock, Arkansas

Note what's really crucial here: The standards don't ask for students to memorize lists of words out of context, but ask them to acquire the skills necessary to determine meanings in context, while reading.

Mr. Crawford realized that he'd fallen into the habit of imitating his own high school learning, in which he (a word-smart student to begin with) was able to memorize new words because he had the background knowledge, interest, and working memory he needed to do so. Melissa did not. What's more, Mr. Crawford knew where his list of 10 words came from, because they'd been developed by his grade-level team to accompany a specific reading assignment. But because the students didn't know the origins of the words, the list still seemed random to them.

Take a look at Mr. Crawford's 10-word list in the context from which the words were actually drawn: a single paragraph in Chapter 2 of *The Adventures of Tom Sawyer. Tom Sawyer,* by the way, is a Common Core exemplar text for Grades 6–8, but remember the nature of the exemplar texts—they are *examples*. Mr. Crawford's team had decided the novel fit well with the American literature curriculum of 10th grade in his school, so that's where students encountered the book. Here is the paragraph with the 10 words in bold:

*He took up his brush and went **tranquilly** to work. Ben Rogers **hove** in sight **presently**—the very boy, of all boys, whose ridicule he had been dreading. Ben's **gait** was the hop-skip-and-jump—proof enough that his heart was light and his anticipations high. He was eating an apple, and giving a long, **melodious** whoop, at intervals, followed by a deeptoned ding-dong-dong, ding-dong-dong, for he was **personating** a steamboat. As he drew near, he **slackened** speed, took the middle of the street, leaned far over to **starboard** and rounded to **ponderously** and with laborious **pomp** and circumstance—for he was personating the Big Missouri, and considered himself to be drawing nine feet of water. He was boat and captain and engine-bells combined, so he had to imagine himself standing on his own hurricane-deck giving the orders and executing them.*

Mr. Crawford's team had come up with this list of words, and many other lists like them, before he even began teaching at the school, both as a way of frontloading the reading of the novel and as a means for helping students do a close read of the passage above. Yet, over time, the list had become just another list of words for them to teach.

Indeed, after encountering the 10 words here, we might feel differently about the original list. For one thing, we might consider that a student such as Melissa is likely to encounter this many unknown words in *every paragraph* of the novel, making the task of learning every unfamiliar term in advance positively Herculean.

What's more, we might question whether these are the most appropriate 10 words to remove from context and ask students to learn. The word *personate,* for instance, is far more understandable within Twain's sentences than taken on its own, but it's also an uncommon word that students are unlikely to encounter again. In fact, most students are more likely to have trouble with seemingly simple words such as *drawing* or *rounding to* in Twain's description. Having just such a discussion with students—about which words matter, and why—provokes just the sort of critical thinking about language that the standards aim to foster.

"I realized I was approaching the whole thing backwards," Mr. Crawford said. "It was the same way my own high school teacher approached

Mr. Crawford said, "I was approaching vocabulary study the same way my own high school teacher approached it— learn the words first, apply them in context later. But that wasn't working for my kids, who needed context first."

it—learn the words first, apply them in context later. But that wasn't working for my kids, who needed context first. And then I saw Melissa's math assignment, and I decided to change my whole approach."

From the Word-Rich Classroom to the Word-Rich School

Following is the simple word web created by Melissa in her 10th-grade math class. The math teacher gave each student a term and then posted these student products on a bulletin board near her classroom. Mr. Crawford happened to notice Melissa's web, which used as a root the word *perimeter*.

In this case, Melissa delved into many aspects of a single word, learning the term inside and out. One might charge that this approach steals valuable coverage time for a single word, and if the point were only to learn that one word, this might be true. But in fact this is more than an arts-and-crafts activity; in this case, Melissa learned important ways of both

Melissa's Word Web Based on the Term *Perimeter*

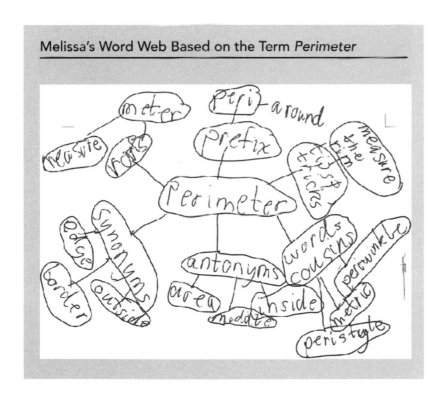

ACTIVE LEARNING

AUTONOMY

looking at and *thinking about* words—through antonyms and synonyms, prefixes and suffixes, roots, and parts of speech—but also a range of other vocabulary words that might be useful to know. *And* she took ownership of her learning by bringing words of her own—those relevant to her work—to the assignment. Melissa, Mr. Crawford realized, was not just learning about the word *perimeter*—she was learning how to learn words in general.

An important point here is that vocabulary study, in particular, cannot reside only in the hands of English teachers. We know that students benefit when all teachers reinforce writing, reading, and usage concepts, but in the area of word study, teachers in most content areas already require students to learn domain-specific words or, sometimes, more general terms. Enlisting *all* teachers in the sort of rich word study Melissa's math teacher introduced can create a wide environment in which students explore and come to understand language. In such a school, we might see:

- A science teacher breaking down the terms *renewable* and *nonrenewable* when teaching about resource use to focus on the prefixes *re-* and *non-* and the adjectival suffix *-able*

RELEVANCE

- A social studies teacher discussing using content clues to help understand words when students read from her text

- An art teacher preloading a lesson by discussing both the denotation and the connotation—and inviting input from students—of domain-specific words such as *perspective* or *saturation*

SCAFFOLDING

- Teachers keeping a shared file such as a Google Document to catalog the words and important roots covered in each discipline so that they can reinforce one another's instruction and the students' learning

In Melissa's case, the visual map reflects her exploration of word mechanics through the exploration of a single word specifically. The detailed description of Standard L.9–10.4 adds that seventh graders should also be prepared to use context clues, Greek and Latin roots, and dictionaries to determine the meaning of new words. The standards, in other words, already steer students and teachers toward the sort of activity Melissa engaged in (including using a dictionary and considering the roots of words) and away from simple memorization.

What About Challenging and Academic Vocabulary?

We're proponents of having students choose words to learn, encounter word study organically and naturally, and operate in a classroom rich with casual encounters with words. But that doesn't mean teachers should never offer explicit instruction or challenge students with advanced words. More to the point, it doesn't mean that teachers should rely only on haphazard and random vocabulary instruction. Just the opposite: Students need to encounter words at all levels, and they need to learn both domain-specific words (e.g., *metaphor* or *photosynthesis*) and generally useful words (e.g., *metamorphosis* or *synthetic*) that are appropriately challenging.

Such learning is particularly important for students who enter school with a smaller bank of words at their disposal than other children, a group that often includes students in poverty. According to one research study (Neuman & Wright, 2013), students in poverty were those least likely to receive instruction in academically challenging words, particularly when teachers relied *only* on casual encounters with words. This discrepancy compounds the gap between students when they enter schools; other research has found that children in welfare families, by age 3, have mastered less than half the number of words children from high-income families accumulate (Hart & Risley, 2003).

Explicit and deliberate instruction can help. But we maintain that it won't work if explicit instruction is delivered through worksheets and quizzes. Explicit instruction includes word study, discussion, and activity. It augments, but does not replace, a word-rich environment that excites students and encourages them to learn.

Imagine if, instead of simply handing students a list of words, Mr. Crawford always approached vocabulary with the end goals of engagement and learning in mind. Thinking along these lines, Mr. Crawford realized he could change his entire approach. He could:

- Sometimes have students help list the words they wished to study, rather than only providing such a list in advance (and out of context)

MULTIPLE LEARNING METHODS

ACTIVE LEARNING

AUTONOMY

RELEVANCE

DIFFERENTIATION

TECHNOLOGY USE

MULTIPLE
LEARNING
METHODS

AUTHENTIC
ASSESSMENT

CHALLENGE AND
SUCCESS

DIFFERENTIATION
AND SCAFFOLDING

- Regularly involve students in choosing words for study, study methods, or assessment methods

- Create a word-rich classroom that featured read-alouds, word walls, and wordplay

- Study words drawn from the texts students are reading or the material they study in all classes, not just his own

- Encourage students to keep personal individual word logs, dictionaries, or word journals

- Use online resources to explore word roots and links and to create and sort personal word lists

- Be certain students heard words as well as saw them on paper

- Assess in a variety of ways that included asking students to apply word meanings in context and to show their understanding of word rules and strategies for understanding meanings

- Seek appropriate instructional texts in which students recognized around 90%–95% of words to model word study

- Scaffold and discuss strategies for reading more challenging texts, including older works, in which students may not recognize at least 90% of the words

ACTIVE LEARNING

"I had to realize that these goals didn't mean giving up more class time, but meant giving up less," Mr. Crawford said. "I no longer had to spend all of Monday introducing the words and all of Friday assessing them. Instead, we embedded vocabulary study—*word* learning—into everything we were already doing. A student would hop up and add a word to our word wall, and then we'd go on with class. Later that day I'd stop and do a quick breakdown of the roots of a new word, then continue with a lesson. It changed everything to build a culture of words this way."

Did this mean that every struggling student was suddenly learning dozens of new words and applying them consistently? Of course not. But Mr. Crawford's word-rich classroom offered so many possibilities for encountering words and how we use them that it not only engaged students in new ways; it almost dared them *not* to participate.

Word Wall

Active Learning and Word Learning

Back to Melissa's learning:

For now, let's assume that Melissa herself noted these 10 unfamiliar terms in the text as she read. That's simple enough—even during a class read-aloud of the passage, Melissa could easily have made a list or marked unfamiliar words. With this scenario in mind and with what we now know about the context of the words, let's revisit some of our "Standards for Motivation and Engagement" and how the Common Core State Standards themselves might affect our thinking about instruction. What has changed about 10 words?

- The words are more *relevant* because Melissa discovered them in actual text—in fact, we're now not just working on vocabulary; we're also working on reading comprehension (and meeting several of the reading standards in the process).

  RELEVANCE

- Melissa has been actively involved and has had some *choice* in the words she studies.

  AUTONOMY

- There was an excellent opportunity here for Mr. Crawford to *scaffold* student learning by connecting word study to reading comprehension.

  SCAFFOLDING

- The words represent a chance to *differentiate* student learning—other students in the class might have come up with different lists of unfamiliar words based on their own needs.

  DIFFERENTIATION

Thus, we cover the *why*—and, in doing so, we increase motivation and ownership of learning. But what about the *how*? What might Melissa's active learning of these 10 words look like?

Our original question at the start of this discussion was this: How would you teach these 10 words to a class of seventh-grade students? Here's where the standards can help. For ninth and tenth graders, for instance, the standards suggest that students:

VOICES FROM THE FIELD

Thoughts About Teaching Vocabulary

"The single most important thing a teacher can do to promote vocabulary growth is to increase students' volume of reading. Any activity which increases reading comprehension, if coupled with the opportunity to read, will result in vocabulary growth."

—William Nagy (1998, p. 19)

"One way to build students' vocabularies is to immerse them in a rich array of language experiences so that they learn words through listening, speaking, reading, and writing."

—Michael Graves (2006)

"To understand a word, it is necessary to see it in as many contexts as possible. To define a word in isolation generally means a futile trip down a blind alley. Examples, by repeated exposure, make for the best vocabulary lessons. Reading is the key."

—Jerry Heverly (2011, p. 100)

"Students learn new words by encountering them in text, either through their own reading or by being read to. Increasing the opportunities for such encounters improves students' vocabulary knowledge, which in turn improves their ability to read more complex text."

—Joan Sedita (2005, p. 35)

"If the goal is an initial familiarity with the meanings of new words, several encounters of a traditional type of instruction may be sufficient. If the goal is higher order processing that involves integrating words and context, then a richer instruction is called for. If the goal is for word meanings to be readily accessible, providing greater influence on comprehension of connected text, then learning activities that extend beyond the classroom are suggested."

—Margaret McKeown, Isabel Beck,
Richard Omanson, and M. T. Pople (1985, p. 534)

> Consult general and specialized reference materials (e.g., dictionaries, glossaries, thesauruses), both print and digital, to find the pronunciation of a word or determine or clarify its precise meaning, its part of speech, or its etymology. (L.9–10.4c)

The standards for students in *seventh* grade—and above—require students to:

> Use the relationship between particular words (e.g., synonym/antonym, analogy) to better understand each of the words. (L.7.5b)

Based on these standards, and keeping in mind our "Standards for Motivation and Engagement," we can start to envision active learning focused on the words from *Tom Sawyer*. Melissa's class could:

- Record unfamiliar words from reading and then work with individual or combined lists of words AUTONOMY

- Attempt, in pairs or groups, to determine word meanings from context by revisiting the text (simultaneously increasing work with the text itself) COLLABORATION

- Use digital or print sources to check their contextual understanding of the words and to find synonyms and antonyms (increasing their exposure to other words in the process) INQUIRY

- Refer to a variety of technological sources to expand their exploration of words, from apps that sound out words to sites such as www.visuwords.com, which creates word webs for users instantly TECHNOLOGY USE

- Construct their own analogies using the words on the list and challenge one another or the class with them ACTIVE LEARNING

- Try to find connections between the words using roots, prefixes, or suffixes INQUIRY

- Change the form of words (for example, converting the word *melodious* to *melody* or *tranquilly* to *tranquil* or *tranquility*) in order to discuss word patterns of parts of speech ACTIVE LEARNING

- Be assessed on any of these tasks rather than a quiz reflecting memorization of words and definitions alone AUTHENTIC ASSESSMENT

BOOKS

Books to Enhance Vocabulary Study

Baseball Haiku: The Best Haiku Ever Written About the Game edited by Cor Van Den Heuvel and Nanae Tamura

With over 200 haikus, this book shows baseball enthusiasts just how important each word can be in describing one of America's enduring sports. What's more, the editors have included a brief description of each poet— and the Japanese haikus are written both in Japanese and in English.

Code Name Verity by Elizabeth Wein

The main character, "Verity," is arrested by the Gestapo when her spy plane crashes in Nazi-occupied France. As Verity cleverly writes her confession, readers must stay alert as they make decisions about which of the many words specific to British wartime activities they need to know and which ones they can skim over and still comprehend the story.

Feed by M. T. Anderson

Imagine a future where a transmitter implanted directly into human brains supplants the need to read, write, or even think. Welcome to Titus's dystopian world where language isn't what it used to be. This novel for mature readers will stretch their concept of communication through mere words alone.

The Lover's Dictionary by David Levithan

Levithan, a popular young adult novelist, has written his first book for adults—or mature high schoolers. The alphabetical entries (in perfect dictionary style) create a moving love story. Teachers who feel the novel is

> Engagement and motivation aren't likely to thrive when memorization alone is the goal.

Memorization, of course, is sometimes necessary, and we don't aim to make it the scapegoat of all troubles with student learning. The point is to claim not that students like Melissa can't or should never memorize, but that engagement and motivation aren't likely to thrive when memorization alone is the goal. Hand a list of words to students on Monday and quiz them on Friday, and you're likely to find that excellent students do well on the quiz but still forget the words later on. Try the same Monday–Friday plan with struggling students, on the other hand, and you're unlikely to see no progress or interest at all.

too mature for their students may want to read certain passages aloud as a way of illustrating ingenious wordplay.

A Northern Light by Jennifer Donnelly

Sixteen-year-old Mattie, the main character in this novel set in 1906, has been accepted to college, but it is not so easy for women to earn a degree in the early 1900s. An aspiring writer, Mattie is in love with words, and, at the beginning of every chapter, the author highlights a word that comes to life later in the text. This riveting murder mystery will keep readers engaged as they add many new words to their vocabulary banks.

Out of My Mind by Sharon Draper

Chapter 1 of this novel for younger readers begins with "Words" written in bold. The 10-year-old narrator, Melody, has words swirling around her "like snowflakes," but she lives a silent life, unable to utter even a single word. As readers come to understand Melody's brilliance, they also begin to appreciate the importance of language in making a person whole.

Why You Say It: The Fascinating Stories Behind Over 600 Everyday Words and Phrases by Webb Garrison

This encyclopedia of words and phrases, along with an engaging explanation about how each came into our language, will cause students to think twice about ordinary words. Use this book as a source of quick read-alouds that will add immensely to students' vocabulary background knowledge.

Final Thoughts

Ultimately, Mr. Crawford began to alter his practice so that he focused, as much as possible, on the engagement of his students. "I'll run short of time," he told us, "and it gets tough. Sometimes I'll have great intentions when I introduce new words, then a week later I'll discover we didn't get the depth I'd hoped for. But in general, I try to approach each class now as a chance to explore words together and to amass vocabulary constantly rather than in once-a-week prescriptions. I'm always on the lookout for engaging activities, but not the silly ones that are just memorization in disguise."

Melissa herself, Mr. Crawford told us, benefitted from such activities. By the end of the year, as he'd begun the transformation of his classroom, Melissa's vocabulary grades, and her learning, showed improvement. She still struggled on assessments and sometimes had trouble recalling words they'd studied in later contexts, but she approached vocabulary learning with a better attitude and, as a result, struggled less in such situations than she had in the first semester of her sophomore year.

And what of Daniel? Daniel graduated from high school and did, in fact, go on to play basketball at a local college. He struggled with language throughout his schooling—in particular, he found the difficult and sometimes centuries-old material he encountered in his senior year especially challenging. He wasn't exempt from senioritis in the last semester of high school, nor did he always complete every assignment. He acted, in fact, like a fairly typical high school student.

But if we think back to Daniel's eighth-grade year and his reluctance and disengagement, we can imagine another direction his life might have taken. He might have dropped out. He might have failed a year of English and had to repeat, or been unable to participate in basketball. He might just have checked out. Credit for his success goes primarily to Daniel himself and to his strong-willed mother; remember, we said that there are no magic bullets in this sort of learning, and we don't want to claim that a particular teacher or activity made all of the difference in Daniel's life. Rather, we see Daniel's learning journey as a process of gradual engagement, one in which he was slowly drawn far enough in by motivating experiences and assignments that appealed to his interests to start learning on his own, for the sake of learning as well as extrinsic rewards.

The Common Core State Standards aren't a magic bullet, either. But they can serve as a guide for what we'd like students such as Daniel, Melissa, and the others we've introduced throughout this book to accomplish by the time they leave high school. They're signposts along the journey reminding us of how far we have to go and where we might need to stop along the way. They remind us that students need to study words, need to understand conventions, need to present and to discuss, to read and to write. Yet although they remind us of the destination, the CCSS don't tell us how to travel there—that part is up to teachers who care about individual students and who are the experts on the learning, motivation, and engagement in the classes they actually encounter each fall, not the classes we wish they had.

Afterword

"Common Core! Oh, no! We can't possibly handle the responsibility, the requirements, or the rigors of those standards! Help!"

Relax. We can do this. With some careful research, some realistic reading, and some thoughtful preparation, implementing a new system of teaching and learning is as obtainable as it is necessary. Major changes are never welcomed because sometimes our comfort zones are shifted, and our standard methods of operation must be modified. As the panic that accompanies a major change touches thousands of teachers and school systems across the country, let's take a few minutes to reflect and regroup. Let's consider where we are, where we need to be, and how we're going to get there. More importantly, let's talk about how we can improve the educational lives of our students.

Our existence is defined through a series of patterns. Winter's anger is softened by spring, which blooms into the fire of summer. Autumn's glory and despair is forgotten with the wrath of winter once again. Historically and traditionally, the end of the bright freedom of summer marks the beginning of a new school year. Freshly waxed hallways, gleaming with expectation and promise, and smelling of chalk dust and challenges, fade into classroom routines and repetitious rhythms. Young minds, like the buds of spring, sprout and bloom with the acquired knowledge of another year, only to return with the fading of the leaves to repeat the cycle once again.

The problem is, however, that some of those buds never sprout, and many of the fallen leaves from the year before lie dusty and trampled on the ground. Those are the adolescents who did not reach minimal success in the past school year, the students who tried, failed, and finally gave up. And some of us as teachers have thrown our hands up in despair as well. How do we motivate these students to learn, to achieve, to master the complexities of the standards? As teachers, where do we start?

It is easy to teach the students who are highly motivated, the ones who walk across the stage proudly at end-of-the-year awards assemblies. But what about the large percentage of students who slouch in their seats during those recognition assemblies? What about the students who have never been recognized for academic excellence, and probably never will be? Traditionally, these kids stumble through school. Teachers make valiant efforts to reach them, but at the end of the school year, the students who survive are simply grateful to be passed along. They deserve better.

But there is hope in your hands. *Common Core CPR: What About the Adolescents Who Struggle . . . or Just Don't Care?* is a powerful text, written for educators by educators, that offers commonsense suggestions for successful work with the standards in all classrooms, especially with students who struggle. Using an interdisciplinary approach to literacy, the authors view the standards not as isolated skills to teach, but as natural outcomes as they scaffold learning.

Because the standards leave room for teachers, curriculum developers, and states to determine how the Common Core goals should be reached and what additional topics should be addressed, teachers are free to provide students with whatever tools their professional judgment and experience identify as most helpful for meeting these goals. So let's take advantage of that freedom and stride forward for our students by making the changes that they so desperately need. Our system of instruction and comprehension must be refined in order to maximize what is imparted to the next generation. Our definitions and interpretation of instruction and education will, of necessity, need to be adjusted, while some things will remain constant.

Magic ceases to exist in a world of reality. Metaphors are lovely, but fail to cover the harsh reality of overcrowded classrooms, bankrupted budgets, political apathy, and increased social responsibility. Teachers struggle to reach lofty goals, to meet the needs of students, to merely reach the end of the day. Very little recognition or reward is given for a job on which rests the knowledge of the past, the responsibility of the present, and the hope of the future. But sometimes assistance is right at our fingertips. *Common Core CPR* is here. Enjoy the journey!

—*Sharon M. Draper*

Appendix A

Standards for Motivation and Engagement With Teacher Tools

Learning Goal	Standard

Active learning

Students interact with material in ways that provoke critical thinking and questioning.

Options for Teachers

- Discussion
- Graphic organizers
- Summaries to reflect understanding
- Movement
- Meaningful projects
- Presentation

Autonomy

Students' encounters with choice and opportunities for input increase their interest and create a sense of control over their own learning.

Options for Teachers

- Individualized reading assignments (choice books)
- Literature circles
- Writing journals and personalized writing topics
- Student-led discussion

Learning Goal	Standard

Relevance

Students form bridges and connections to content even when it may seem, at first, distant from their own lives.

Options for Teachers

- Discussion to explore and connect themes and characters

- Writing prompts that connect material to real life

- Research of similar, connected events (e.g., modern slavery and pre–Civil War slavery)

Collaboration

Learning takes place in pairs and groups in which multiple participants and points of view are engaged.

Options for Teachers

- Discussions in pairs and small groups

- Structured whole-class discussion

- Online blogs, wikis, Google Documents, discussion forums, etc.

- Students' presentations with group feedback or discussion

Technology use

Students use technology not as a toy or distraction but as a tool to increase learning opportunities and to increase depth of study.

Options for Teachers

- The Internet (research and interaction)

- Audio and video files

- Presentation software (PowerPoint, Prezi, Glogster, etc.)

- Graphic design software

Learning Goal	**Standard**

Technology use (continued)

- Shared resource software (blogs, wikis, websites, etc.)
- Social discussion and networking sites
- Online quiz software
- Online citation and note-taking programs

Multiple learning methods

Students encounter material in a variety of ways that increase "stickiness," appeal to various learning preferences, and connect disciplines.

Options for Teachers

Use multiple approaches from the following list to teach one concept:

- Note-taking during a teacher or student presentation
- Researching and presenting
- Student teaching another student
- Creating a song, artwork, a skit, or movement
- Discussion and collaborative exploration
- Creating questions
- Constructing flowcharts, diagrams, or webs
- Concept mapping
- Interviewing
- Persuasive or analytical writing
- Narrative writing and journaling

Challenge and success

When learning, all students feel both challenged and successful in ways that increase self-efficacy.

Options for Teachers

- Frequent rewriting and revision
- Varied formats of assessment that cater to different strengths

Learning Goal	**Standard**
Challenge and success (continued)	• Assignments that allow students to explore their own interests
	• Setting small, achievable goals in the short run (and larger goals in the long run)
	• Positive feedback combined with meaningful and useful criticism
Differentiation and scaffolding	*Instruction is individualized, builds upon prior knowledge, and is carefully structured so that each student learns deeply and at an appropriate rate for the class and material.*
	Options for Teachers
	• Individualized writing prompts and problems
	• Metacognitive and reflective activities that help students learn from mistakes and successes
	• Individually assigned, developmentally appropriate reading selections
	• Writing assignments of various lengths
	• Projects with options and choice built in
	• Problem-based learning that allows for increasing depth of response
	• Conferencing that address a student's specific needs, including reteaching
Inquiry	*Assignments and topics promote a sense of curiosity and a love of learning through problem solving and open-ended questioning.*
	Options for Teachers
	• Open-ended questions
	• Student-generated questions and topics
	• Meaningful projects

Learning Goal	Standard
Inquiry (continued)	• Research • Discussion
Feedback and authentic assessment	*A variety of assessments (formative, summative, and self-directed) and a variety of timely responses (conferences, rubrics, written comments, and peer feedback) ensure that student learning capitalizes on strengths, limits or corrects weaknesses, and motivates ongoing learning.*

Options for Teachers

- Formal tests
- Essays
- Graded discussions
- Presentations
- Pretests
- Revision
- Conferences
- Written reflections
- Peer evaluations
- Self-evaluations
- Student-teacher conferences

Appendix B

Books for . . . Lists

Some Other Favorite Contemporary Young Adult Books

Barry's List

Al Capone Does My Shirts by Gennifer Choldenko

The Book Thief by Markus Zusak

The Knife of Never Letting Go and sequels by Patrick Ness

Nation by Terry Pratchett

Cinder by Marissa Meyer

The Perks of Being a Wallflower by Stephen Chbosky

The Scorpio Races by Maggie Stiefvater

The Total Tragedy of a Girl Named Hamlet by Erin Dionne

Seraphina by Rachel Hartman

Dash and Lily's Book of Dares by David Levithan

ReLeah's List

I Am the Cheese by Robert Cormier

Boot Camp by Todd Strasser

The Chosen One by Carol Lynch Williams

The Curious Incident of the Dog in the Night-Time by Mark Haddon (and for younger readers a great novel on the same topic: *Mockingbird* by Kathryn Erskine)

How They Croaked: The Awful Ends of the Awfully Famous by Georgia Bragg and Kevin O'Malley

Looking for Alaska by John Green

Luna by Julie Anne Peters

Purple Heart by Patricia McCormick

Red Kayak by Priscilla Cummings

Out of the Easy by Ruta Sepetys

Chapter 1: Books for Connecting Language Arts and Social Studies

The Astonishing Life of Octavian Nothing, Traitor to the Nation: Volume I: The Pox Party and *The Astonishing Life of Octavian Nothing: Traitor to the Nation, Volume II: Kingdom on the Waves* by M. T. Anderson

Between Shades of Gray by Ruta Sepetys

Bomb: The Race to Build—and Steal—the World's Most Dangerous Weapon by Steve Sheinkin

A Break With Charity: A Story About the Salem Witch Trials by Ann Rinaldi

Chains: Seeds of America and *Forge: Seeds of America* by Laurie Halse Anderson

Claudette Colvin: Twice Toward Justice by Phillip Hoose

Hitler Youth and *The Boy Who Dared* by Susan Campbell Bartoletti

T4 by Ann Clare LeZotte

Titanic: Voices From the Disaster by Deborah Hopkinson

Words in the Dust by Trent Reedy

Chapter 2: Picture Books for Scaffolding the Teaching of Theme

Blues Journey by Walter Dean Myers

The Butterfly by Patricia Polacco

14 Cows for America by Carmen Deedy

Fox by Margaret Wild and Ron Brooks

The Man Who Walked Between the Towers by Mordicai Gerstein

Planting the Trees of Kenya: The Story of Wangari Maathai by Claire A. Nivola

Patrol: An American Soldier in Vietnam by Walter Dean Myers

Smoky Night by Eve Bunting

The Wolves in the Walls by Neil Gaiman

Chapter 3: Books for Teaching Informational Text

Amistad: A Long Road to Freedom by Walter Dean Myers

The Boy Kings of Texas: A Memoir by Domingo Martinez

They Call Themselves the KKK: The Birth of an American Terrorist Group by Susan Campbell Bartoletti

Getting Away With Murder: The True Story of the Emmett Till Case by Chris Crowe

The Great Fire by Jim Murphy

The Immortal Life of Henrietta Lacks by Rebecca Skloot

Moonbird: A Year on the Wind With the Great Survivor B95 by Phillip Hoose

We've Got a Job: The 1963 Birmingham Children's March by Cynthia Y. Levinson

Chapter 4: Young Adult Novels Useful for Teaching Critical Literacy and Encouraging Deep Thinking

The Chocolate War by Robert Cormier

Copper Sun by Sharon Draper

Double Helix by Nancy Werlin

Jumped by Rita Williams-Garcia

Lions of Little Rock by Kristin Levine

Never Fall Down by Patricia McCormick

Shine by Lauren Myracle

The Sledding Hill by Chris Crutcher

Smashed by Lisa Luedeke

Chapter 5: Dystopian Novels for an Inquiry Unit on Creating a Sustainable Future

Ashfall and *Ashen Winter* (series) by Mike Mullin

Birthmarked (trilogy) by Caragh O'Brien

Divergent (Book 1) and *Insurgent* (Book 2) by Veronica Roth

The House of the Scorpion by Nancy Farmer

Life as We Knew It (series) by Susan Beth Pfeffer

The Maze Runner (series) by James Dashner

Oryx and Crake by Margaret Atwood

Ship Breaker by Paolo Bacigalupi

Son by Lois Lowry

Chapter 6: Books That Inspire Meaningful Presentations

Beyond Courage: The Untold Story of Jewish Resistance During the Holocaust by Doreen Rappaport

Chew on This: Everything You Don't Want to Know About Fast Food by Charles Wilson and Eric Schlosser

One Crazy Summer by Rita Williams-Garcia

The Fault in Our Stars by John Green

The 9/11 Report: A Graphic Adaptation by Sid Jacobson and Ernie Colon

Photo by Brady: A Picture of the Civil War by Jennifer Armstrong

Skinny by Donna Cooner

Stiff: The Curious Lives of Human Cadavers by Mary Roach

Chapter 7: Books Representative of Various Periods, Cultures, and Worldviews

The Absolutely True Diary of a Part-time Indian by Sherman Alexie

The Breadwinner by Deborah Ellis

Crossing the Wire by Will Hobbs

Fallen Angels or *Sunrise Over Fallujah* by Walter Dean Myers

Fire From the Rock by Sharon Draper

I Am Nujood, Age 10 and Divorced by Nujood Ali, Delphine Minoui, and Linda Coverdale

Inside Out and Back Again by Thanhha Lai

The Kite Runner by Khaled Hosseini

A Long Walk to Water: Based on a True Story by Linda Sue Park

Sold by Patricia McCormick

Chapter 7: Ms. Buchanan's Sixth Grade: Choices in Historical Fiction

The Boy in the Striped Pajamas by John Boyne

Elijah of Buxton by Christopher Paul Curtis

Fever 1793 by Laurie Halse Anderson

Goddess of Yesterday by Caroline Cooney

Iron Thunder by Avi

Milkweed by Jerry Spinelli

New Boy by Julian Houston

Out of the Dust by Karen Hesse

Soldier's Heart: Being the Story of the Enlistment and Due Service of the Boy Charley Goddard in the First Minnesota Volunteers by Gary Paulsen

Under a War-Torn Sky by L. M. Elliott

Chapter 8: Books to Enhance Vocabulary Study

Baseball Haiku: The Best Haiku Ever Written About the Game edited by Cor Van Den Heuvel and Nanae Tamura

Code Name Verity by Elizabeth Wein

Feed by M. T. Anderson

The Lover's Dictionary by David Levithan

A Northern Light by Jennifer Donnelly

Out of My Mind by Sharon Draper

Why You Say It: The Fascinating Stories Behind Over 600 Everyday Words and Phrases by Webb Garrison

References

Allington, R. (2002, November). You can't learn much from books you can't read. *Educational Leadership, 60*(3), 16–19.

Alvermann, D. (2003). *Seeing themselves as capable and engaged readers: Adolescents and instruction.* Retrieved from http://www.ldonline.org/article/19364/

Anderson, J. (2006). Zooming in and zooming out: Putting grammar in context into context. *The English Journal, 95*(5), 28–34.

Anderson, R. C., Wilson, P. T., & Fielding, L. G. (1988). Growth in reading and how children spend their time outside of school. *Reading Research Quarterly, 23,* 285–303.

Asher, J. (2011). *Thirteen reasons why.* New York, NY: Razorbill.

Barrell, J. (2007). *Problem-based learning: An inquiry approach.* Thousand Oaks, CA: Corwin.

Baumann, J. F., Edwards, E. C., Boland, E. M., Olejnik, S., & Kame'enui, E. J. (2003). Vocabulary tricks: Effects of instruction in morphology and context on fifth-grade students' ability to derive and infer word meanings. *American Educational Research Journal, 40*(2), 447–494.

Beatty-Martinez, A. (2013). *Reading instruction for all students: A Policy Research Brief produced by the National Council of Teachers of English.* Retrieved from http://www.academia.edu/2137573/Reading_Instruction_for_All_Students

Beck, I. L., McKeown, M. G., & Kucan, L. (2002). *Bringing words to life: Robust vocabulary instruction.* New York, NY: Guilford.

Becker, W. C. (1977). Teaching reading and language to the disadvantaged: What we have learned from field research. *Harvard Educational Review, 47,* 518–543.

Beers, K., & Probst, R. E. (2013). *Notice and note: Strategies for close reading.* Portsmouth, NH: Heinemann.

Behrman, E. H. (2006). Teaching about language, power, and text: A review of classroom practices that support critical literacy. *Journal of Adolescent & Adult Literacy, 49*(6), 490–498.

Bender, W. N. (2012). *Project-based learning: Differentiating instruction for the 21st century.* Thousand Oaks, CA: Corwin.

Berger, J. (2006). Transforming writers through grammar study. *The English Journal, 95*(5), 53–59.

Biemiller, A. (1999). *Language and reading success.* Cambridge, MA: Brookline.

Blachowicz, C. L., Fisher, P. J. L., Ogle, D., & Watts-Taffe, S. (2006). Vocabulary: Questions from the classroom. *Reading Research Quarterly, 41*(4), 524–539.

Black, P., & Wiliam, D. (1998). Assessment and classroom learning. *Assessment in Education, 5*(1), 7–74.

Borman, G. D., & Rachuba, L. T. (2001). *Academic success among poor and minority students: An analysis of competing models of school effects.* Center for Research on the Education of Students Placed at Risk (CRESPAR). Baltimore, MD: Johns Hopkins University.

Boston, C. (2002). The concept of formative assessment. *Practical Assessment, Research & Evaluation.* Retrieved from http://PAREonline.net/getvn. asp?v=8&n=9

Boyles, N. (December 2012–January 2013). Closing in on close reading. *Educational Leadership, 70*(4), 36–41.

Cambourne, B. (1995). Toward an educationally relevant theory of literacy learning: Twenty years of inquiry. *The Reading Teacher, 49,* 182–190.

Coleman, D., & Pimentel, S. (2012, April 12). *Revised publishers' criteria for the Common Core State Standards in English Language Arts and Literacy, Grades 3–12.* Retrieved from http://www.corestandards.org/assets/Publishers_Criteria_for_3-12.pdf

Copeland, M. (2005). *Socratic circles: Fostering critical and creative thinking in middle and high school.* Portland, ME: Stenhouse.

Darling-Hammond, L. (2010). *The flat world and education: How America's commitment to equity will determine our future.* New York, NY: Teachers College Press.

Dean, D. (2011). Shifting perspectives about grammar: Changing what and how we teach. *English Journal, 100*(4), 20–26.

Dressman, M., Wilder, P., & Connor, J. J. (2005). Theories of failure and the failure of theories: Cognitive/sociocultural/macrostructural study of eight struggling students. *Research in the Teaching of English, 40,* 8–61.

Ellis, E. S., Worthington, L., & Larkin, M. J. (n.d.). *Executive summary of the research synthesis on effective teaching principles and the design of quality tools for educators.* Retrieved from http://idea.uoregon.edu

Fielding, L. G., Wilson, P. T., & Anderson, R. C. (1986). A new focus on free reading: The role of trade books in reading instruction. In T. E. Raphael (Ed.), *Contexts of school-based literacy.* New York, NY: Random House.

Fine, M. (1988). De-institutionalizing educational inequity. In Council of Chief State School Officers (Ed.), *School success for students at risk* (pp. 88–119). New York, NY: Harcourt Brace Jovanovich.

Gallagher, J. D. (2012). Being a "reader" in new times: A case study examining the construction of a reader in a ninth-grade English class. *Reading & Writing Quarterly, 28*(3), 201–228.

Gallagher, K. (2009). *Readicide: How schools are killing reading and what you can do about it.* Portland, ME: Stenhouse.

Gilmore, B. (2008). *Plagiarism: Why it happens and how to prevent it.* Portsmouth, NH: Heinemann.

Graves M. F. (2006). *The vocabulary book.* New York, NY: Teachers College Press.

Graves, M. F. (2009). *Teaching individual words: One size does not fit all.* New York, NY: Teachers College Press.

Guthrie, J. T. (Ed.). (2008). *Engaging adolescents in reading.* Thousand Oaks, CA: Corwin.

Guthrie, J. T., & Anderson, E. (1999). Engagement in reading: Processes of motivated, strategic, knowledgeable, social readers. In J. T. Guthrie & D. E. Alvermann (Eds.), *Engaged reading: Processes, practices, and policy implications* (pp. 17–45). New York, NY: Teachers College Press.

Hart, B., & Risley, T. (2003). The early catastrophe: The 30 million word gap. *American Educator, 27,* 4–9.

Henry, L. A., Castek, J., O'Byrne, W. I., & Zawilinski, O. (2012). Using peer collaboration to support online reading, writing, and communication: An empowerment model for struggling readers. *Reading & Writing Quarterly, 28*(3), 279–306.

Heverly, J (2011). Why I no longer teach vocabulary. *English Journal, 100*(4), 98–100.

Hogan, K., & Pressley, M. (Eds.). (1997). *Scaffolding student learning: Instructional approaches and issues.* Cambridge, MA: Brookline.

Ivey, G., & Fisher, D. (2006). *Creating literacy-rich schools for adolescents.* Alexandria, VA: ASCD.

Ivey, S. J., & Guthrie, J. T. (2008). Struggling readers: Boosting motivation in low achievers. In J. T. Guthrie (Ed.), *Engaging adolescents in reading* (pp. 115–129). Thousand Oaks, CA: Corwin.

Klem, A. M., & Connell, J. P. (2004). Relationships matter: Linking teacher support to student engagement and achievement. *Journal of School Health, 74*(7), 262–273.

Kooser, T. (2012). *House held up by trees.* Somerville, MA: Candlewick Press.

Krashen, S. D. (2004). *The power of reading: Insights from the research.* Westport, CT: Libraries Unlimited.

Krashen, S. (2009). Anything but reading. *Knowledge Quest, 37*(5), 19–25.

Langer, J. A. (1984). Examining background knowledge and text comprehension. *Reading Research Quarterly, 19*(4), 468–481.

Langer, J., Close, E., Angelis, J., & Preller, P. (2000). *Teaching middle school and high school students to read and write well: Six features of effective instruction.* Albany: Center on English Learning and Achievement (CELA), State University of New York.

Lee, C. D., & Spratley, A. (2010). *Reading in the disciplines: The challenges of adolescent literacy.* New York: Carnegie Corporation of New York.

Lent, R., & Pipkin, G. (2012). *Keep them reading: An anti-censorship handbook for educators.* New York, NY: Teachers College Press.

Lesesne, T. (2010). *Reading ladders: Leading students from where they are to where we'd like them to be.* Portsmouth, NH: Heinemann.

Luke, A., & Freebody, P. (1997). The social practices of reading. In S. Muspratt, A. Luke, & P. Freebody (Eds.), *Constructing critical literacies* (pp. 1985–225). Creskill, NJ: Hampton Press.

Margolis, H., & McCabe, P. P. (2004). Self-efficacy: A key to improving the motivation of struggling learners. *The Clearing House, 77*(6), 241–249.

Marzano, R. J. (2004). *Building background knowledge for academic achievement: Research on what works in schools.* Alexandria, VA: ASCD.

McKeown, M. G., Beck, I. L., Omanson, R. C., & Pople, M. T. (1985). Some effects of the nature and frequency of vocabulary instruction on the knowledge and use of words. *Reading Research Quarterly, 20*(5), 522–535.

McLaughlin, M. W., & Talbert, J. E. (2006). *Building school-based teacher learning communities: Professional strategies to improve student achievement.* New York, NY: Teachers College Press.

Miller, G. A., & Gildea, P. M. (1987). How children learn words. *Scientific American, 257*(3), 94–99.

Nagy, W. (1998, August). *Technical Report No. 431: Vocabulary instruction and reading comprehension.* Center for the Study of Reading, University of Illinois at Urbana-Champaign. Retrieved from https://www.ideals.illinois .edu/bitstream/handle/2142/17756/ctrstreadtechrepv01988i00431_opt .pdf?sequence=1

Nagy, W. E. (2003). *Teaching vocabulary to improve reading comprehension.* Urbana, IL: National Council of Teachers of English.

Nagy, W. E., & Anderson, R. C. (1984). How many words are there in printed school English? *Reading Research Quarterly, 19,* 303–330.

National Governors Association Center for Best Practices and Council of Chief State School Officers. (2010). *Common Core State Standards.* Retrieved from http://www.corestandards.org/the-standards

Neuman, S. B. (1999). Books make a difference: A study of access to literacy. *Reading Research Quarterly.*

Neuman, S. B., & Wright, T. S. (2013). Vocabulary instruction in commonly used kindergarten core reading curricula. *The Elementary School Journal, 113*(3), 386–408.

Padak, N., Newton, E., Rasinski, T., & Newton, R. M. (2008). Getting to the root of word study: Teaching Latin and Greek word roots in elementary and middle grades. In A. E. Farstrup & S. Samuels (Eds.), *What research has to say about vocabulary instruction* (pp. 6–31). Newark, DE: International Reading Association.

Pajares, F. (1996). Self-efficacy beliefs in academic settings. *Review of Educational Research, 66,* 543–578.

Paraskevas, C. (2006). Grammar apprenticeship. *The English Journal, 95*(5), 65–70.

Parks, R. (with J. Haskins). (1992). *Rosa Parks: My story.* New York, NY: Puffin Books.

Pink, D. (2011). *Drive: The surprising truth about what motivates us.* New York, NY: Riverhead Books.

Prensky, M. (2001). Digital natives, digital immigrants. *On the Horizon,* (9)5. Retrieved from http://www.marcprensky.com/writing/Prensky%20-%20 Digital%20Natives,%20Digital%20Immigrants%20-%20Part1.pdf

Rawlings, J. K. (1998). *Harry Potter and the Sorcerer's Stone.* New York, NY: A. A. Levine Books.

Roberts, T., & Billings, L. (2011). *Teaching critical thinking: Using seminars for 21st century literacy.* Larchmont, NY: Eye on Education.

Romano, T. (2000). *Blending genre, altering style: Writing multigenre papers.* Portsmouth, NH: Heinemann.

Rosenblatt, L. (1995). *Literature as exploration.* New York, NY: Modern Language Association of America.

Routman, R. (2003). *Reading essentials: The specifics you need to teach reading well.* Portsmouth, NH: Heinemann.

Rowling, J. K. (1997). *Harry Potter and the sorcerer's stone.* New York, NY: Arthur A. Levine Books.

Sadler, D. R. (1989). Formative assessment and the design of instructional systems. *Instructional Science, 8*(2), 119–144.

Schrefer, E. (2012). *Endangered.* New York, NY: Scholastic Press.

Schulten, K. (2012). Engaging nonfiction: The times, the Common Core and a question for you. *The Learning Network: Teaching and Learning With The New York Times.* Retrieved from http://learning.blogs.nytimes. com/2012/06/26/engaging-nonfiction-the-times-the-common-core-and-a-question-for-you/

Schunk, D. H., & Zimmerman, B. J. (1997). Developing self-efficacious readers and writers: The role of social and self-regulatory processes. In J. T. Guthrie & A. Wigfield (Eds.), *Reading engagement: Motivating readers through integrated instruction* (pp. 34–50). Newark, DE: International Reading Instruction.

Sedita, J. (2005). Effective vocabulary instruction. *Insights on Learning Disabilities, 2*(1), 33–45.

Serafini, F., & Giorgis, C. (2004). *Reading aloud and beyond: Fostering the intellectual life with older readers.* Portsmouth, NH: Heinemann.

Should *NY Post* have printed photo of man about to die? (2012). *USA Today,* December 4. Retrieved from http://www.usatoday.com/story/news/ nation/2012/12/04/nyc-subway-death-push/1744875/

Smagorinsky, P., Wilson, A. A., & Moore, C. (2011). Teaching grammar and writing: A beginning teacher's dilemma. *English Education, 43*(3), 262–292.

Smagorinsky, P., Wright, L., Murphy Augustine, S., O'Donnell-Allen, C., & Konopak, B. (2007). *Student engagement in the teaching and learning of grammar: A case study of an early-career secondary school English teacher.* Retrieved from http://digitalcommons.calpoly.edu/cgi/viewcontent.cgi?article=1002&context=coe_dean

Southwest Educational Development Laboratory. (1997). Professional learning communities: What are they and why are they important? *Issues About Change, 6(1).* Retrieved from http://www.sedl.org/pubs/catalog/items/cha35.html

Stahl, S., & Fairbanks, M. (1986). The effects of vocabulary instruction: A model-based meta-analysis. *Review of Educational Research, 56*, 72–110.

Sternberg, R. J. (1985). Implicit theories of intelligence, creativity, and wisdom. *Journal of Personality and Social Psychology, 49*, 607–627.

Sternberg, R. J. (1987). Most vocabulary is learned in context. In M. G. McKeown & M. E. Curtis (Eds.), *The nature of vocabulary acquisition* (pp. 89–105). Hillsdale, NJ: Erlbaum.

Stevens, K. C. (1980). The effect of background knowledge on the reading comprehension of ninth graders. *Journal of Reading Behavior, 12*(2), 151–154.

Strangman, N., Hall, T., & Meyer, A. (2009, November 2). *Background knowledge with UDL.* Retrieved from http://www.cast.org/publications/ncac/ncac_backknowledgeudl.html

Strong, W. (1994). *Sentence combining: A composing book.* New York, NY: McGraw-Hill.

Strong, W. (2001). *Coaching writing: The power of guided practice.* Portsmouth, NH: Heinemann.

Student Achievement Partners. (n.d.). *Achieve the Core: Common Core close reading sample lessons.* Retrieved from http://www.achievethecore.org/steal-these-tools/close-reading-exemplars

Tangney, J. P., Baumeister, R. F., & Boone, A. L. (2004). High self-control predicts good adjustment, less pathology, better grades, and interpersonal success. *Journal of Personality, 72*(2), 271–322.

Tobias, S. (1994). Interest, prior knowledge, and learning. *Review of Educational Research, 64*(1), 37–54.

William, D. (2011). *Embedded formative assessment.* Bloomington, IN: Solution Tree Press.

Wood, D., Bruner, J. S., & Ross, G. (1976). The role of tutoring in problem solving. *Journal of Psychology and Psychiatry, 17*(2), 89–100.

Wozniak, C. L. (2011). Reading and talking about books: A critical foundation for intervention. *Voices From the Middle, 19*(2), 17–21.

Index

About the Authors

An international consultant, **ReLeah Cossett Lent** was a secondary teacher before becoming a founding member of a statewide literacy project at the University of Central Florida. The author of eight books—including *Overcoming Textbook Fatigue*—and chair of the National Council of Teachers of English's Standing Committee Against Censorship, she is the recipient of the American Library Association's Intellectual Freedom Award, NCTE's Intellectual Freedom Award, the PEN/Newman's Own First Amendment Award, and, most recently, the Florida Council of Teachers of English President's Award.

Barry Gilmore is the middle school head at Hutchison School in Memphis, Tennessee. A National Board Certified Teacher, he taught English and social studies for nearly 20 years. Barry is the author of six literacy books and former president of the Tennessee Council of Teachers of English. Awards for his teaching have come from NCTE, TCTE, the U.S. Department of Education, and the Tennessee Holocaust Commission.

CORWIN LITERACY

ALSO AVAILABLE

CORWIN

A SAGE Company

The Corwin logo—a raven striding across an open book—represents the union of courage and learning. Corwin is committed to improving education for all learners by publishing books and other professional development resources for those serving the field of PreK–12 education. By providing practical, hands-on materials, Corwin continues to carry out the promise of its motto: **"Helping Educators Do Their Work Better."**